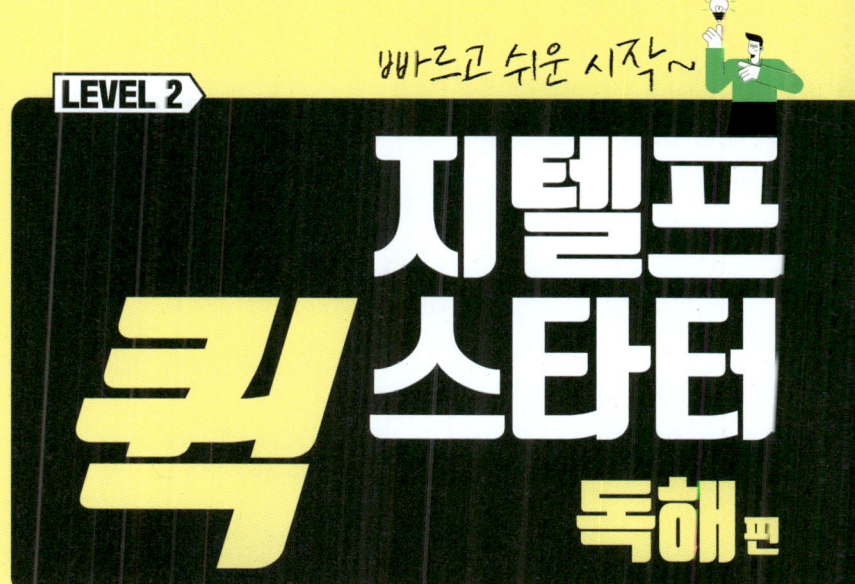

G-TELP 영어연구소

G-TELP 영어연구소는 국내외 영어 콘텐츠 전문 연구진들로 이루어진 조직으로서, G-TELP 시험들을 전문적으로 분석 및 연구해오고 있습니다. 다년간 쌓아온 디지털 데이터베이스와 정확한 데이터를 분석하는 도구를 기반으로 G-TELP의 모든 시험을 대비할 수 있는 수험서, 일반 영어, 비즈니스 영어, 전문 영어 등 다양한 분야의 영어학습서를 기획, 집필, 편집, 출간하고 있습니다.

지텔프 퀵 스타터
독해 편

초 판	2021년 08월 23일
발행인	김현중
출판사	G-TELP KOREA 출판사업본부
저자	G-TELP 영어연구소
검수	안수진, 곽미경, 강지현, 고명수
ISBN	978-89-91164-57-4
정가	18,900원

도서 문의 안내

PHONE	1577-3836
FAX	02-454-2137

이 책의 내용과 포맷은 저작권법에 따라 보호받고 있으므로 무단 복제와 무단 전재를 금합니다.

지텔프 퀵 스타터 - 독해 편
PREFACE

안녕하세요. G-TELP 연구소입니다.

G-TELP는 1985년 ITSC 주관으로 개발 검증된 이래 세계 여러 나라 정부 기관과 기업에서 영어 활용 능력 평가 도구로 활용되고 있는 국제 공인 영어 시험입니다.

G-TELP Level 2 시험은 국내 650여개 기업의 채용 및 승진 시험과 경찰, 군무원, 공무원 채용뿐만 아니라 국가자격증 시험 등에서 영어능력검정 대체시험으로 활용되고 있습니다. G-TELP는 상대적으로 적은 문항 수와 짧은 시험시간으로 시험에 대한 부담이 적고 단기간에 원하는 목표 점수에 도달할 수 있기에 최근 G-TELP 수험자 및 응시자가 급격하게 늘어나고 있습니다.

"지텔프 퀵 스타터 독해편"은 지텔프 독해의 전반적인 내용을 다루며, 특히 영어 입문자들에게 효율적인 지텔프 독해 학습 전략을 제시합니다.

"독해 왕초보를 위한 지텔프 독해 학습법 제시"
지텔프 독해 Part 별 출제 패턴 분석을 통해 필수-기초-심화 공략 포인트로 나누어 단계별 학습 전략을 제시하고 있습니다. 영어 입문 수험자들도 지텔프 독해 영역을 자신의 수준에 맞게 단계적으로 학습이 가능합니다.

"출제기관에서 엄선한 독해 지문 수록"
"지텔프 퀵 스타터 독해 편"은 지텔프 공식주관사에서 최신 출제 경향을 철저히 분석한 자료들을 토대로 수험자에게 도움이 될 수 있는 지문을 수록했습니다. 특히, 엄선된 독해 주제로 입문 학습자들도 접근 가능한 Mini Test를 개발했으며, 최신 출제 경향을 반영한 기출유형 모의고사도 2회도 수록했습니다

"효과적인 지텔프 학습을 위한 다양한 보조 학습 자료"
품사별로 분류한 500개 어휘 목록, 지텔프 독해 비법을 정리한 노트, 학습 플랜과 학습 체크로 구성된 학습 가이드라인 등 학습에 도움이 되는 다양한 자료들을 준비했습니다.

"지텔프 퀵 스타터 독해편"으로 G-TELP 입문자부터 고득점을 목표로 하는 수험자까지, 모두가 원하는 바를 이룰 수 있길 기원합니다.

G-TELP 영어연구소 올림

CONTENTS

교재 구성 및 특징   6

시험 소개   10
- 출제기관
- GLT(G-TELP Level Test 지텔프 등급 시험)란?
- G-TELP Level 2 란?
- 정시 시험 프로세스

시험 전 확인하기   19

학습 가이드라인   20
- 학습 플랜
- 학습 체크

해설집
- Mini Test   4
- 실전모의고사   40

CHAPTER 1. 독해

Part 1.
Biography Article — 24
필수 공략 포인트	26
기초 공략 포인트	28
심화 공략 포인트	34
Mini Test	46
Vocabulary	52

Part 2.
Magazine Article — 56
필수 공략 포인트	58
기초 공략 포인트	60
심화 공략 포인트	65
Mini Test	76
Vocabulary	82

Part 3.
Encyclopedia Article — 88
필수 공략 포인트	90
기초 공략 포인트	92
심화 공략 포인트	98
Mini Test	110
Vocabulary	116

Part 4.
Business or Formal Letter — 122
필수 공략 포인트	124
기초 공략 포인트	126
심화 공략 포인트	132
Mini Test	142
Vocabulary	148

CHAPTER 2. 실전 모의고사

실전 모의고사 1회	155
실전 모의고사 2회	167

CHAPTER 3. 부록

핵심 보카 500	180
시크릿 노트 G	

교재 구성 및 특징

지텔프 개요

- 출제기관, 소개, 시험 소개, 성적 활용 현황, 성적표 분석 등 지텔프에 관련 정보를 간결하게 정리

- 시험에 대한 이해도 향상으로 체계적인 시험 대비 가능

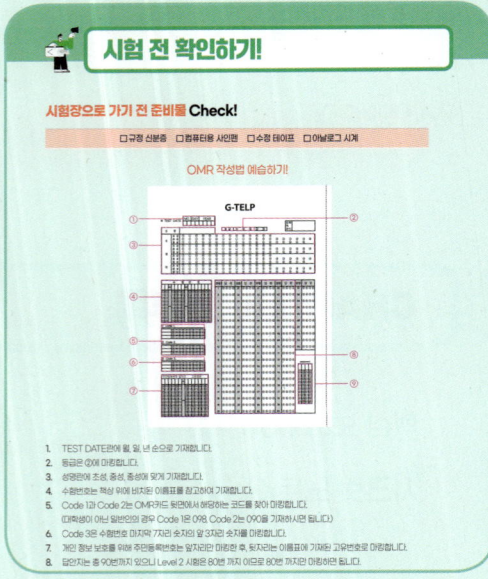

시험장 가기 전 필수 확인 사항 안내

- 규정 신분증, 컴퓨터용 사인펜 등 시험 당일 필수 준비물 체크표

- OMR카드 분석으로 실제 시험일에 당황하지 않고 답안지 작성을 할 수 있도록 완벽 대비

지텔프 퀵 스타터 - 독해 편

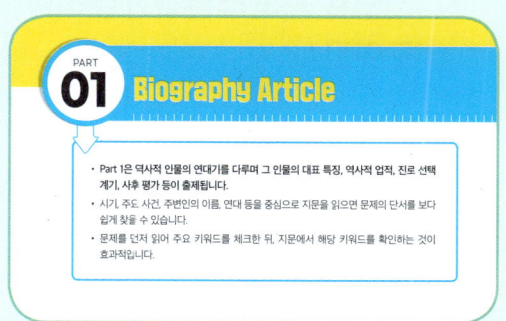

파트별 출제 경향 소개

- 해당 파트 마다 출제 경향을 간략하게 소개하여 출제 유형을 한 눈에 이해할 수 있도록 깔끔하게 정리

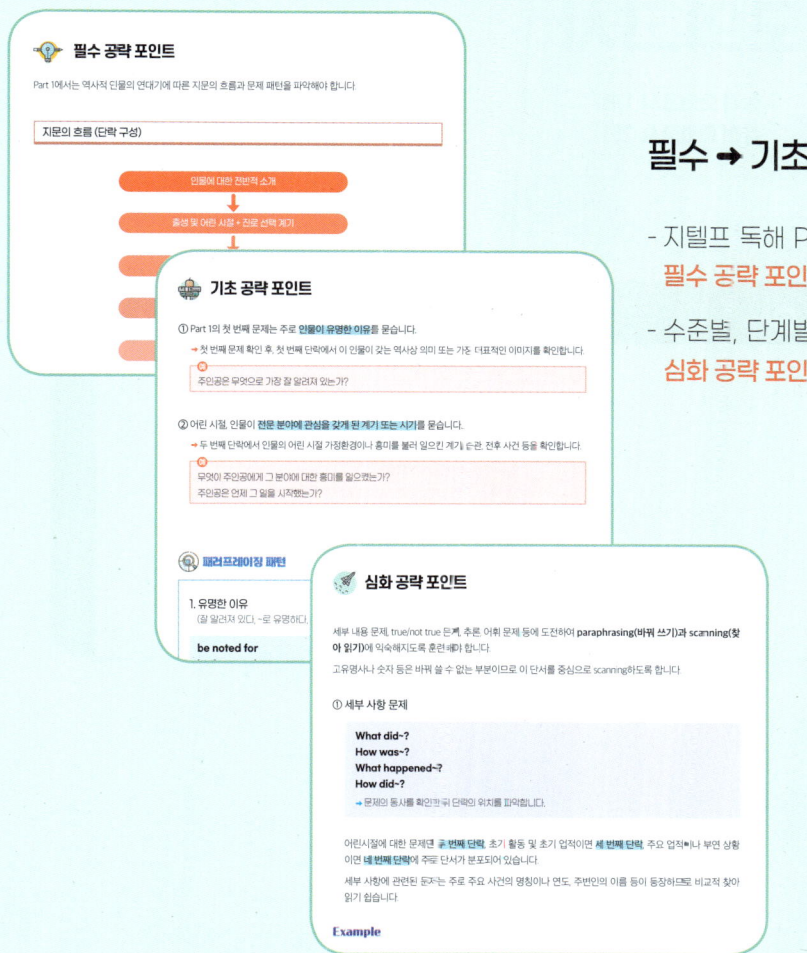

필수 → 기초 → 심화 공략 포인트

- 지텔프 독해 Part 별 출제 패턴 분석으로 **필수 공략 포인트** 파악
- 수준별, 단계별로 학습할 수 있도록 **기초, 심화 공략 포인트**로 나누어 제시

지텔프 공식 주관사가 분석한 모의고사

- 지텔프 공식주관사에서 최신 출제 경향을 철저히 분석한 자료들을 토대로 개발
- 입문 학습자들도 접근 가능한 Mini Test를 파트별로 제공
- 최신 출제 경향을 반영한 기출유형 모의고사 2회 수록

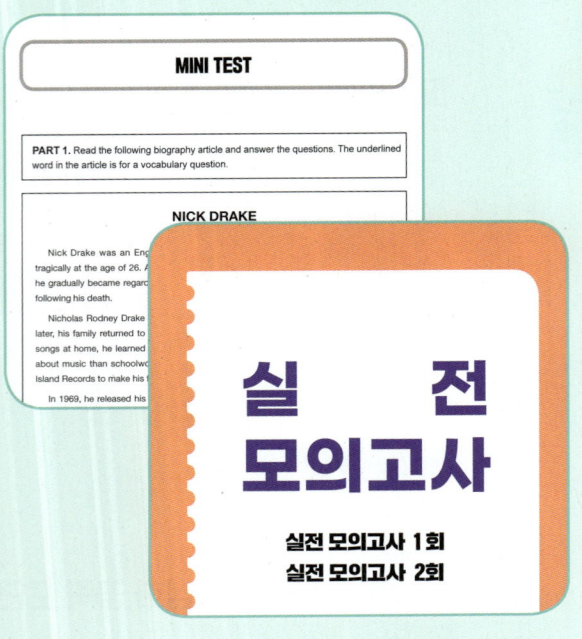

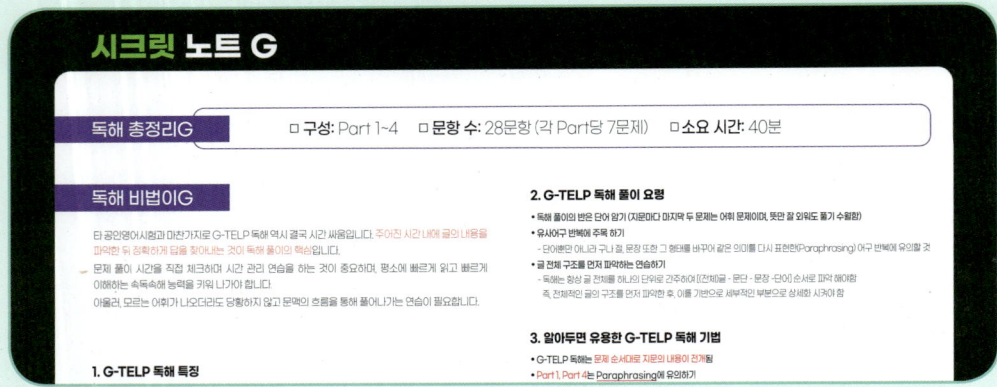

시크릿 노트 G

- 지텔프 독해 문항 분석 및 접근 전략을 한 눈에 볼 수 있는 비법 노트
- 언제 어디서든 펼쳐서 참고할 수 있도록 부록 형태로 제작

지텔프 퀵 스타터 - 독해 편

학습 가이드라인

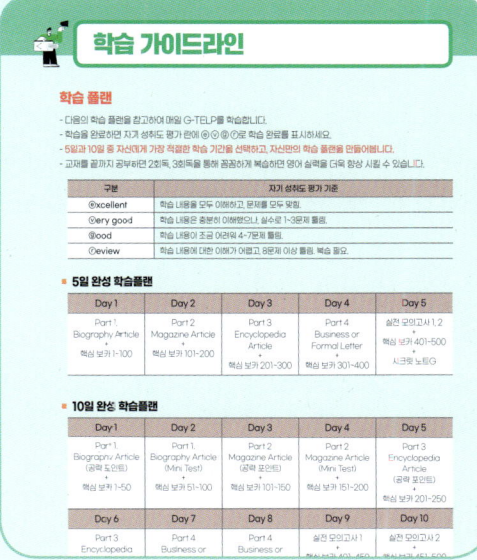

- 학습 진도를 참고하여 자신에게 가장 알맞은 학습 기간을 선택하고, 최적화된 학습을 계획할 수 있는 **학습 플랜표**

- 계획한 학습내용을 토대로 스스로의 학습상태를 확인 할 수 있는 **학습 체크표**

핵심 보카 500

- 학습에 용이하도록 품사별, 알파벳 순서로 분류

- 지텔프 독해 해석 및 어휘 문제 공략에 도움이 되는 단어 모음집

시험 소개

출제 기관

지텔프 코리아는 신뢰성, 타당성, 실용성을 갖춘 종합적인 영어평가라는 모토 아래 ITSC (International Testing Service Center)의 글로벌 파트너로서 1985년부터 G-TELP 시험을 주관하는 어학평가, 교육, 출판 전문 기업입니다. 지텔프코리아는 업무 협약을 통해 한국 내 G-TELP 시험의 시행, 마케팅, 홍보, 출판, 교육에 대한 운영을 담당하고 있습니다.

지텔프 코리아는 지난 30여 년 동안 영어학습자의 영어능력을 보다 정확하고 세밀하게 분석할 수 있는 평가도구 개발에 끊임없이 노력해 왔습니다. 2006년부터 2019년 1월까지 12년 동안 국가자격시험인 항공영어구술증명시험(EPTA)을 시행하였으며, 평가영역별, 레벨별, 목적별, 연령별 등으로 구분된 아래의 다양한 시험을 정기적으로 시행하고 있습니다.

- 문법과 듣기, 읽기 능력을 평가하는 5단계의 G-TELP Level Test
- 실생활과 관련된 영어 말하기/작문 능력을 평가하는 G-TELP Speaking Test, G-TELP Writing Test
- 비즈니스 말하기/작문 수행능력 평가인 G-TELP Business Speaking Test, G-TELP Business Writing Test
- 영어 초급자 및 초등학생과 중학생의 영어 능력을 평가하는 G-TELP Junior

주니어부터 성인까지 영어를 종합적으로 평가할 수 있는 완성된 평가 교육 시스템을 갖추고, 전문 분야별 영어 활용 능력 평가 도구 개발에 쏟아온 투자와 열정이 신뢰성과 타당성, 실용성을 갖춘 종합적인 평가 시스템 구축을 위한 밑거름이 되었으리라 믿으며, 단순히 우열을 가르는 평가가 아닌 학습자에게 개인의 능력을 분석 진단하여 학습 동기를 제공하고, 학습 과정으로써 진정한 평가가 될 수 있도록 최선의 노력을 다할 것입니다.

GLT(G-TELP Level Test 지텔프 등급 시험)란?

G-TELP(General Tests of English Language Proficiency)는 미국 국제 테스트 연구원(ITSC, International Testing Services Center)에서 주관하여 University of California Los Angeles, Georgetown University, San Diego State University, Lado International College 등의 저명 교수진이 연구/개발하였고, 국내외 저명한 언어학자, 평가전문가들이 참여하여 국제적으로 시행하는 글로벌 영어능력 평가 인증 시험입니다. GLT는 Level 1부터 Level 5까지 다섯 등급으로 나뉘어진 등급 시험이며, 문제는 모두 4지 선다형의 객관식 형태로 출제됩니다. 문법/청취/독해 및 어휘로 이루어져 있으며, 각 영역에서 모두 75%이상을 획득한 경우에 해당 응시 등급을 Mastery한 것으로 여겨집니다.

■ 시험 특징

- 5단계(Level 1~5)의 수준별로 구분된 시험
- 문법/청취/독해 및 어휘 3가지 영역의 종합 영어 능력 평가 → 객관식 사지선다형
  (단, Level 1은 청취/독해 및 어휘 2가지 영역만 중점 평가)
- 절대 평가 방식
- 빠른 성적 확인 → 응시일로부터 일주일 이내 빠른 성적 발표
- 정기 시험: Level 2 시험 → Level 2 정기 시험에 국가고시/국가자격시험/기업체 채용 시험에 주로 활용
  수시 시험: Level 1~5 시험

■ 등급별 시험 구성

구분	출제 방식 및 시간	평가 기준	합격자의 영어 구사 능력	응시자격
Level 1	청취: 30문항/약 30분 독해 및 어휘: 70문항/70분 합계: 100문항/약 100분	Native Speaker에 준하는 영어 능력: 상담, 토론 가능	• 모국어로 하는 외국인과 거의 대등한 의사소통이 가능 • 국제회의 통역도 가능한 수준	Level 2 Mastery (영역별 75점 이상)
Level 2	문법: 26문항/20분 청취: 26문항/약 30분 독해 및 어휘: 28문항/40분 합계: 80문항/약 90분	다양한 상황에서 대화 가능: 업무 상담 및 해외연수 등이 가능한 수준	• 일상생활 및 업무 상담 등에서 어려움 없이 의사 소통 할 수 있는 수준 • 외국인과의 회의 및 세미나 참석, 해외 연수 등이 가능한 수준	제한 없음
Level 3	문법: 22문항/20분 청취: 24문항/약 20분 독해 및 어휘: 24문항/40분 합계: 70문항/80분	간단한 의사소통과 친숙한 상태에서의 단순 대화 가능	• 간단한 의사소통과 친숙한 상태에서의 단순한 대화가 가능한 수준 • 해외여행과 단순한 업무 출장을 할 수 있는 수준	제한 없음
Level 4	문법: 20문항/20분 청취: 20문항/약 15분 독해 및 어휘: 20문항/25분 합계: 60문항/약 60분	기본적인 문장을 통해 최소한의 의사소통이 가능한 수준	• 기본적인 어휘와 짧은 문장을 통해 최소한의 의사소통이 가능한 수준 • 외국인이 자주 반복하거나 부연설명을 해주어야 이해할 수 있는 수준	제한 없음
Level 5	문법: 16문항/15분 청취: 16문항/약 15분 독해 및 어휘: 18문항/25분 합계: 50문항/약 55분	극히 초보적인 수준의 의사 소통 가능	• 영어 초보자 • 일상의 인사/소개 등을 듣고, 이해할 수 있는 수준 • 말 또는 글을 통한 자기표현은 거의 불가능한 수준	제한 없음

G-TELP Level 2 란?

■ 시험 구성

영역	내용	지문 수 (개)	문항 수 (개)	배점 (점)	시간 (분)
Grammar (총 26문항)	가정법, 시제, 조동사, To부정사, 동명사, 접속사, 관계사	-	26	100	20
Listening (총 26문항)	Part 1. Interesting Story 자신의 경험담을 주변 사람들과 나누기	1	6~7	100	약 30
	Part 2. Speech 특정 주제에 대한 전문가의 설명	1	6~7		
	Part 3. Conversation 특정 주제나 문제에 대한 의견 제시 및 충고 요청	1	6~7		
	Part 4. Presentation 특정 주제에 대한 연사의 설명 및 발표	1	6~7		
Reading & Vocabulary (총 28문항)	Part 1. Biography Article 역사적 사건을 특정 인물을 중심으로 소개한 글	1	7	100	40
	Part 2. Magazine Article 시사적인 사회적, 기술적 현상을 설명하는 기사글	1	7		
	Part 3. Encyclopedia Article 일반적이고 비전문적인 백과사전 내용	1	7		
	Part 4. Business or Formal Letter 설명적이고 설득력 있는 상업 통신문	1	7		
Total			80	300	약 90

★ 시험 시간을 특정 영역에 제한을 두지는 않으므로, 주어진 시간 내에 다른 영역의 문제풀이 가능
★ 각 영역 100점 만점으로 총 300점이며, 세 개 영역의 평균 값으로 성적 산출

■ 출제 분야

● 문법 (Grammar)

이 등급에 해당되는 수험자는 다음과 같은 기본적인 문법구조와 아울러 어느 정도 복잡한 문장구조를 이해하는 사람입니다.
- 가정법: 가정법 과거, 가정법 과거완료 등
- 시제: 진행형, 완료형, 완료진행형 등
- 조동사: 다양한 조동사의 쓰임 및 요구/제안/명령 동사와 should 생략 등
- To 부정사와 동명사: 역할 및 목적어로 취하는 동사들 등
- 접속사: 종속접속사, 등위접속사, 접속부사
- 관계사: 관계대명사, 관계부사 등

● 청취 (Listening)

이 등급의 수험자는 영어를 모국어로 사용하는 사람이 정상속도로 말하지만, 다소 쉽게 변형하여 부연 설명해서 말하는 아래의 내용과 같은 것을 이해합니다.
- 개인적인 이야기
- 어떤 결정에 이르고자 하는 비공식적인 협상 등의 대화
- 어떤 특정한 행동의 진행상황을 설명하거나 특정한 상품을 추천하는 공식적인 담화
- 일반적인 어떤 일의 진행이나 과정에 대한 설명

● 독해 및 어휘 (Reading & Vocabulary)

이 등급에 해당되는 수험자는 실제 혹은 다소 쉽게 변형된 일반적인 아래와 같은 내용의 글을 읽고 이해합니다.
- 과거 역사 속의 사건이나 현시대의 이야기
- 최근의 사회적이고 기술적인 묘사에 초점을 맞춘 잡지나 신문의 기사
- 전문적인 것이 아닌 일반적인 내용의 백과사전
- 어떤 것을 설명하거나 설득하는 상업서신

FAQ

Q1. 지텔프 시험의 적용 범위는?
- 정기 시험(Level 2)의 경우 세무사, 노무사, 군무원, 공무원 등 국가고시의 영어시험 대체 점수로 활용 가능합니다.
- 수시 시험(Level 1~5)은 일반 기업체 채용 및 승진, 대학교 졸업인증 등 수시 시험도 인정하는 경우에 한해서 활용 가능하며, 수시 시험 인정 여부는 반드시 미리 확인하시기 바랍니다.

Q2. 공무원 임용, 군무원, 각종 자격증 영어시험 대체 수시 성적도 유효 한가요?
- 정기 시험(Level 2)만 인정되는 경우가 대부분입니다. 수시 시험 인정 여부는 해당 기관에 별도로 문의 하시기 바랍니다.

Q3. Mastery, Near Mastery, No Mastery 는 무엇을 의미하나요?
- **Mastery** : 세개의 영역(문법, 청취, 독해 및 어휘) 모두 75% 이상 획득한 경우
- **Near Mastery** : 세개의 영역(문법, 청취, 독해 및 어휘)중 두개 영역에서 75% 이상 획득한 경우
- **No Mastery** : 세가지 영역(문법, 청취, 독해 및 어휘) 중 한 개 이하의 영역만 75% 이상인 경우

Q4. 시험 필기도구 및 낙서 규정은 어떻게 되나요?
시험 필기 도구는 컴퓨터용 수성 사인펜만 가능하며, OMR 답안지에는 반드시 수성사인펜으로 작성해야 합니다. 공정하고 정확한 평가를 위해서 시험 중 문제지에 낙서하는 행위를 금지하고 있습니다. 단, 본인만 볼 수 있는 정도의 작은 표시는 허용(글씨 크기 10pt 정도)은 하고 있습니다.

Q5. 파트 별 시험시간 규정은 따로 있나요?
현재 파트 별 시험시간 제한 규정은 없습니다. 시험 시작부터 종료시간까지 어떤 파트를 풀던지 상관없습니다. 예를 들어, 문법 시간에 독해 문제를 풀어도 됩니다.

Q6. 중도 퇴실 했는데 풀었던 문제까지는 성적 주나요?
중도 퇴실은 시험을 포기한 것으로 0점 처리 됩니다.

■ 성적표

G-TELP의 개인성적표는 그 등급의 Mastery(합격) 여부를 표시하는 Overall Proficiency(전체 등급 능숙도)와 Skill Area Score(문법, 청취, 독해 및 어휘 점수) 그리고 Task/Structure Score(각 기능의 세분화된 부분의 점수 및 문제 형태)에 대한 정보를 알려줍니다.

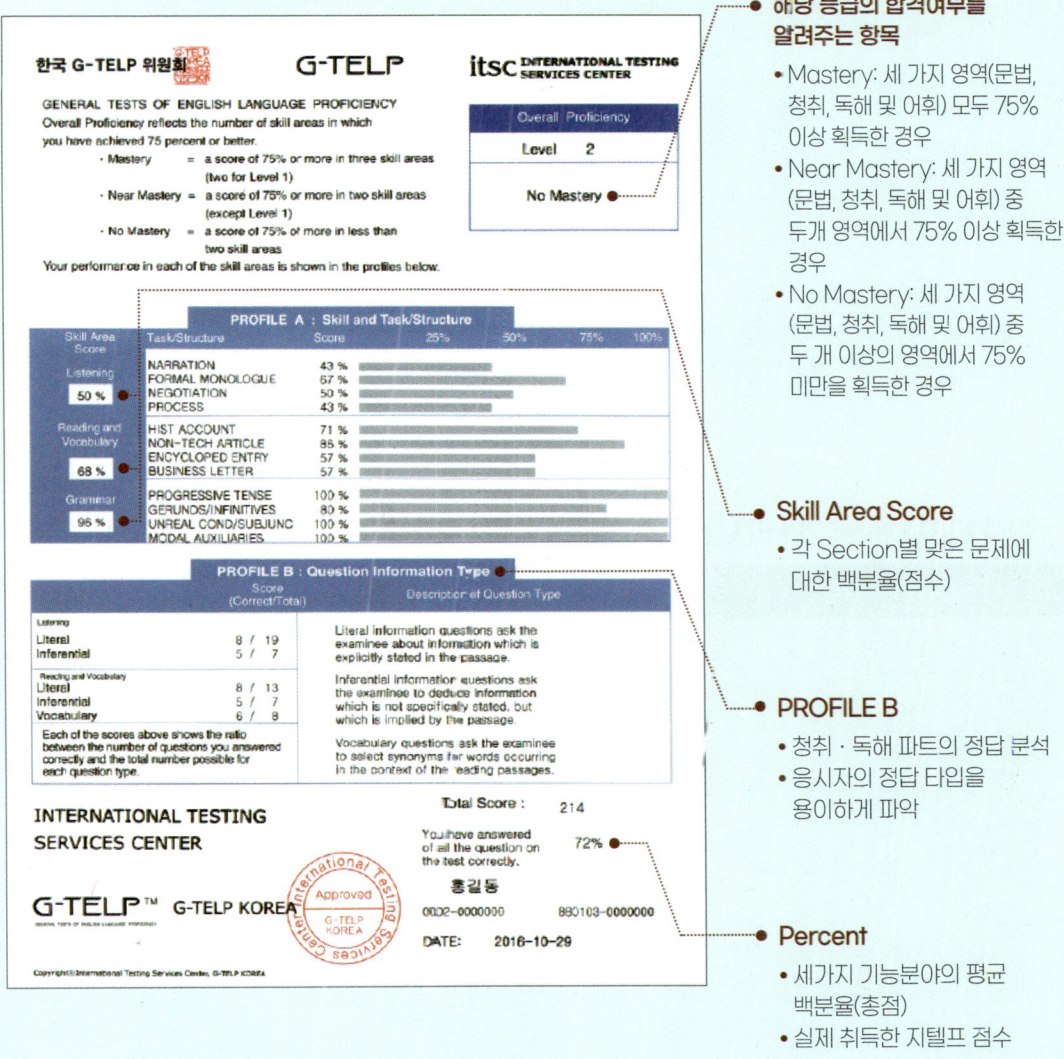

- 해당 등급의 합격여부를 알려주는 항목
  - Mastery: 세 가지 영역(문법, 청취, 독해 및 어휘) 모두 75% 이상 획득한 경우
  - Near Mastery: 세 가지 영역(문법, 청취, 독해 및 어휘) 중 두개 영역에서 75% 이상 획득한 경우
  - No Mastery: 세 가지 영역(문법, 청취, 독해 및 어휘) 중 두 개 이상의 영역에서 75% 미만을 획득한 경우

- Skill Area Score
  - 각 Section별 맞은 문제에 대한 백분율(점수)

- PROFILE B
  - 청취·독해 파트의 정답 분석
  - 응시자의 정답 타입을 용이하게 파악

- Percent
  - 세가지 기능분야의 평균 백분율(총점)
  - 실제 취득한 지텔프 점수

■ Mastery 기준

문법(Grammar), 청취(Listening), 독해 및 어휘(Reading & Vocabulary) 모두 75%이상 획득한 경우, Mastery 한 것으로 인정됨으로 영어 능력을 종합적으로 평가하여 수험자의 정확한 영어 활용 수준을 판단할 수 있습니다.

Section	점수 비율	Mastery 기준
문법	100점 만점	* Mastery: 세 가지 영역(문법, 청취, 독해 및 어휘) 모두 75% 이상 획득한 경우
청취	100점 만점	
독해 및 어휘	100점 만점	* Near Mastery: 세 가지 영역(문법, 청취, 독해 및 어휘) 중 두개 영역에서 75% 이상 획득한 경우
총점	총 300점 만점	
평균	100점 (성적표상 You have answered 100% of all the question in the test correctly 부분)	* No Mastery: 세 가지 영역(문법, 청취, 독해 및 어휘) 중 두 개 이상의 영역에서 75% 미만을 획득한 경우 ** 국내에서는 대개 Level 2시험의 특정 평균 점수 이상을 획득하면 영어 대체 시험 합격점으로 인정

■ G-TELP Level 2와 타시험 점수 대비표

G-TELP 점수	TOEIC 점수	TOEFL(IBT) 점수
99	969	111~112
95	940	106~108
90	903	105
85	867	100
80	830	94~95
75	793	88~89
70	757	83
65	713	76
60	676	72~73
50	603	64

지텔프 퀵 스타터 - 독해 편

■ G-TELP Level 2와 타시험 점수 대비표

활용 기관 및 시험	G-TELP Level 2 점수 (점)	TOEIC 점수 (점)
군무원	9급 32 7급 47 5급 65	9급 470 7급 570 5급 700
호텔서비스사	39	490
경찰공무원 영어 시험 대체 * 2022년 시행 예정	43	550
소방 간부 후보생	50	625
경찰 간부 후보생	50	625
5급 공채	65	700
7급 공채	65	700
입법 고시(국회)	65	700
법원행정고시(법원)	65	700
세무사	65	700
공인노무사	65	700
감정평가사	65	700
공인회계사	65	700
호텔관리사	66	700
카투사	73	780
관광통역안내사	74	760
7급(외무영사직렬)	77	790
변리사	77	775
호텔 경영사	79	800
외교관 후보자	88	870

정기 시험 프로세스

■ 시험접수

- 월 2회 일요일 격주로 시행
  (*정기 시험의 시행 일정, 지역, 고사장, 응시료는 변동될 수 있으므로 한국지텔프 홈페이지에서 해당 정보 확인)
- www.g-telp.co.kr에서 인터넷 접수 또는 지정 접수처에 직접 방문하여 접수
- 응시료(2020년 기준) : 정기접수기간 금액 / 추가접수기간 금액
  - 일   반 : 60,300원 / 64,700원
  - 졸 업 인 증 : 41,600원 / 46,000원
  - 군 인 할 인 : 30,200원 / 34,600원
  - 한 국 장 학 재 단 : 43,100원 / 47,500원
  - 기 초 생 활 수 급 자 : 20,000원 / 22,000원 (정상가 결제 후 환급)
  - 중 · 고 등 학 생 : 30,000원 / 30,000원 (정상가 결제 후 환급, 정기 접수/추가 접수 금액 동일)
- 결제 방법 : 신용카드, 온라인 계좌이체, 무통장 입금, 페이코 등 중에서 선택
- 환불 :
  - 접수 기간 내 또는 접수(결제)일 포함 8일 이내 → 전액 환불
  - 접수 기간 만료~ 당 회차 시험 수험번호 공지 전일 → 50% 환불
  - 수험번호 공지일~시험 시행 전 수요일 → 30% 환불

■ 시험 응시

- 입실가능시간 : 13시20분~14시50분 (* 14시50분 입실 통제 후 절대 입실 불가)
- 오리엔테이션 시작 시간 : 14시25분
- 고사장 입구에서 고사장 확인, 고사장에서는 지정자리에서 응시
- 규정 신분증, 필기도구, 아날로그 손목시계 이외의 개인 소지품 소지는 불허
  - 소지품 및 전원을 끈 전자기기는 가방에 넣어 교실 앞에 제출
  - 규정 신분증: 주민등록증, 여권(기간 만료 전인 여권), 운전면허증, 장애인등록증(주민등록번호 포함), 군신분증(군인), 중고생인 경우 학생증, 외국인인 경우 여권, 외국인등록증 (단, 대학생의 경우 학생증 불허)
  - 허용 필기도구: 컴퓨터용 사인펜, 수정 테이프 (단, 수정액은 사용 불가)

■ 성적 확인

- 성적 결과 통보 : 온라인 성적 확인 → 응시일로부터 5일 이내
  원본 성적표 발송 → 온라인 출력은 확인 직후부터/우편 발송은 성적 발표 후 다음주 화요일 일반 우편으로 발송
- 성적표 수령 방법 : 온라인 직접 출력 또는 우편으로 수령 (* 최초 1회 발급은 무료)
- 성적 유효 기간 : 응시일을 기준으로 만 2년간 유효

시험 전 확인하기!

시험장으로 가기 전 준비물 Check!

☐ 규정 신분증　☐ 컴퓨터용 사인펜　☐ 수정 테이프　☐ 아날로그 시계

OMR 작성법 예습하기!

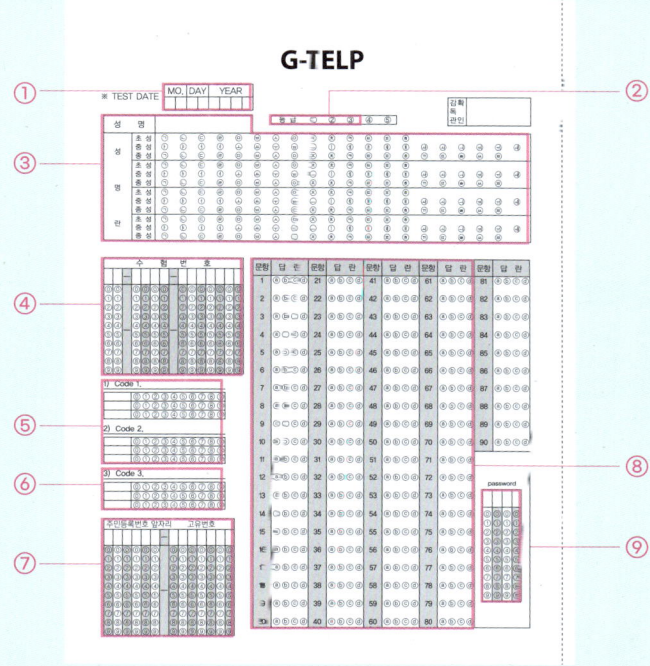

1. TEST DATE란에 월, 일, 년 순으로 기재합니다.
2. 등급은 ②에 마킹합니다.
3. 성명란에 초성, 중성, 종성에 맞게 기재합니다.
4. 수험번호는 책상 위에 비치된 이름표를 참고하여 기재합니다.
5. Code 1과 Code 2는 OMR카드 뒷면에서 해당하는 코드를 찾아 마킹합니다.
   (대학생이 아닌 일반인의 경우 Code 1은 098, Code 2는 090을 기재하시면 됩니다.)
6. Code 3은 수험번호 마지막 7자리 숫자의 앞 3자리 숫자를 마킹합니다.
7. 개인 정보 보호를 위해 주민등록번호는 앞자리만 마킹한 후, 뒷자리는 이름표에 기재된 고유번호로 마킹합니다.
8. 답안지는 총 90번까지 있으니 Level 2 시험은 80번 까지 이므로 80번 까지만 마킹하면 됩니다.
9. Password는 인터넷 성적 확인 시 필요한 번호로 네 자리 숫자이며, 마킹 후 반드시 기억하도록 합니다.

*** 시험 시간에는 별도의 답안지 마킹 시간이 주어지지 않습니다 ***

학습 가이드라인

학습 플랜

■ 5일 완성 학습플랜

Day 1	Day 2	Day 3	Day 4	Day 5
Part 1. Biography Article + 핵심 보카 1~100	Part 2 Magazine Article + 핵심 보카 101~200	Part 3 Encyclopedia Article + 핵심 보카 201~300	Part 4 Business or Formal Letter + 핵심 보카 301~400	실전 모의고사 1, 2 + 핵심 보카 401~500 + 시크릿 노트G

■ 10일 완성 학습플랜

Day 1	Day 2	Day 3	Day 4	Day 5
Part 1. Biography Article (공략 포인트) + 핵심 보카 1~50	Part 1. Biography Article (Mini Test) + 핵심 보카 51~100	Part 2 Magazine Article (공략 포인트) + 핵심 보카 101~150	Part 2 Magazine Article (Mini Test) + 핵심 보카 151~200	Part 3 Encyclopedia Article (공략 포인트) + 핵심 보카 201~250
Day 6	**Day 7**	**Day 8**	**Day 9**	**Day 10**
Part 3 Encyclopedia Article (Mini Test) + 핵심 보카 251~300	Part 4 Business or Formal Letter (공략 포인트) + 핵심 보카 301~350	Part 4 Business or Formal Letter (Mini Test) + 핵심 보카 351~400	실전 모의고사 1 + 핵심 보카 401~450 + 시크릿 노트G	실전 모의고사 2 + 핵심 보카 451~500 + 시크릿 노트G

학습 체크

Part 1. Biography Article	문제집	해설집	학습체크
필수 공략 포인트	p. 26		☐
기초 공략 포인트	p. 28		☐
심화 공략 포인트	p. 34		☐
Mini Test	p. 46	p. 4	☐
Vocabulary	p. 52		☐

Part 2. Magazine Article	문제집	해설집	학습체크
필수 공략 포인트	p. 58		☐
기초 공략 포인트	p. 60		☐
심화 공략 포인트	p. 65		☐
Mini Test	p. 76	p. 13	☐
Vocabulary	p. 82		☐

Part 3. Encyclopedia Article	문제집	해설집	학습체크
필수 공략 포인트	p. 90		☐
기초 공략 포인트	p. 92		☐
심화 공략 포인트	p. 98		☐
Mini Test	p. 110	p. 22	☐
Vocabulary	p. 116		☐

Part 4. Business or Formal Letter	문제집	해설집	학습체크
필수 공략 포인트	p. 124		☐
기초 공략 포인트	p. 126		☐
심화 공략 포인트	p. 132		☐
Mini Test	p. 142	p. 31	☐
Vocabulary	p. 148		☐

CHAPHER

지텔프 독해 스타터

General Tests of English Language Proficiency

독해

PART 1. Biography Article

PART 2. Magazine Article

PART 3. Encyclopedia Article

PART 4. Business or Formal Letter

PART 1

지텔프 독해 스타터

General Tests of English Language Proficiency

Biography
Article

PART 01 Biography Article

- Part 1은 역사적 인물의 연대기를 다루며 그 인물의 대표 특징, 역사적 업적, 진로 선택 계기, 사후 평가 등이 출제됩니다.
- 시기, 주요 사건, 주변인의 이름, 연대 등을 중심으로 지문을 읽으면 문제의 단서를 보다 쉽게 찾을 수 있습니다.
- 문제를 먼저 읽어 주요 키워드를 체크한 뒤, 지문에서 해당 키워드를 확인하는 것이 효과적입니다.

필수 공략 포인트

Part 1에서는 역사적 인물의 연대기에 따른 지문의 흐름과 문제 패턴을 파악해야 합니다.

지문의 흐름 (단락 구성)

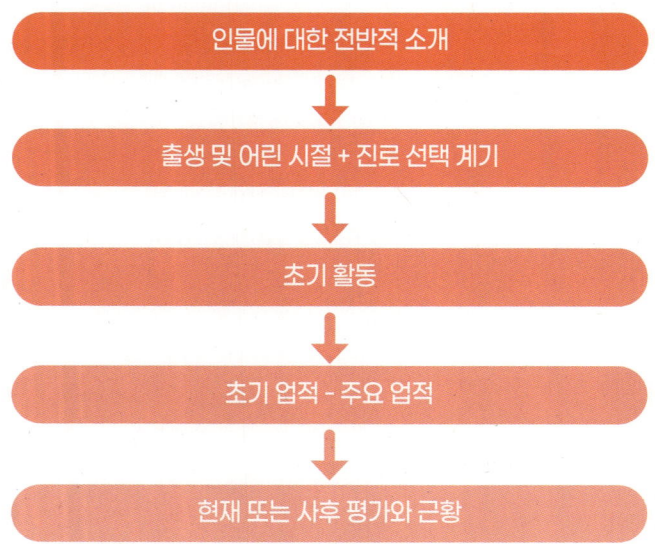

 **문제 패턴**

단락 구성 순서	단락별 대표 유형	대표 문제 패턴
인물 소개	유명한 이유	be noted for be famous for be best known for be recognized for
출생 및 어린 시절	분야에 대한 관심 계기 또는 진로 선택 시기	what inspired what made what contributed what motivated when first when start
초기 업적	세부 사항 세부 사항/추론	what why when true/not true how
주요 업적	세부 사항	
근황 또는 평가	평가 유추	what said how spend days what do

기초 공략 포인트

① Part 1의 첫 번째 문제는 주로 인물이 유명한 이유를 묻습니다.
　→ 첫 번째 문제 확인 후, 첫 번째 단락에서 이 인물이 갖는 역사상 의미 또는 가장 대표적인 이미지를 확인합니다.

　주인공은 무엇으로 가장 잘 알려져 있는가?

② 어린 시절, 인물이 전문 분야에 관심을 갖게 된 계기 또는 시기를 묻습니다.
　→ 두 번째 단락에서 인물의 어린 시절 가정환경이나 흥미를 불러 일으킨 계기, 습관, 전후 사건 등을 확인합니다.

　무엇이 주인공에게 그 분야에 대한 흥미를 일으켰는가?
　주인공은 언제 그 일을 시작했는가?

 패러프레이징 패턴

1. 유명한 이유
(잘 알려져 있다, ~로 유명하다, ~로 인정받다)

be noted for	be best known for
be famous for	be recognized for/as

- James Dean **was recognized for** his sensitive performances as an actor.
  제임스 딘은 배우로서 그의 감성 있는 연기**로 인정받았다**.

- Goethe **is well known as** a great writer who brought German literature to a wider audience.
  괴테는 독일 문학을 일반적인 독자에게 가져온 위대한 작가**로 잘 알려져 있다**.

- Charles Schultz **is famous for** the comic strip *Peanuts*.
  찰스 슐츠는 연재만화 「Peanuts」**로 유명하다**.

2-1. 어린 시절 계기
(동기 부여, 흥미, 고무, 소개)

motivate	contribute
inspire	introduce
arouse one's interest	

- Visiting Paris <u>aroused his interest</u> in French literature for the first time.
  파리 방문은 처음으로 프랑스 문학에 대한 <u>그의 관심을 불러일으켰다</u>.

- The newspaper comics he enjoyed <u>inspired him to draw</u> Peanuts.
  그가 즐겨보던 신문 연재 만화는 그가 「Peanuts」를 <u>그리도록 영감을 주었다</u>.

2-2. 첫 시기
(언제 시작했는지, 언제가 처음인지)

when	before
start	later
first	after
at the age of	since

- He <u>started drawing</u> Peanuts in 1950 <u>after serializing</u> Li'l Folks.
  그는 <u>「릴 포크스」를 연재한 뒤</u> 1950년부터 「Peanuts」를 <u>그리기 시작했다</u>.

- <u>At the age of three,</u> he spoke for the first time.
  <u>세 살 때</u>, 그는 처음으로 말을 했다.

 Exercise

Tim Burton

Tim Burton is an American film director, illustrator, and producer. He is the eighth highest-grossing director of all time. He is best known for his dark-humored fantasy films, like *Beetlejuice* (1988), and blockbusters, like *Batman* (1989). Burton's works are usually a combination of animation and horror.

Timothy Walter Burton was born on August 25, 1958, in Burbank, California. His parents are Jean Burton, a shop owner, and William "Bill" Burton, a former baseball player and an employee at the city's parks and recreation department. When Burton was young, he was amused watching Roger Corman's horror films, and that inspired him to make his own short films. He also spent time drawing characters during his childhood. He then studied character animation at the California Institute of the Arts.

53. What is Tim Burton most famous for?
    (a) his immense wealth
    (b) his humorous yet disturbing films
    (c) being a great movie illustrator
    (d) being the most successful U.S. director

54. How did Burton become interested in making films?
    (a) by seeing horror films when he was a child
    (b) by studying animation courses in college
    (c) by illustrating his own original characters
    (d) by working for a movie production company

 단서

Tim Burton

Tim Burton is an American film director, illustrator, and producer. He is the eighth highest-grossing director of all time. 53) **He is best known for his dark-humored fantasy films,** like *Beetlejuice* (1988), and blockbusters, like *Batman* (1989). Burton's works are usually a combination of animation and horror.

Timothy Walter Burton was born on August 25, 1958, in Burbank, California. His parents are Jean Burton, a shop owner, and William "Bill" Burton, a former baseball player and an employee at the city's parks and recreation department. 54) **When Burton was young, he was amused watching Roger Corman's horror films, and that inspired him to make his own short films.** He also spent time drawing characters during his childhood. He then studied character animation at the California Institute of the Arts.

팀 버튼

팀 버튼은 미국 영화 감독이자, 일러스트레이터이며, 제작자이다. 그는 역대 8번째로 높은 수익을 올린 감독이다. 53) 그는 「비틀쥬스」(1988)와 같은 어두운 유머의 공상 과학 영화와 「배트맨」(1989)과 같은 블록버스터로 가장 잘 알려져 있다. 버튼의 작품들은 일반적으로 애니메이션과 호러의 조합이다.

티모시 월터 버튼은 1958년 8월 25일 캘리포니아 주 버뱅크에서 태어났다. 그의 부모는 상점 주인인 진 버튼과 전직 야구 선수이자 도시 공원 및 유락 시설 관리부 직원인 윌리엄 "빌" 버튼이다. 54) 버튼이 어렸을 때, 그는 로저 코먼의 공포 영화를 보는 것을 즐겼고, 그것이 그가 단편 영화를 만들도록 영감을 주었다. 그는 또한 어린 시절에 캐릭터를 그리며 시간을 보냈다. 그런 다음 캘리포니아 예술 대학에서 캐릭터 애니메이션을 공부했다.

 단어

film director n. 영화감독
producer n. 제작자
be best known for v. ~로 가장 잘 알려져 있다
shop owner n. 점주
employee n. 고용인, 종업원
amuse v. 즐겁게 하다, 재미있게 하다
spend time v. 시간을 보내다

illustrator n. 일러스트레이터, 삽화가
highest-grossing adj. 높은 수익을 올린
combination n. 조합, 결합, 연합
former adj. 이전의
department n. 부서
inspire v. 영감을 주다

📝 문제풀이

53. What is Tim Burton **most famous for**?

    (a) his immense wealth
    (b) his humorous yet disturbing films
    (c) being a great movie illustrator
    (d) being the most successful U.S. director

53. 팀 버튼은 무엇으로 **가장 유명한**가?

    (a) 그의 막대한 부
    (b) 그의 유머러스하지만 충격적인 영화들
    (c) 대단한 영화 일러스트레이터가 된 것
    (d) 가장 성공한 미국의 감독이 된 것

 Tip! 문제의 most famous for을 확인한 뒤 첫 단락에서 동일 표현(best known for)을 찾는다.

 해설

그가 「비틀쥬스」와 같은 어두운 유머의 공상과학 영화와 「배트맨」과 같은 블록버스터로 가장 잘 알려져 있다는 설명을 통해 그가 유머러스하지만 충격적인 영화로 유명하다는 것을 알 수 있다. 따라서 **(b) his humorous yet disturbing films**가 정답이다.

▸ paraphrasing point

dark-humored fantasy films → humorous yet disturbing films

단어 immense wealth n. 막대한 부, 거대한 부   disturbing adj. 충격적인, 불안감을 주는
successful adj. (어떤 일에) 성공한, 성공적인

54. How did Burton become **interested in making films**?

   (a) by **seeing horror films** when he was a child
   (b) by studying animation courses in college
   (c) by illustrating his own original characters
   (d) by working for a movie production company

54. 버튼은 어떻게 영화 제작에 흥미를 갖게 되었나?

   (a) 그가 어렸을 때 공포 영화를 봄으로써
   (b) 대학에서 애니메이션을 전공함으로써
   (c) 자신의 독창적인 캐릭터를 그림으로써
   (d) 영화 제작사에서 일함으로써

 문제의 become interested를 확인하고 두 번째 단락에서 대응 표현 amused와 inspired를 찾아 읽는다.

그가 어렸을 때 로저 코먼의 공포 영화를 즐겨봤고 그것이 그에게 단편 영화에 대한 영감을 주었다는 내용을 통해 버튼이 영화 제작에 흥미를 느낀 것은 어렸을 때 공포 영화를 봤기 때문이라는 것을 알 수 있다. 따라서 **(a) by seeing horror films when he was a child**가 정답이다.

▶ paraphrasing point

watching Roger Corman's horror films → seeing horror films

단어 course n. 과목, 강의, 강좌   production company n. 제작사

 **심화 공략 포인트**

세부 내용 문제, true/not true 문제, 추론, 어휘 문제 등에 도전하여 **paraphrasing(바꿔 쓰기)과 scanning(찾아 읽기)**에 익숙해지도록 훈련해야 합니다.

고유명사나 숫자 등은 바꿔 쓸 수 없는 부분이므로 이 단서를 중심으로 scanning하도록 합니다.

① 세부 사항 문제

> What did~?
> How was~?
> What happened~?
> How did~?
> ➡ 문제의 동사를 확인한 뒤 단락의 위치를 파악합니다.

어린시절에 대한 문제면 두 번째 단락, 초기 활동 및 초기 업적이면 세 번째 단락, 주요 업적이나 부연 상황이면 네 번째 단락에 주로 단서가 분포되어 있습니다.

세부 사항에 관련된 문제는 주로 주요 사건의 명칭이나 연도, 주변인의 이름 등이 등장하므로 비교적 찾아 읽기 쉽습니다.

Example

Mother Teresa taught geography at the Convent of Maria's affiliated school. But **in 1946, she decided to leave the convent** when she heard a divine voice asking her to go out of the congregation and to take care of the poor Indians suffering in the streets.	테레사 수녀는 성 마리아 수녀원의 부속 학교에서 지리학을 가르쳤다. 그러나 **1946년, 그녀는** 수도회를 나가 거리에서 고통받는 인도의 가난한 사람들을 돌보라는 신의 목소리를 들었을 때 **수녀원을 떠나기로 결심했다**.

Q. What happened to Mother Teresa **in 1946**?

(a) She suffered because of poverty.
(b) She entered the convent of Maria.
(c) She started teaching geography.
(d) She decided to leave her congregation.

Q. 1946년에 테레사 수녀에게 무슨 일이 일어났는가?

(a) 그녀는 가난 때문에 고통받았다.
(b) 그녀는 성 마리아 수녀원에 입소했다.
(c) 그녀가 지리학을 가르치기 시작했다.
(d) 그녀는 수녀원을 떠나기로 결심했다.

 **Tip!** 문제의 1946년을 확인하고 지문의 1946을 찾아 읽는다.

해설

1946년 기차 안에서 신의 목소리를 듣고 수녀원을 떠나기로 결심했다는 내용을 통해 (d) She decided to leave her congregation 가 정답임을 알 수 있다.

단어
geography n. 지리학	convent n. 수녀원
affiliated adj. 부속의, 산하의, 소속된	decide v. 결정하다
divine adj. 신의, 신성의	congregation n. 수도회
take care of v. ~을 돌보다, ~의 책임을 지다	suffer v. (질병·고통·슬픔·결핍 등에) 시달리다, 고통받다

② True or Not True 문제

> **Which ~ not describe?**
> **Which ~ done?**
> **Which ~ true?**
> **Which ~ happen?**
> ➜ 문제와 보기를 먼저 확인하고, 언급된 사건을 키워드로 단락을 대조하며 보기를 소거해 나가야 합니다.

Example

The Pulitzer Prize, recognized as **(b) one of the most prestigious awards in the world**, is given **(a) to journalists and cultural figures in the United States.** (c) The prize is awarded by the Pulitzer Prize Committee of Columbia University for the most outstanding achievements in the United States that year, (d) and the committee pays $10,000 to the winner.

(b) 세계에서 가장 권위있는 상 중 하나로 인정받는 풀리처상은 (a) 미국 내 언론 및 문화인들에게 주어진다. (c) 상은 컬럼비아 대학의 풀리처상 위원회로부터 그 해 미국에서 가장 뛰어난 업적을 이룬 인물에게 수여되고, (d) 위원회는 수상자에게 1만달러를 지급한다.

Q. **Which** does **NOT** describe the Pulitzer Prize?

(a) It is awarded to outstanding cultural figures around the world.
(b) It is the most prestigious cultural award in the world.
(c) The Pulitzer Prize Committee of Columbia University determines the winners.
(d) The winner is paid $10,000.

Q. 퓰리처 상을 묘사하지 않는 것은 무엇인가?

(a) 전세계의 뛰어난 문화인들에게 수여된다.
(b) 세계에서 가장 권위있는 문화 상이다.
(c) 컬럼비아 대학의 퓰리처상 위원회가 수상자를 결정한다.
(d) 수상자는 1만달러를 지급 받는다.

 문제를 읽고 키워드인 'Pulitzer'와 'not describe'를 확인하고 단락에서 보기에 해당되는 것들을 소거해 나간다.

퓰리처 상은 미국 내 언론 및 문화인들에게 수여되는 상이라는 내용을 통해 전세계의 뛰어난 문화인들에게 수여된다는 것은 사실이 아님을 알 수 있다. 따라서 (a) It is awarded to outstanding cultural figures around the world가 정답이다.

단어
journalist n. 언론인, 저널리스트, (신문·방송·잡지사의) 기자
figure n. 인물 v. 중요하다
prestigious adj. 권위있는, 명망 있는, 일류의
achievement n. 성과, 성취, 달성, 업적
cultural adj. 문화의, 문화와 관련된
recognized adj. 인정된, 알려진
outstanding adj. 뛰어난, 탁월한

③ 추론/유추 문제

Based on the article~
According to the article~
Why most likely~
What most likely~
probably~

→ 추론/ 유추 문제를 풀기 위해서는 단락을 읽고, 종합적으로 사고를 해야합니다.
본문에서 정답의 직접적인 단서를 찾기 어려우므로, 글 전체 내용과 흐름에 대한 이해가 요구됩니다.
문제에서 언급하는 키워드를 찾아 그 주변부를 읽고 답을 유추해야 합니다.

Example

Although she was the best player in the world, **she wasn't free from her contract with the club**. Years later, she **had to return** to her original club, leaving better opportunities behind.	비록 그녀는 세계 최고의 선수였지만, **구단과의 계약으로부터 자유롭지 못했다**. 몇 년 뒤, 그녀는 더 좋은 기회를 뒤로 한 채, 원래의 구단으로 **돌아와야 했다**.

Q. **Why** most likely did she **return** to the original club?

(a) because she was a patriot
(b) because she wanted to meet more fans
(c) because of her contract issues with the club
(d) because she had to compete in the Olympics

Q. 그녀는 왜 원래의 구단으로 돌아왔는가?

(a) 그녀가 애국자였기 때문에
(b) 그녀는 더 많은 팬들을 만나고 싶었기 때문에
(c) 구단과의 그녀의 계약 문제 때문에
(d) 그녀는 올림픽에 출전해야 했기 때문에

 **Tip!** 문제의 사건이 일어날 수밖에 없었던 환경을 묘사하는 부분을 찾는다.

 해설

그녀가 구단과의 계약으로부터 자유롭지 못했다는 단서를 통해 정답이 (c) because of her contract issues with the club임을 알 수 있다.

단어	contract n. 계약	original adj. 원래의, 본래의
	club n. 구단	leave A behind v. A를 두고 가다, 뒤로 하다
	patriot n. 애국자	compete v. 출전하다, 참가하다

④ 어휘

> **In the context of the passage, A means _____.**
>
> → Part 1뿐 아니라 Part 2, Part 3, Part 4에 각각 2문제씩 등장합니다.
> 사전적 의미 보다는 아니라 문맥적 의미를 유추하는 문제로, 평소 유의어 학습을 충분히 해 두는 것이 좋습니다.

 **Exercise**

Tim Burton

Tim Burton is an American film director, illustrator, and producer. He is the eighth highest-grossing director of all time. He is best known for his dark-humored fantasy films, like *Beetlejuice* (1988), and blockbusters, like *Batman* (1989). Burton's works are usually a combination of animation and horror.

Timothy Walter Burton was born on August 25, 1958, in Burbank, California. His parents are Jean Burton, a shop owner, and William "Bill" Burton, a former baseball player and an employee at the city's parks and recreation department. When Burton was young, he was amused watching Roger Corman's horror films, and that inspired him to make his own short films. He also spent time drawing characters during his childhood. He then studied character animation at the California Institute of the Arts.

After graduating, Burton became an apprentice at Walt Disney Studios. He assisted in creating animations and concept art while he was there. In 1982, Burton made *Vincent*, a six-minute animated film about a seven-year-old boy who wants to be like actor Vincent Price, Burton's childhood idol. The film was a success, winning several awards. In 1984, Burton made *Frankenweenie*, a unique version of the Frankenstein story. However, the film went unreleased until 1992 because it was seen by the company as too scary for children. Moreover, after the completion of the film, Burton was let go by Disney because his works did not fit the company.

It was in 1985 when Burton got his first shot at directing a full-length film. He was commissioned to direct *Pee-wee's Great Adventure*, and the film's success led him to direct more full-length feature films. With the success of *Beetlejuice* in 1988, he finally became an established director, and in 1989, Warner Bros. entrusted him with directing *Batman*. It earned $100 million in its first 10 days of showing, making it the fifth-highest grossing film in history at that time. The film also received several nominations and awards.

Burton continued to make films with his signature gothic, quirky style from then on. Most notably, these include *Edward Scissorhands* (1990), one of his most emotional and artistic films; *Batman Returns* (1992), the sequel to his phenomenal *Batman*; and *Charlie and the Chocolate Factory* (2005), a musical fantasy-comedy. Burton is also an accomplished artist. His paintings and drawings have been exhibited in many museums around the world.

55. What is Burton's movie, *Vincent*, all about?

   (a) It is a retelling of the original Frankenstein story.
   (b) It is based on Burton's own childhood.
   (c) It is about a kid who dreams of being like Burton's hero.
   (d) It is a film about a Frankenstein-like child.

56. Why most likely did Disney decide to fire Burton?

   (a) He didn't have enough animation skills.
   (b) He could only make short animated films.
   (c) His films were too unexciting for children.
   (d) His films were inappropriate for Disney's audience.

57. According to the article, which describes the movie *Batman Returns*?

   (a) It was a follow-up to a hit movie.
   (b) It is one of his most touching movies.
   (c) It was his first full-length movie.
   (d) It was a record-breaking movie.

58. In the context of the passage, fit means _____.

   (a) differ
   (b) adapt
   (c) set
   (d) suit

59. In the context of the passage, accomplished means _____.

   (a) sharp
   (b) skillful
   (c) failed
   (d) clever

 단서

Tim Burton

Tim Burton is an American film director, illustrator, and producer. He is the eighth highest-grossing director of all time. 53) **He is best known for his dark-humored fantasy films,** like *Beetlejuice* (1988), and blockbusters, like *Batman* (1989). Burton's works are usually a combination of animation and horror.

Timothy Walter Burton was born on August 25, 1958, in Burbank, California. His parents are Jean Burton, a shop owner, and William "Bill" Burton, a former baseball player and an employee at the city's parks and recreation department. 54) **When Burton was young, he was amused watching Roger Corman's horror films, and that inspired him to make his own short films.** He also spent time drawing characters during his childhood. He then studied character animation at the California Institute of the Arts.

After graduating, Burton became an apprentice at Walt Disney Studios. He assisted in creating animations and concept art while he was there. In 1982, 55) **Burton made Vincent, a six-minute animated film about a seven-year-old boy who wants to be like actor Vincent Price,** Burton's childhood **idol**. The film was a success, winning several awards. In 1984, Burton made *Frankenweenie*, a unique version of the Frankenstein story. However, the film went unreleased until 1992 because it was seen by the company as too scary for children. Moreover, after the completion of the film, 56) **Burton was let go by Disney because his works did not** 58) **fit the company**.

팀 버튼

팀 버튼은 미국 영화 감독이자, 일러스트레이터이며, 제작자이다. 그는 역대 8번째로 높은 수익을 올린 감독이다. 53) 그는 「비틀쥬스」(1988)와 같은 어두운 유머의 공상과학 영화와 「배트맨」(1989)과 같은 블록버스터로 가장 잘 알려져 있다. 버튼의 작품들은 일반적으로 애니메이션과 호러의 조합이다.

티모시 월터 버튼은 1958년 8월 25일 캘리포니아 주 버뱅크에서 태어났다. 그의 부모는 상점 주인인 진 버튼과 전직 야구 선수이자 도시 공원 및 유락 시설 관리부 직원인 윌리엄 "빌" 버튼이다. 54) 버튼이 어렸을 때, 그는 로저 코먼의 공포 영화를 보는 것을 즐겼고, 그것이 그가 단편 영화를 만들도록 영감을 주었다. 그는 또한 어린 시절에 캐릭터를 그리며 시간을 보냈다. 그런 다음 캘리포니아 예술 대학에서 캐릭터 애니메이션을 공부했다.

졸업 후, 버튼은 월트 디즈니 스튜디오에서 견습생이 되었다. 그는 그곳에 있는 동안 애니메이션과 컨셉 아트 제작을 도왔다. 55) 1982년 버튼은 그의 어린 시절 우상인 배우 빈센트 프라이스처럼 되고 싶어하는 7살 소년에 관한 6분짜리 애니메이션 영화 「빈센트」를 만들었다. 이 영화는 여러 상을 수상하며 성공했다. 1984년 버튼은 프랑켄슈타인 이야기의 독특한 버전인 「프랑켄위니」를 만들었다. 그러나, 이 영화는 회사에 의해 아이들에게 너무 무서운 것으로 보여졌기 때문에, 1992년까지 개봉되지 않았다. 게다가 영화를 완성한 후, 56) 버튼은 그의 작품이 회사에 58) 맞지 않는다는 이유로 디즈니에서 쫓겨났다.

It was in 1985 when Burton got his first shot at directing a full-length film. He was commissioned to direct *Pee-wee's Great Adventure*, and the film's success led him to direct more full-length feature films. With the success of *Beetlejuice* in 1988, he finally became an established director, and in 1989, Warner Bros. entrusted him with directing *Batman*. It earned $100 million in its first 10 days of showing, making it the fifth-highest grossing film in history at that time. The film also received several nominations and awards.

Burton continued to make films with his signature gothic, quirky style from then on. Most notably, these include *Edward Scissorhands* (1990), one of his most emotional and artistic films; 57) **Batman Returns (1992), the sequel to his phenomenal Batman;** and *Charlie and the Chocolate Factory* (2005), a musical fantasy-comedy. Burton is also an 59) **accomplished** artist. His paintings and drawings have been exhibited in many museums around the world.

단어

apprentice n. 견습생
success n. 성공, 성과
unique adj. 독특한, 특이한, 특별한
completion n. 완성
shot n. 촬영, 시도
commission v. 맡기다, 위임하다, 주문하다
entrust (A with B) v. (A에게 B를) 맡기다, 위임하다
receive v. 받다
continue v. 계속하다, 계속되다
quirky adj. 기이한, 별난
sequel n. (책·영화·연극 등의) 속편
accomplished adj. 기량이 뛰어난, 재주가 많은

assist v. 돕다, 거들다
award n. 상
unreleased adj. 미개봉의, 공개되지 않은
fit v. 알맞다, 적합하다
full-length film n. 장편영화
established adj. 인정받는, 존경받는
earn v. 돈을 벌다, 수익을 올리다
nomination n. 추천, 지명
signature n. 특징
emotional adj. 감정적인, 정서의
phenomenal adj. 경이로운
exhibit v. 전시하다

문제풀이

55. What is Burton's movie, *Vincent*, all about?

(a) It is a retelling of the original Frankenstein story.
(b) It is based on Burton's own childhood.
(c) It is about a kid who dreams of being like Burton's hero.
(d) It is a film about a Frankenstein-like child.

55. 버튼의 영화 「빈센트」는 무엇에 관한 내용인가?

(a) 원래의 프랑켄슈타인을 각색한 것이다.
(b) 버튼 자신의 어린 시절에 기초한다.
(c) 버튼의 영웅처럼 되기를 꿈꾸는 아이에 관한 것이다.
(d) 프랑켄슈타인과 같은 아이에 관한 영화이다.

해설

영화 「빈센트」는 6분짜리 애니메이션 영화로, 버튼의 어린 시절 우상이었던 빈센트 프라이스처럼 되고 싶어하는 7살 소년에 관한 영화라는 내용을 통해 (c) It is about a kid who dreams of being like Burton's hero가 정답임을 알 수 있다.

paraphrasing point

idol → hero

단어 original adj. 원래의, 본래의   childhood n. 어린 시절

---

56. Why most likely did Disney decide to fire Burton?

(a) He didn't have enough animation skills.
(b) He could only make short animated films.
(c) His films were too unexciting for children.
(d) His films were inappropriate for Disney's audience.

56. 왜 디즈니는 버튼을 해고하기로 결정했을 것 같은가?

(a) 그가 충분한 애니메이션 기술을 갖고 있지 않아서
(b) 그가 단편 애니메이션 영화만 만들 수 있어서
(c) 그의 영화가 어린이들에게 너무 흥미롭지 않아서
(d) 그의 영화가 디즈니의 관객들에게 부적절해서

버튼의 작품들이 회사에 맞지 않는다는 이유로 디즈니에서 쫓겨났다는 언급을 통해 디즈니사의 관객들에게 부적절하다는 것이 해고 이유임을 알 수 있다. 따라서 **(d) His films were inappropriate for Disney's audience**가 정답이다.

paraphrasing point

not fit → inappropriate

let go → fire

단어 **unexciting** adj. 흥미롭지 않은, 재미있지 않은, 따분한   **inappropriate** adj. 부적절한, 부적합한
audience n. 관객, 청중

---

57. According to the article, which describes the movie *Batman Returns*?

(a) It was a follow-up to a hit movie.
(b) It is one of his most touching movies.
(c) It was his first full-length movie.
(d) It was a record-breaking movie.

57. 글에 따르면, 영화 「배트맨 리턴즈」를 묘사한 것은 무엇인가?

(a) 히트작의 속편이었다.
(b) 그의 가장 감동적인 영화 중 하나다.
(c) 그의 첫 장편 영화였다.
(d) 기록을 깬 영화였다.

「배트맨 리턴즈」가 경이로운 「배트맨」의 속편이라고 언급했으므로 **(a) It was a follow-up to a hit movie**가 정답임을 알 수 있다.

paraphrasing point

sequel → follow-up

단어 **follow-up** n. 후속편   **touching** adj. 감동적인   **record-breaking** adj. 기록을 깨는

58. In the context of the passage, fit means _____.

(a) differ
(b) adapt
(c) set
(d) suit

58. 글의 문맥에 따르면, fit은 _____를 의미한다.

(a) 다르다
(b) 적응하다
(c) 자리잡다
(d) 어울리다

> 해설

문맥상 버튼이 회사에 '맞지 않는다'는 이유로 쫓겨났다는 내용을 통해 fit이 '**어울리다, 알맞다**'의 의미임을 알 수 있다. 따라서 **(d) suit**가 정답이다.

59. In the context of the passage, accomplished means _____.

(a) sharp
(b) skillful
(c) failed
(d) clever

59. 글의 문맥에 따르면, accomplished는 _____를 의미한다.

(a) 예리한
(b) 뛰어난
(c) 실패한
(d) 영리한

> 해설

그의 그림들이 전 세계의 많은 박물관에서 전시되고 있다는 것으로 미루어 보아 버튼을 '**뛰어난**' 예술가라고 표현한 것임을 알 수 있다. 따라서 **(b) skillful**이 정답이다.

MINI TEST

PART 1. Read the following biography article and answer the questions. The underlined word in the article is for a vocabulary question.

NICK DRAKE

Nick Drake was an English folk singer who released three albums before dying tragically at the age of 26. Although his music received little attention during his lifetime, he gradually became regarded as an influential figure to other musicians in the decades following his death.

Nicholas Rodney Drake was born on June 19, 1948 in Rangoon, Burma. Two years later, his family returned to England. Motivated by his mother, who wrote and recorded songs at home, he learned to play the piano at a young age. As a teen, he cared more about music than schoolwork and dropped out of college after signing a contract with Island Records to make his first album.

In 1969, he released his debut *Five Leaves Left* to mixed reviews and poor sales. He continued to work on his music until he died by apparent suicide in 1974. He was <u>largely</u> forgotten until the 1980s when a new generation of songwriters started to cite him as an inspiration. Drake's music finally achieved something close to mainstream recognition in 1999 when his song "Pink Moon" was used in a Volkswagen commercial, sparking a new wave of interest. His now much-imitated style is characterized by soft vocals, haunting melodies, and simple arrangements.

01 Based on the text, what is notable about Nick Drake's musical career?

(a) He became more famous after death.
(b) He became successful at a young age.
(c) He influenced musicians during his lifetime.
(d) He received much attention after his first album.

02 What most likely inspired Drake to become a musician?

(a) learning to play piano at school
(b) living abroad at a young age
(c) receiving an album contract offer
(d) listening to his mother's songs

03 In the context of the passage, <u>largely</u> means _____.

(a) massively
(b) mostly
(c) grandly
(d) generously

RICHARD MATHESON

Richard Matheson was a prolific American writer of novels, short stories, and screenplays who published most of his works in the mid- to late-20th century. His writing style was notable for <u>synthesizing</u> elements of science fiction, fantasy, and horror.

Matheson was born on February 20, 1926, in Allendale, New Jersey. He developed an interest in writing at a young age, publishing his first short story in the local newspaper when he was only eight years old. He started writing novels after he graduated from college with a degree in journalism.

He became successful not long after his first novel was published in 1953. The next year, he released the post-apocalyptic vampire novel *I am Legend*, which would go on to inspire three film adaptations, including the 2007 blockbuster of the same name. In total, seven of his books were adapted into Hollywood films. In the late 60's he started writing screenplays for films and popular television shows even as he continued to write and publish novels. The stories that he penned throughout his career had a huge impact on other contemporary writers, especially the legendary horror writer Stephen King, who has frequently praised Matheson's work.

04 When did Matheson first start writing?

(a) when he got a job as a journalist
(b) after he graduated from college
(c) when he was a very young boy
(d) after he joined the school newspaper

05 According to the article, what is most likely true about Matheson's career?

(a) He had a lasting influence in the world of horror fiction.
(b) He had several failed film adaptations of his books.
(c) He achieved his lifelong goal of working in Hollywood.
(d) He quit writing novels in favor of screenplays.

06 In the context of the passage, synthesizing means _____.

(a) arranging
(b) cooperating
(c) inventing
(d) mixing

JOSEPH LISTER

Joseph Lister was a British surgeon and professor whose research led to a reduction in post-operation fatalities. He is now known as the "father of modern surgery" due to his use of antiseptics, which revolutionized surgical sterilization.

Lister was born in Upton, England on April 5, 1827. His father, who was interested in plant and animal cells, designed a new kind of lens that improved the performance of microscopes. Joseph Lister developed an early passion for science and medicine, owing in part to his father. He attended medical school and in 1860 became a professor of surgery at the University of Glasgow.

At the time, most doctors were unaware of the existence of germs and believed that illnesses were caused by "bad air." Surgeons rarely took precautions such as handwashing or sterilizing surgical tools, which frequently led to severe or fatal infections in patients. After learning about bacteria, Lister started to experiment with carbolic acid as a potential antiseptic. He observed that infections decreased and wounds healed more quickly when carbolic acid was applied. In 1867, he published his findings, but other medical professionals remained dubious about his ideas. However, as doctors began to see positive results for themselves, the practice of using antiseptics gradually became more widespread.

07 What contributed to Lister's desire to become a medical professional?

(a) a need for better microscopes
(b) his classes in medical school
(c) new discoveries about animal cells
(d) his father's scientific work

08 What mostly likely happened when other doctors used antiseptics during their surgical procedures?

(a) Carbolic acid supplies at hospitals ran low.
(b) Wounds healed at the same rate as before.
(c) Fewer patients died following operations.
(d) They published articles about their findings.

09 In the context of the passage, dubious means _____.

(a) doubtful
(b) problematic
(c) unreliable
(d) ambiguous

Vocabulary

한눈에 보는 Part 1 보카

abroad ad. 해외에, 해외로	**accomplished** adj. 기량이 뛰어난, 재주가 많은
achievement n. 성과, 성취, 달성, 업적	**adaptation** n. 각색, 적용
affiliated adj. 부속의, 산하의, 소속된	**decide** v. 결정하다
amuse v. 즐겁게 하다, 재미있게 하다	**immense wealth** n. 막대한 부, 거대한 부
antiseptic n. 소독제, 살균제	**apparent** adj. 명백한, 분명한
apprentice n. 견습생	**arrangement** n. 편곡, 배열
assist v. 돕다, 거들다	**attention** n. 집중, 주의, 주목, 관심
audience n. 관객, 청중	**award** n. 상
be best known for v. ~로 가장 잘 알려져 있다	**be unaware of** v. ~을 알지 못하다, 모르다
be regarded as v. ~로 여겨지다	**carbolic acid** n. 석탄산 (살균제, 소독제로 쓰는 화학물질)
career n. 경력, 직업	**childhood** n. 어린 시절
club n. 구단	**college** n. 대학
combination n. 조합, 결합, 연합	**commercial** n. (상업)광고
commission v. 맡기다, 위임하다, 주문하다	**compete** v. 출전하다, 참가하다
completion n. 완성	**congregation** n. 수도회
contemporary adj. 동시대의	**continue** v. 계속하다, 계속되다
contract n. 계약	**contribute** v. 기여하다, 기부하다, ~의 원인이 되다
convent n. 수녀원	**course** n. 과목, 강의, 강좌
cultural adj. 문화의, 문화와 관련된	**decade** n. 10년
degree n. 학위	**department** n. 부서
develop v. 발달하다, 성장하다, 성장시키다	**discovery** n. 발견

cell n. 세포	disturbing adj. 충격적인, 불안감을 주는
divine adj. 신의, 신성의	drop out v. 중퇴하다
dubious adj. 의심하는, 미심쩍어 하는	earn v. 돈을 벌다, 수익을 올리다
emotional adj. 감정적인, 정서의	employee n. 고용인, 종업원
entrust (A with B) v. (A에게 B를) 맡기다, 위임하다	established adj. 인정받는, 존경받는
exhibit v. 전시하다	experiment v. 실험하다 n. 실험
fatal adj. 치명적인, 죽음을 초래하는	fatality n. 사망률
figure n. 인물 v. 중요하다	film director n. 영화감독
fit v. 알맞다, 적합하다	follow-up n. 속편
former adj. 이전의	frequently ad. 자주, 흔히
full-length film n. 장편영화	geography n. 지리학
germ n. 세균, 미생물	graduate v. 졸업하다, 학위를 받다
haunting adj. 잊혀지지 않는	heal v. 치유되다, 낫다, 상처가 아물다
operation n. 운영, 가동, 수술	highest-grossing adj. 높은 수익을 낸
illustrator n. 일러스트레이터, 삽화가	imitate v. 모방하다, 본뜨다
improve v. 향상시키다, 개선하다	inappropriate adj. 부적절한, 부적합한
infection n. 감염	influential adj. 영향력 있는
inspire v. 영감을 주다	journalism n. 저널리즘, 신문학
journalist n. 언론인, 저널리스트, (신문·방송·잡지사의) 기자	lasting adj. 지속적인, 영구적인
leave A behind v. A를 두고 가다, 뒤로 하다	mainstream n. 주류
microscope n. 현미경	new wave n. 새 물결
nomination n. 추천, 지명	notable adj. 유명한
original adj. 원래의, 본래의	outstanding adj. 뛰어난, 탁월한
patriot n. 애국자	pen v. 쓰다
phenomenal adj. 경이로운	post-operation adj. 수술 후의

praise v. 칭찬하다	**precaution** n. 예방조치
prestigious adj. 권위 있는, 명망 있는, 일류의	**procedure** n. 수술, 절차
producer n. 제작자	**production company** n. 제작사
prolific adj. 다작의, 다작하는	**publish** v. 게재하다, 출간하다
quirky adj. 기이한, 별난	**receive** v. 받다
recognition n. 인정, 인식, 표창	**recognized** adj. 인정된, 알려진
record-breaking adj. 기록을 깨는	**release** v. 발표하다, 출시하다
retreat n. 피정, 수행	**revolutionize** v. 혁신을 일으키다
screenplay n. 시나리오	**sequel** n. (책·영화·연극 등의) 속편
shop owner n. 점주	**shot** n. 촬영, 시도
signature n. 특징	**spark** v. 불러일으키다, 발화시키다
spend time v. 시간을 보내다	**sterilization** n. 소독, 살균
sterilize v. 살균하다, 소독하다	**success** n. 성공, 성과
successful adj. (어떤 일에) 성공한, 성공적인	**suffer** v. (질병·고통·슬픔·결핍 등에) 시달리다, 고통받다
suicide n. 자살	**supply** n. 공급량, 비축량
surgeon n. 외과의사	**surgical** adj. 외과의, 수술의
synthesize v. 합성하다	**take care of** v. ~을 돌보다, ~의 책임을 지다
touching adj. 감동적인	**tragically** ad. 비극적으로
treatment n. 대우, 처우	**unexciting** adj. 흥미롭지 않은, 재미있지 않은, 따분한
unique adj. 독특한, 특별한, 특이한	**unreleased** adj. 미개봉의, 공개되지 않은
widespread adj. 널리 퍼진, 광범위한	**wound** n. 상처

 Quiz

빈칸에 각 단어의 뜻을 적으시오.

① contemporary _____   ⑥ arrangement _____

② attention _____   ⑦ amuse _____

③ continue _____   ⑧ retreat _____

④ award _____   ⑨ completion _____

⑤ figure _____   ⑩ publish _____

정답 ① 동시대의 ② 관심 ③ 계속하다, 계속되다 ④ 상 ⑤ 인물, 중요하다 ⑥ 편곡, 배열
⑦ 즐겁게 하다, 재미있게 하다 ⑧ 피정, 수행 ⑨ 완성 ⑩ 게재하다, 출간하다

PART 2

지텔프 독해 스타터

General Tests of English Language Proficiency

Magazine Article

PART 02 Magazine Article

- Part 2는 사회/과학/환경/기술/역사적 발견/의학 등 다양한 주제에 관한 사회적 이슈를 다루는 정보 기사 글이 출제됩니다.
- 연구 결과, 계기, 소재에 대한 특징, 시사점 등 세부 사항에 관한 문제가 주로 다뤄집니다.
- 제목을 통해 주제를 비롯한 문제의 힌트를 쉽게 얻을 수 있습니다.

 필수 공략 포인트

Part 2는 잡지나 신문 등의 기사 형태로 정보를 전달하는 글입니다. 글을 읽기 전에 제목을 통해 글의 주제와 흐름을 어느정도 파악이 가능하므로 제목을 먼저 읽도록 합니다.

지문의 흐름 (단락 구성)

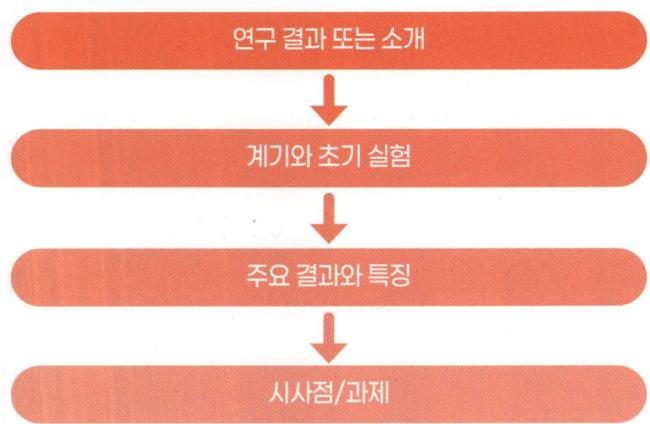

🔍 문제 패턴

단락 구성 순서	단락별 대표 유형	대표 문제 패턴
제목	주제	what is the (main) topic? what is the article all about? what is the article mainly about?
연구 결과 또는 소개	연구 결과/ 연구 목적	researchers find out that~ discovered that~ a study shows that~ experts say that~ announced that~
계기와 초기 실험	연구 계기 관련 인물 등 세부사항	what how which true/not When Where why most likely to~
주요 결과와 특징	연구 방법 차이점 등 세부사항	
시사점	시사점	what shows what discovers
현황/과제/한계	유추하기	what will~ what could be~

기초 공략 포인트

① Part 2의 첫 번째 문제는 주로 주제나 발견 사실을 묻습니다.

➡ 먼저 주제를 묻는 문제인 경우, 제목에서 큰 단서를 얻을 수 있습니다.

이 글은 무엇에 관한 것인가?
이 글의 주제는 무엇인가?

② 첫 문제로 주제가 나오지 않는다면, 연구 결과나 발견 사실을 묻습니다.

➡ 첫 단락에서 새롭게 발견한 사실을 찾아 관련 내용을 확인합니다.

연구자들이 발견한 것은 무엇인가?
이 연구가 보여주는 것은 무엇인가?

 패러프레이징 패턴

1. 주제
(주제는 무엇인가?, 무엇에 관한 글인가?, ~란 무엇인가?)

- What is the article all about?
- What is the topic of the article?
- What is the (중심 소재)?

➡ 글의 제목에서 확인할 수 있어요!

[제목] **How Processed Food Impacts Child Obesity**
가공 음식이 어떻게 어린이의 비만에 영향을 미치는가

➡ 주제가 가공 음식이 어린이 비만에 미치는 영향이라는 것을 알 수 있습니다.

[제목] **Next-Generation Wi-Fi 6 Technology Designed to Improve Home Networks**
가정용 네트워크 향상을 위해 고안된 차세대 Wi-Fi 6 기술

➡ 주제가 홈 네트워크를 개선하는 차세대 Wi-Fi 6기술이라는 것을 알 수 있습니다.

2. 발견
(연구자들은 발견했다, 전문가들이 말한다, 연구에 따르면 등)

- researchers found ~
- a new study/experiment shows ~
- experts say ~
- scientists/archeologists discovered ~

➡ 첫 단락에서 확인할 수 있어요!

• **Archaeologists have discovered** mummies that can help them study clothing from the Bronze Age.
<u>고고학자들은</u> 그들이 청동기 시대 의복을 연구하는 것을 도울 수 있는 미라<u>를 **발견했다**</u>.
➡ 고고학자들이 새로 발견한 미라를 통해 청동기 시대 의복을 연구하게 되었다는 것을 알 수 있습니다.

• **Researchers have found that** psychological changes also affect body temperature and hormonal cycles.
<u>연구자들은</u> 심리 변화가 체온과 호르몬 주기에도 영향을 미친다는 것<u>을 **발견했다**</u>.
➡ 심리 변화가 체온과 호르몬 주기에 영향을 미친다는 사실을 알 수 있습니다.

 **Exercise**

STUDY SAYS CHIMPANZEES' WORKING MEMORY IS SIMILAR TO HUMANS

A study discovered that humans and chimpanzees have a similar working memory process. Researchers from the United Kingdom, Germany, and Austria collaborated to test how the working memory of chimpanzees functions. Since humans and chimpanzees share almost the same genetic pattern, making them biologically alike, the researchers were interested in finding out if their working memories function similarly.

60. What did the researchers find out?

   (a) that chimpanzees share similar memory traits with humans
   (b) that primates and humans have identical memories
   (c) how chimpanzees collaborate with humans
   (d) how chimpanzees differ genetically from humans

 단서

STUDY SAYS CHIMPANZEES' WORKING MEMORY IS SIMILAR TO HUMANS

[60)] **A study discovered that humans and chimpanzees have a similar working memory process**. Researchers from the United Kingdom, Germany, and Austria collaborated to test how the working memory of chimpanzees functions. Since humans and chimpanzees share almost the same genetic pattern, making them biologically alike, the researchers were interested in finding out if their working memories function similarly.

침팬지의 작업 기억력이 인간과 비슷하다는 연구 결과

[60)] 한 연구에서 인간과 침팬지의 작업 기억 과정이 유사하다는 것을 발견했다. 영국, 독일, 오스트리아의 연구원들은 침팬지의 작업 기억이 어떻게 기능하는지 테스트하기 위해 협력했다. 인간과 침팬지가 거의 같은 유전적 패턴을 가지고 있어서 생물학적으로 비슷하기 때문에, 연구원들은 그들의 작업 기억이 유사하게 기능하는지 알아내는 데 관심이 있었다.

 단어

similar adj. 비슷한, 유사한, 닮은
process n. 과정, 진행, 방법
function v. 기능하다
genetic adj. 유전의, 유전적인

discover v. 발견하다
collaborate v. 협력하다
biologically ad. 생물학적으로

 **문제풀이**

60. What did the researchers **find out**?

   (a) **that chimpanzees share similar memory traits with humans**
   (b) that primates and humans have identical memories
   (c) how chimpanzees collaborate with humans
   (d) how chimpanzees differ genetically from humans

60. 연구자들은 무엇을 알아 냈는가?

   (a) 침팬지가 인간과 유사한 기억 특성을 공유한다는 것
   (b) 영장류와 인간은 동일한 기억을 가지고 있다는 것
   (c) 어떻게 침팬지가 인간과 협력하는지
   (d) 침팬지가 인간과 유전적으로 어떻게 다른지

 첫 번째 문제에서 연구자들이 발견한 것(find out)을 묻는 문제임을 확인하고 첫 단락에서 관련 표현인 discover(발견하다)을 확인한다.
that절에서도 비슷한 키워드 문구(a similar working memory process → similar memory traits)가 반복되는 것을 볼 수 있다.

 해설

첫 단락에서 한 연구에서 인간과 침팬지의 작업 기억 과정이 유사하다는 것을 발견했다고 언급하고 있으므로 **(a) that chimpanzees share similar memory traits with humans**가 정답이다.

단어   trait n. 특성   identical adj. 동일한, 똑같은   differ (from) v. (~와) 다르다

🚀 심화 공략 포인트

Part 2에서는 하나의 중심 소재가 있고, 그 소재에 대한 연구 소개, 연구 과정, 연구 결과와 시사점, 그리고 평가와 향후 방향을 예측하는 지문으로 구성되어 있습니다.

이 때 연구내용에 관한 세부사항을 출제하게 되는데, 연구 내용 및 소재는 다른 말로 대체하기 어려워 **그대로 쓰여지는** 경향이 있으므로, scanning을 할 때 주요 키워드가 됩니다.

① 연구 계기와 과정, 실험 내용과 결과 등에 관한 세부 내용

> **What help~?**
> **Which is true~?**
> **How did researchers~?**
> **What is~?**
> **Where ~differ?**
> **What difference?**
> **비교급~than?**
>
> ➡ 실험 또는 연구의 세부 내용 문제는 주로 방법/시기/요소를 묻거나 발견 사실 또는 소재의 특징에 관해 true/not true 문제로 묻습니다.
> 실험 방식이나 주요 요소(실험자, 실험대상, 실험 환경과 과정 등)와 비교 및 차이점에 주목할 필요가 있습니다.

Example

Researchers **assumed** that reducing data downloads decreases chances of causing environmental damage **because** data processing uses electricity, and when electricity is produced, carbon, water and land footprints are created.

연구원들은 데이터 다운로드를 줄이면 데이터 처리 과정에서 전기를 사용하기 **때문에** 환경적 피해가 발생할 가능성이 줄어들고, 전기가 생산될 때 탄소, 물 및 토지 발자국이 생성된다고 **가정했다**.

Q. Why did the researchers **assume** that reducing data downloads prevents damage to the environment?

(a) because data processing is expensive
(b) because the environment is harmed when generating electricity
(c) because the carbon footprint is the result of environmental damage
(d) because insufficient electricity affects data output

Q. **왜** 연구원들은 데이터 다운로드를 줄이는 것이 환경 피해를 방지한다고 **가정했을까**?

(a) 데이터 처리에 비용이 많이 들기 때문에
(b) 전기를 생산할 때 환경이 해를 입기 때문에
(c) 탄소 발자국이 환경 피해의 결과이기 때문에
(d) 전기 부족은 데이터 생산량에 영향을 미치기 때문에

해설

데이터 처리가 전기를 사용하고, 전기가 생산될 때 탄소, 물 및 토지 발자국이 생성되기 때문에 데이터 다운로드를 줄여 전기 사용을 줄이는 것이 환경 피해를 방지한다고 가정할 수 있었다는 것을 확인할 수 있다. 따라서 **(b) because the environment is harmed when generating electricity**가 정답이다.

단어

assume v. 가정하다, 추정하다
decrease v. 줄다, 감소하다
carbon n. 탄소
processing n. 과정, 절차
insufficient adj. 부족한, 불충분한

reduce v. 줄이다, 낮추다
electricity n. 전기
footprint n. 발자국
environmental adj. 환경의

② 연구의 시사점

(연구는 ~을 밝힌다, ~을 시사한다, ~를 알려준다)

> The study sheds light on~
> The finding suggests~
> The discovery shows~

- an environmental <u>study sheds light on</u> how increased Internet use leads to bigger water, land, and carbon footprints

환경 연구는 <u>어떻게</u> 증가된 인터넷 사용이 더 많은 물과 땅, 그리고 탄소 발자국으로 이어지는지를 <u>밝혀준다</u>.

③ 한계점/추후 과제/예상

(~일 것이다, ~할 수 있다, ~일지도 모른다)

> will~
> could be~
> may~

- Although advances in science and medicine allow many diseases to be cured, there can be negative consequences as well. By prolonging the human lifespan, such advances <u>may</u> actually make humans more susceptible to infectious diseases.

과학과 의학의 발전으로 많은 질병이 치료된다고 하더라도, 부정적인 결과도 있을 수 있다. 인간의 수명을 연장함으로써, 그러한 발전은 실제로 인간을 전염병에 더 취약하게 만들<u>지도 모른다</u>.

 **Exercise**

STUDY SAYS CHIMPANZEES' WORKING MEMORY IS SIMILAR TO HUMANS

A study discovered that humans and chimpanzees have a similar working memory process. Researchers from the United Kingdom, Germany, and Austria collaborated to test how the working memory of chimpanzees functions. Since humans and chimpanzees share almost the same genetic pattern, making them biologically alike, the researchers were interested in finding out if their working memories function similarly.

Working memory is a cognitive process associated with the ability to gather and retain pieces of information and use them in decision-making. Because of this, working memory allows species to continuously update present information and make better decisions. Humans have an <u>extended</u> duration of working memory. On the other hand, based on their short attention span, many animals store recently acquired information for less than half a minute before they forget.

The research team tested a group of chimpanzees by displaying a set of boxes while food was being hidden inside some of them. After the boxes were covered, each chimpanzee had to guess which among the boxes contained food. The chimpanzees could enjoy the food as their <u>reward</u> if they chose correctly. After each round, the boxes were shuffled and hidden for 15 seconds. With every correct guess, the number of boxes increased.

The best chimpanzees identified at least four boxes correctly. However, when they were asked to perform another task at the same time, their results were not as impressive. According to the researchers, the chimpanzees performed similarly to how a human might perform while multitasking. For example, remembering a new address can be difficult if one is also concentrating on trying to cook a meal. When the chimpanzees were faced with a similar challenge, their scores declined.

The researchers concluded that a chimpanzee's working memory capacity is comparable to that of a seven-year-old child. However, chimpanzees are more likely to search the boxes randomly, while humans are more likely to use a simple search strategy, like investigating from one side to the other. Overall, the study suggests that the working memories of chimpanzees and humans are similar when it comes to updating information.

61. According to the article, what is "working memory"?

    (a) It is a set of cognitive tests.
    (b) It is a unique trait that humans use to make decisions.
    (c) It is a process of updating and using information.
    (d) It is the unit of memory that works the hardest.

62. How did the researchers test the working memory of chimpanzees?

    (a) by diverting their attention to different foods
    (b) by making them play a guessing game
    (c) by allowing them to cover the boxes that contain rewards
    (d) by letting them decide which food they want to eat

63. Why most likely were the multitasking scores not as high?

    (a) The chimpanzees were distracted by food.
    (b) Only humans are capable of multitasking.
    (c) The number of boxes was increased.
    (d) The chimpanzees faced the same difficulties as humans.

64. According to the study, where do humans and chimpanzees differ in applying their working memory?

    (a) in search strategy
    (b) in multitasking performance
    (c) in childhood development
    (d) in information recall

65. In the context of the passage, extended means _____.

    (a) given
    (b) prolonged
    (c) broad
    (d) delayed

66. In the context of the passage, reward means _____.

    (a) prize
    (b) welfare
    (c) punishment
    (d) salary

 단서

STUDY SAYS CHIMPANZEES' WORKING MEMORY IS SIMILAR TO HUMANS

60) **A study discovered** that humans and chimpanzees have **a similar working memory process**. Researchers from the United Kingdom, Germany, and Austria collaborated to test how the working memory of chimpanzees functions. Since humans and chimpanzees share almost the same genetic pattern, making them biologically alike, the researchers were interested in finding out if their working memories function similarly.

61) **Working memory is a cognitive process associated with the ability to gather and retain pieces of information and use them in decision-making.** Because of this, working memory allows species to continuously update present information and make better decisions. Humans have an 65) <u>extended</u> duration of working memory. On the other hand, based on their short attention span, many animals store recently acquired information for less than half a minute before they forget.

62) **The research team tested a group of chimpanzees by displaying a set of boxes while food was being hidden** inside some of them. After the boxes were covered, **each chimpanzee had to guess** which among the boxes contained food. The chimpanzees could enjoy the food as their 66) <u>reward</u> if they chose correctly. After each round, the boxes were shuffled and hidden for 15 seconds. With every correct guess, the number of boxes increased.

연구는 침팬지의 작업 기억이 인간과 비슷하다고 밝히다

한 연구에서 인간과 침팬지의 작업 기억 과정이 유사하다는 것을 발견했다. 영국, 독일, 오스트리아의 연구원들은 침팬지의 작업 기억이 어떻게 기능하는지 테스트하기 위해 협력했다. 인간과 침팬지가 거의 같은 유전적 패턴을 가지고 있어서 생물학적으로 비슷하기 때문에, 연구원들은 그들의 작업 기억이 유사하게 기능하는지 알아내는 데 관심이 있었다.

61) 작업 기억은 정보 조각을 수집 및 유지하고 의사 결정에 사용하는 능력과 관련된 인지 과정이다. 이것 때문에, 작업 기억은 종들이 현재 정보를 지속적으로 업데이트하고 더 나은 결정을 내릴 수 있게 해준다. 인간은 65) 확장된 작업 기억 기간을 가지고 있다. 반면에, 짧은 주의력을 바탕으로 많은 동물들은 최근 습득한 정보를 그들이 잊기 전 30초도 안되는 시간 동안만 저장한다.

62) 연구팀은 일부 상자들 안에 음식이 숨겨지는 동안, 상자들을 보여줌으로써 침팬지 그룹을 테스트했다. 상자를 덮은 후, 각각의 침팬지는 상자 중 어떤 것이 음식을 포함하고 있는지를 추측해야 했다. 침팬지들은 그들이 올바르게 선택하면 66) 보상으로 음식을 먹을 수 있었다. 각 라운드가 끝나면 상자들을 섞어서 15초 동안 숨겼다. 정확한 추측을 할 때마다 상자 수가 증가했다.

The best chimpanzees identified at least four boxes correctly. However, when they were asked to perform another task at the same time, **their results were not as impressive. According to the researchers,** [63) **the chimpanzees performed similarly to how a human might perform while multitasking.** For example, remembering a new address can be difficult if one is also concentrating on trying to cook a meal. When the chimpanzees were faced with a similar challenge, their scores declined.

The researchers concluded that a chimpanzee's working memory capacity is comparable to that of a seven-year-old child. However, chimpanzees are more likely to search the boxes randomly, [64) **while humans are more likely to use a simple search strategy, like investigating from one side to the other.** Overall, the study suggests that the working memories of chimpanzees and humans are similar when it comes to updating information.

최고의 침팬지는 최소한 네 개의 상자를 정확하게 식별했다. 그러나 그들이 동시에 다른 작업을 수행하라는 요청을 받았을 때, 결과는 그다지 인상적이지 않았다. 연구원에 따르면, 63) 침팬지는 인간이 멀티태스킹을 할 때 하는 방식과 유사하게 수행한다. 예를 들어, 음식을 만드는 데 집중한다면, 새 주소를 기억하는 것은 어려울 수 있다. 침팬지들이 비슷한 도전에 직면했을 때, 그들의 점수는 떨어졌다.

연구자들은 침팬지의 작업 기억 능력이 7세 어린이의 작업 기억 능력과 비슷하다고 결론지었다. 그러나 침팬지는 상자를 무작위로 찾을 가능성이 더 높은 반면, 64) 인간은 한쪽에서 다른 쪽으로 찾는 것과 같은 간단한 탐색 전략을 사용할 가능성이 더 높다. 전반적으로, 이 연구는 정보를 업데이트 할 때 침팬지와 인간의 작업 기억이 비슷하다는 것을 시사한다.

단어

working memory n. 작업 기억
be associated with v. ~와 관련되다
decision-making n. 의사결정
species n. 종
present adj. 현재의
extend v. 확대하다, 확장하다, 연장하다
attention n. 집중, 주의, 주목, 관심
store v. 저장하다, 보관하다
acquire v. 습득하다
display v. 보여주다, 전시하다
cover v. 덮다
shuffle v. 뒤섞다
perform v. 수행하다
concentrate (on) v. (~에) 집중하다
decline n. 감소 v. 감소하다, 거절하다
capacity n. 능력, 용량, 수용력
randomly ad. 무작위로, 임의로
investigate v. 조사하다, 수사하다, 살피다

cognitive adj. 인지의
retain v. 유지하다, 보유하다
allow v. 허락하다, 허용하다
continuously ad. 연달아, 끊임없이
decision n. 결정, 판단
duration n. 지속되는 시간, 기간
span n. 범위, 기간
recently ad. 최근에
half a minute n. 30초, 아주 짧은 시간
hidden adj. 숨겨진
among prep. ~에 둘러싸인, ~의 가운데어
identify v. 식별하다, 구별하다
impressive adj. 인상적인
face v. 직면하다, 직면하게 하다
conclude v. 결론짓다
comparable adj. 비교할 수 있는
strategy n. 전략

문제풀이

61. According to the article, what is "**working memory**"?

(a) It is a set of cognitive tests.
(b) It is a unique trait that humans use to make decisions.
(c) It is a process of updating and using information.
(d) It is the unit of memory that works the hardest.

61. 기사에 따르면, "**작업 기억**"이란 무엇인가?

(a) 일련의 인지 테스트다.
(b) 인간이 결정을 내리는 데 사용하는 독특한 특성이다.
(c) 정보를 업데이트하고 사용하는 과정이다.
(d) 가장 견고하게 작용하는 기억 단위다.

 인용 표현("")은 paraphrasing으로 바꿀 수 없는 표현이므로 본문에서 working memory가 언급된 곳을 찾아 읽는다.

 작업 기억이 정보를 수집, 유지하고 의사결정에 사용하는 능력과 관련된 인지 과정이라는 내용을 통해 정보를 업데이트하고 사용하는 과정임을 알 수 있다. 따라서 **(c) It is a process of updating and using information**이 정답이다.

단어 cognitive adj. 인지의, 인식의   unique adj. 독특한, 특이한, 특별한   trait n. 특성

---

62. How did the researchers **test the working memory of chimpanzees**?

(a) by diverting their attention to different foods
(b) by making them play a guessing game
(c) by allowing them to cover the boxes that contain rewards
(d) by letting them decide which food they want to eat

62. 연구원들은 침팬지의 작업 기억을 어떻게 테스트했는가?

(a) 다른 음식에 주의를 돌림으로써
(b) 추측 게임을 하도록 함으로써
(c) 보상이 담긴 상자를 덮을 수 있도록 허용함으로써
(d) 그들이 어떤 음식을 먹고 싶은지를 결정하게 함으로써

 문제에서 언급된 test the working memory를 본문에서 찾는다.
실험 방법(how)을 묻는 질문이므로 관련 내용을 scanning하면 본문에 언급된 guess와 보기의 guessing game의 연관성을 확인할 수 있다.

해설

침팬지가 어떤 상자에 음식이 들어있는지를 추측하게 하는 테스트를 했다는 내용을 통해 (b) by making them play a guessing game이 정답임을 알 수 있다.

단어   divert v. 다른 데로 돌리다, 전환시키다   contain v. ~이 들어있다

---

63. Why most likely were the **multitasking** scores **not as high**?

    (a) The chimpanzees were distracted by food.
    (b) Only humans are capable of multitasking.
    (c) The number of boxes was increased.
    (d) The chimpanzees faced the same difficulties as humans.

63. 멀티태스킹 점수가 그다지 높지 않은 이유는 무엇인가?

    (a) 침팬지는 음식에 주의가 산만해져서
    (b) 인간만이 멀티태스킹을 할 수 있어서
    (c) 상자 수가 증가해서
    (d) 침팬지가 인간과 같은 난관에 직면해서

 문제에서 언급된 multitasking을 본문에서 찾아 읽는다.

 해설

본문에서 침팬지의 멀티태스킹 결과가 인상적이지 않았고, 인간이 멀티태스킹을 할 때와 유사했다는 내용을 통해 (d) The chimpanzees faced the same difficulties as humans가 정답임을 알 수 있다.

단어   distracted adj. 산만해진   be capable of v. ~할 수 있다   increase v. 증가하다, 늘다

64. According to the study, where do humans and chimpanzees **differ** in applying their working memory?

    (a) in search strategy
    (b) in multitasking performance
    (c) in childhood development
    (d) in information recall

64. 연구에 따르면, 인간과 침팬지는 작업 기억을 적용하는 데 있어 어떤 **차이가 있는가**?

    (a) 탐색 전략
    (b) 멀티태스킹 성능
    (c) 아동 발달
    (d) 정보 회수

 **Tip!** 인간과 침팬지의 차이점을 비교하는 표현(differ, on the other hand, while 등)을 찾아 읽는다.

 해설

침팬지는 상자를 무작위로 찾을 가능성이 더 높은 반면, 인간은 한쪽에서 다른 쪽으로 찾는 것과 같은 간단한 탐색 전략을 사용할 가능성이 더 높다는 내용을 통해 탐색 전략의 차이가 있다는 것을 알 수 있다. 따라서 **(a) in search strategy**가 정답이다.

단어 **apply** v. 적용하다, 쓰다, 신청하다, 지원하다   **strategy** n. 전략
performance n. 성능, 성과, 실적   **development** n. 발달, 성장, 개발

65. In the context of the passage, <u>extended</u> means _____.

    (a) given
    (b) prolonged
    (c) broad
    (d) delayed

65. 글의 문맥에 따르면, <u>extended</u>는 _____을 의미한다.

    (a) 주어진
    (b) 장기의
    (c) 넓은
    (d) 지연

해설

인간은 extended한 기억 기간을 가졌고 반면에 동물들은 짧은 시간 정보를 기억한다는 내용을 통해 본문의 extend가 short의 대조되는 의미임을 알 수 있다. 따라서 **(b) prolonged**가 정답이다.

66. In the context of the passage, reward means
    _____.

    (a) prize
    (b) welfare
    (c) punishment
    (d) salary

66. 글의 문맥에 따르면, reward는 _____을 의미한다.

    (a) 상품
    (b) 복지
    (c) 처벌
    (d) 급여

> 해설

침팬지가 올바르게 추측할 경우 보상으로 그 음식을 먹을 수 있었다는 내용이므로, 문맥상 '상, 상품'이라는 의미가 가장 비슷하다. 따라서 정답은 (a) prize이다.

MINI TEST

PART 2. Read the following magazine article and answer the questions. The underlined word in the article is for a vocabulary question.

THE RISE AND FALL OF MEAL KIT DELIVERY SERVICES

In 2012, startup company Blue Apron popularized a new kind of service: the delivery of high-quality meal kits directly to customers each week. People using the service could make a home-cooked meal in 30 minutes or less, using fresh ingredients that had already been measured and chopped. The kits even included simple instructions for cooking and assembling the meal. People could say goodbye to the hassle of meal-planning and grocery shopping.

Following Blue Apron's success, dozens of similar businesses sprang up around the country. A meal kit service now exists for any consumer's taste preferences or dietary restrictions. Many of these services can provide food that is organic, vegetarian, or vegan. People with food allergies and people who want to lose weight can now find plans that cater to their needs.

However, the meal kit delivery industry is now in <u>dire</u> condition. Many companies are already bankrupt and the survivors have been losing money for years. A key factor in this downfall is the massive cost of such an operation. The companies need to purchase premium ingredients and hire large staffs to prepare and deliver the kits.

01 According to the article, why most likely did meal kit services become popular?

(a) because of the convenience
(b) because of their low prices
(c) because of the daily deliveries
(d) because of their gourmet meals

02 How can meal kits be useful for people who have dietary restrictions?

(a) Customers can order fewer meals per week.
(b) Customers can personalize the contents of a kit.
(c) All of the kits are made from organic produce.
(d) All of the plans are good for people on a diet.

03 In the context of the passage, dire means _____.

(a) gruesome
(b) cruel
(c) poor
(d) vital

THE MYTH OF THE SUGAR HIGH

Parents have long believed that their children become more energetic and harder to control when they consume more sugar. They call the effect a "sugar high." However, the sugar high is largely a myth that was debunked by a series of scientific studies in the mid-1990s.

A study in 1994 tested three groups of children. One group was given a diet that included real sugar, and the other two groups were each given a different artificial sweetener. Parents were not told which type of diet their children were consuming during the observation period. At the end of the study, parents and researchers did not record any significant differences in behavior among the three groups.

So why has the sugar high remained such a persistent myth despite evidence to the contrary? One possible explanation is that children tend to consume more sugar on special occasions, such as birthday parties and holiday gatherings, when feelings of elation are already at their peak. In that case, the rise in energy levels is caused by the situation and not by sugar. Because of the parents' belief in the sugar high, they perceive their children's hyperactivity to be connected to the consumption of cakes, candy, and sugary beverages.

04 What most likely did scientists conclude about sugar at the end of the 1994 study?

(a) It is superior to artificial sweeteners.
(b) It has little or no effect on behavior.
(c) It has a greater effect on the parents.
(d) It is not suitable for most children.

05 According to the article, why would children behave differently if they go to a party?

(a) because of their parents' attitudes
(b) because they consume more food
(c) because of increased excitement
(d) because they have too much sugar

06 In the context of the passage, <u>debunked</u> means _____.

(a) disproved
(b) insulted
(c) confirmed
(d) disliked

NO SUCH THING AS A PERFECT UMBRELLA

Devices made to shield us from the rain have existed in some form since the ancient times. The lightweight folding model that is most familiar to us first appeared in the early 1700s, but it seems we haven't been able to improve on it much since then. The perfectly circular umbrella with a collapsible structure on the underside has endured for centuries but still poses a number of problems for the user.

The wind is a common threat, frequently catching the umbrella from the wrong angle and turning it inside out. Traditional umbrellas can also be burdensome as the user tries to avoid hitting other people on crowded streets while carrying bags or attempting to make phone calls with only one hand. An additional concern is the lack of protection from water splashed by passing cars. An umbrella can keep your hair dry, but what about your legs?

A number of inventors have tried to offer solutions to these problems. Several products released in the last few years have played with shape to make umbrellas that are wind-resistant. One such innovation is the aerodynamic Senz umbrella that can withstand winds of more than 60 miles per hour. However, due to the odd shape—with a short, wide front and a long, narrow tail—two people cannot comfortably share the same umbrella.

07 What is an advantage of the traditional umbrella?

(a) keeping one's legs from getting wet
(b) letting one use both hands for certain tasks
(c) protecting one's head from the rain
(d) sheltering one from strong winds

08 Based on the article, why is the Senz umbrella not ideal for all situations?

(a) It is unable to shield more than one person.
(b) It will not fit comfortably into a bag.
(c) Its odd shape makes it hard to hold.
(d) Its water-resistance is weak in heavy rain.

09 In the context of the passage, poses means _____.

(a) pretends
(b) arranges
(c) presents
(d) models

Vocabulary

한눈에 보는 Part 2 보카

acquire v. 습득하다	additional adj. 추가적인
aerodynamic adj. 공기 역학의	allergy n. 알레르기
allow v. 허락하다, 허용하다	among prep. ~에 둘러싸인, ~의 가운데에
shuffle v. 뒤섞다	ancient adj. 고대의
appear v. 나타나다, 생기다, 발생하다, 등장하다	apply v. 적용하다, 쓰다, 신청하다, 지원하다
artificial sweetener n. 인공 감미료	be associated with v. ~와 관련되다
assume v. 가정하다, 추정하다	attempt v. 시도하다
attention n. 집중, 주의, 주목, 관심	attitude n. 태도, 자세, 사고방식
avoid v. 피하다	be connected to v. ~와 관련 있다
behave v. 행동하다	behavior n. 행동, 행실, 태도
beverage n. 음료	biologically ad. 생물학적으로
burdensome adj. 부담이 되는	be capable of v. ~할 수 있다
capacity n. 능력, 용량, 수용력	carbon n. 탄소
cater v. 음식을 공급하다	chop v. 다지다, 썰다
circular adj. 원형의	cognitive adj. 인지의, 인식의
collaborate v. 협력하다	collapsible adj. 접이식의
common adj. 흔한, 일반적인	comparable adj. 비교할 수 있는
concentrate (on) v. (~에) 집중하다	concern n. 문제, 염려, 우려
conclude v. 결론짓다	consume v. 먹다, 소모하다, 섭취하다, 소비하다

consumption n. 섭취, 소비, 소비량, 소모	continuously ad. 연달아, 끊임없이
contrary adj. ~와는 다른, 반대되는	cover v. 덮다
crowded adj. 붐비는	debunk v. (생각·믿음 등이) 틀렸음을 드러내다, 밝히다
decision-making n. 의사결정	decision n. 결정, 판단
decline n. 감소 v. 감소하다, 거절하다	decrease v. 줄다, 감소하다
despite prep. ~에도 불구하고	diet n. 식단, 식사
dietary restriction n. 식단 제한	differ (from) v. (~와) 다르다
dire adj. 몹시 나쁜, 심각한, 끔찍한	discover v. 발견하다
display v. 보여주다, 전시하다	distracted adj. 산만해진
divert v. 다른 데로 돌리다, 전환시키다	contain v. ~이 들어있다
downfall n. 몰락, 몰락의 원인	duration n. 지속되는 시간, 기간
effect n. 영향, 효과	elation n. (큰)행복감, 기쁨, 의기양양
electricity n. 전기	endure v. 지속하다
energetic adj. 활기찬, 혈기 왕성한	environmental adj. 환경의
evidence n. 증거	exist v. 존재하다, 실존하다 n. 존재, 실존
extend v. 확대하다, 확장하다	face v. 직면하다, 직면하게 하다
factor n. 요인, 요소	fold v. 접다
footprint n. 발자국	function v. 기능하다
gathering n. 모임	genetic adj. 유전의, 유전적인
gourmet meal n. 고급 음식, 고급 식료품	grocery n. 식료품점
half a minute n. 30초, 아주 짧은 시간	hidden adj. 숨겨진
hyperactivity n. 과잉 행동	identical adj. 동일한, 똑같은

identify v. 식별하다, 구별하다	**impressive** adj. 인상적인
improve v. 개선하다	**increase** v. 증가하다, 늘다
ingredient n. (특히 요리 등의) 재료	**innovation** n. 혁신
instruction n. 설명 (=directions)	**insufficient** adj. 부족한, 불충분한
inventor n. 발명가	**investigate** v. 조사하다, 수사하다, 살피다
lack n. 부족, 결핍	**lightweight** adj. 경량의
massive adj. 거대한, 엄청나게 큰	**myth** n. 근거 없는 믿음, 신화
observation n. 관찰	**occasion** n. 경우, 때
odd adj. 이상한	**operation** n. 운영, 가동, 수술
organic adj. 유기농의	**peak** n. 최고조, 꼭대기
perceive v. 인식하다	**perform** v. 수행하다
performance n. 성능, 성과, 실적	**development** n. 발달, 성장, 개발
period n. 기간	**persistent** adj. 지속적인
personalize v. 개인화하다, 개인에 맞추다	**produce** v. 생산하다
popularize v. 대중화하다, 많은 사람들에게 알리다	**preference** n. 선호
present adj. 현재의	**process** n. 과정, 진행, 방법
processing n. 과정, 절차	**randomly** ad. 무작위로, 임의로
recently ad. 최근에	**reduce** v. 줄이다, 낮추다
release v. 발표하다, 출시하다	**resistant** adj. 저항하는, 저항의
retain v. 유지하다, 보유하다	**shelter** n. 대피, 피신 v. (비·바람으로부터) ~을 보호하다
shield v. 보호하다, 막다	**significant** adj. 큰, 상당한
similar adj. 비슷한, 유사한, 닮은	**span** n. 범위, 기간

species n. 종	**splash** v. 물을 튀기다
spring up v. 갑자기 생겨나다, 나타나다	**startup company** n. 스타트업 회사
store v. 저장하다, 보관하다	**strategy** n. 전략
structure n. 구조	**suitable** adj. 적합한, 알맞은
taste n. 입맛, 맛	**tend to v** v. ~하는 경향이 있다
threat n. 위협	**traditional** adj. 전통적인, 전통의
trait n. 특성	**turn inside out** v. (안에서 밖으로) 뒤집다
underside adj. 밑면의	**unique** adj. 독특한, 특이한
vegan n. 엄격한 채식주의, 채식주의자	**vegetarian** n. 채식주의자
weak adj. 약한, 힘이 없는	**weight** n. 무게, 체중
wet adj. 젖은	**withstand** v. 견디다
working memory n. 작업 기억	

 **Quiz**

빈칸에 각 단어의 뜻을 적으시오.

① evidence _____	⑥ acquire _____

② cognitive _____	⑦ display _____

③ avoid _____	⑧ biologically _____

④ traditional _____	⑨ strategy _____

⑤ occasion _____	⑩ despite _____

정답 ① 증거 ② 인지의, 인식의 ③ 피하다 ④ 전통적인, 전통의 ⑤ 경우, 때
⑥ 습득하다 ⑦ 보여주다, 전시하다 ⑧ 생물학적으로 ⑨ 전략 ⑩ ~에도 불구하고

PART 3

지텔프 독해 스타터
General Tests of English Language Proficiency

Encyclopedia Article

PART 03 Encyclopedia Article

- Part 3는 다양한 분야에서 한 가지 소재를 정해 집중적으로 다루는 정보 글입니다.
- 과학, 인문, 환경, 사회, 문화, 역사적 소재와 관련하여 소재의 정의와 형성과정, 기원과 특징에 관한 문제를 출제합니다.

필수 공략 포인트

Part 3는 지식백과의 형식으로, 정보를 전달하는 성격을 지닌 지문이 출제됩니다.
해당 파트에서 정의와 기원에 관한 전형적인 문제는 반드시 출제되므로 주요 공략 포인트 입니다.

지문의 흐름 (단락 구성)

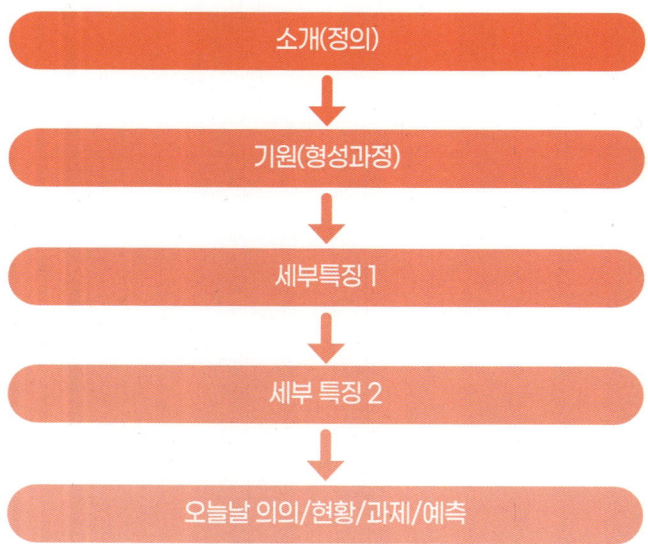

 **문제 패턴**

단락 구성 순서	단락별 대표 유형	대표 문제 패턴
소개	정의	What is~?
기원(형성과정)	기원	When was it found~? Why ~arise? How ~made first? What does the origin?
세부 특징1	대표 특징 초기 특징 변화 과정	How~? Why~? Which ~not/True?
세부 특징2	세부 특징 최근 특징 변화 후기	
현황/의의/과제	현황, 추론	What could~? What most likely to~?

기초 공략 포인트

① Part 3의 첫 번째 문제는 주로 소재의 정의를 묻습니다.
  ➜ 첫 번째 단락에서 해당 근거를 확인할 수 있습니다.

  ~란 무엇인가?
  ~는 무엇으로 알려져 있는가?

② 소재의 기원 및 형성과정을 묻는 문제가 출제됩니다.
  ➜ 주로 두 번째 단락에서 확인할 수 있습니다.

  언제 처음 발견 되었는가?
  어떻게 형성되었는가?
  왜 대두 되었는가?

 패러프레이징 패턴

1. 소재
   (~란 무엇인가?, ~는 무엇으로 알려져 있는가?, ~는 무슨 의미인가?)

   - What is ~?
   - What is the most remarkable about~?
   ➜ 첫 단락에서 소재에 대한 정의를 찾을 수 있습니다.

   • **What is** Big Brother?
   Big Brother는 <u>무엇인가</u>?

   • **What is most remarkable about** the rain gauge of Chosen?
   조선의 측우기에 <u>대해 가장 주목할 점은 무엇인가</u>?

   • **What is** dolmen?
   고인돌이란 <u>무엇인가</u>?

2. 기원(형성과정)

(~는 어떻게 처음 만들어졌는가?, ~는 언제 처음 발견되었는가?, ~의 기원은 무엇인가?, 왜~ 가 대두되었는가?)

- When did the need for ~ arise/emerge?
- When was/were ~ first found/discovered?
- How did ~ contribute to ~ ?

- What is the origin of astrology?
  점성술의 기원은 무엇인가?

- When did the need for the Internet first emerge?
  언제 인터넷의 필요성이 처음 대두되었는가?

- When were the ancient Mayan settlements first discovered?
  언제 고대 마야인의 정착지가 처음 발견되었는가?

- How did polar temperatures contribute to the formation of ice caps?
  극지방의 온도는 어떻게 만년설의 형성에 기여했는가?

 **Exercise**

GREAT PACIFIC GARBAGE PATCH

The Great Pacific Garbage Patch (GPGP) is an area in the North Pacific Ocean where human-produced waste floats and gathers together due to ocean currents. Also known as the "Pacific trash vortex," the GPGP is the largest accumulation of waste, mostly plastics, among the five offshore garbage patches in the world's oceans.

In 1988, the National Oceanic and Atmospheric Administration (NOAA) published a paper predicting the presence of a garbage patch in the North Pacific Ocean. The GPGP was confirmed nine years later when marine researcher Charles Moore sailed in a transpacific yacht race. Upon returning from his voyage, he reported seeing large stretches of floating waste debris in the Pacific Ocean between California and Hawaii.

67. What is the Great Pacific Garbage Patch?

    (a) Pacific Ocean currents that produce toxic waste
    (b) a place where people around the Pacific dump waste
    (c) a place in the Pacific Ocean where waste piles up
    (d) a place where marine debris turns into plastic

68. When was the actual existence of the GPGP verified?

    (a) after a transpacific exploration
    (b) after an eyewitness report by a scientist
    (c) upon the publication of an oceanic study
    (d) when plastic waste started disappearing

 단서

GREAT PACIFIC GARBAGE PATCH

태평양 거대 쓰레기 지대

67) **The Great Pacific Garbage Patch (GPGP) is an area in the North Pacific Ocean where human-produced waste floats and gathers together due to ocean currents.** Also known as the "Pacific trash vortex," the GPGP is the largest accumulation of waste, mostly plastics, among the five offshore garbage patches in the world's oceans.

In 1988, the National Oceanic and Atmospheric Administration (NOAA) published a paper predicting the presence of a garbage patch in the North Pacific Ocean. 68) **The GPGP was confirmed nine years later when marine researcher Charles Moore sailed in a transpacific yacht race.** Upon returning from his voyage, he reported seeing large stretches of floating waste debris in the Pacific Ocean between California and Hawaii.

67) 태평양 거대 쓰레기 지대(GPGP)는 해류로 인해 인간이 생산한 폐기물이 떠다니고 모이는 북태평양 지역이다. "태평양 쓰레기 소용돌이"라고도 알려진 GPGP는 전 세계 바다의 5대 쓰레기 지대 중 가장 큰 폐기물 축적물로, 대부분 플라스틱이다.

1988년, 국립해양대기국(NOAA)은 북태평양에 쓰레기 지대가 존재한다는 것을 예측하는 논문을 발표했다. 68) GPGP는 9년 후 해양연구원 찰스 무어가 태평양 횡단 요트 경주에서 항해했을 때 확인되었다. 항해에서 돌아오자마자, 그는 캘리포니아와 하와이 사이의 태평양에 광범위하게 뻗은 떠있는 폐기물 잔해들을 보았다고 보고했다.

단어

Pacific adj. 태평양의 n. 태평양
waste n. 쓰레기
gather v. 모이다, 모으다
vortex n. 소용돌이
offshore adj. 앞바다의
publish v. 발표하다, 출판하다, 게재하다
presence n. 존재
marine adj. 바다의, 해양의
voyage n. 항해

garbage patch n. 쓰레기 지대(잔뜩 모여 섬 같은 형상을 이룬 해양 쓰레기 더미)
float v. 떠다니다, 표류하다, 부유하다
current n. 해류
accumulation n. 축적물
National Oceanic and Atmospheric Administration n. 국립해양대기청
predict v. 예측하다
confirm v. 확인하다
transpacific adj. 태평양 횡단의, 태평양 저편의
stretch n. 구간, 지역

문제풀이

67. What is the Great Pacific Garbage Patch?

(a) Pacific Ocean currents that produce toxic waste
(b) a place where people around the Pacific dump waste
(c) a place in the Pacific Ocean where waste piles up
(d) a place where marine debris turns into plastic

67. 태평양 거대 쓰레기 지대는 무엇인가?

(a) 독성 폐기물을 생성하는 태평양 해류
(b) 태평양 주변 사람들이 쓰레기를 버리는 장소
(c) 태평양에서 쓰레기가 쌓이는 장소
(d) 해양 잔해가 플라스틱으로 변하는 장소

 GPGP의 정의를 묻는 질문이므로 첫 단락에서 정의를 확인한다.

해설

본문에서 GPGP는 해류로 인해 인간이 생산한 쓰레기가 떠다니고 모이는 북태평양 지역이라고 언급하고 있으므로 **(c) a place in the Pacific Ocean where waste piles up**가 정답이다.

paraphrasing point

an area → a place
waste floats and gathers together → waste piles up

단어
current n. 해류
dump v. 버리다, ~을 떠넘기다
debris n. 쓰레기, 잔해
toxic adj. 독성의
pile up v. 쌓다

68. When was the actual existence of the GPGP verified?

   (a) after a transpacific exploration
   (b) after an eyewitness report by a scientist
   (c) upon the publication of an oceanic study
   (d) when plastic waste started disappearing

68. GPGP의 실제 존재는 언제 확인되었는가?

   (a) 태평양 횡단 탐사 후
   (b) 과학자에 의한 목격자 보고 후
   (c) 해양 연구를 발표한 직후
   (d) 플라스틱 폐기물이 사라지기 시작했을 때

해설

1988년에 GPGP의 존재를 예측하는 논문이 나왔고, 9년 뒤 해양연구원인 Charles Moore가 태평양 횡단 요트 경주에서 항해했을 때 확인되었다는 내용을 통해 **(b) after an eyewitness report by a scientist**가 정답임을 알 수 있다.

▸ paraphrasing point

confirmed → an eyewitness report
marine researcher → scientist

existence n. 존재, 실재
eyewitness n. 목격자, 증인
disappear v. 사라지다, 없어지다
exploration n. 탐사
publication n. 발표, 공개

심화 공략 포인트

Part 3에서는 다양한 분야에서 선별한 특정 소재에 대해 **역사적 배경, 형성과정, 변화 과정, 현황 등**에 관한 세부 사항을 출제하며, 주로 **시기와 방법, 이유**에 대해 묻고 있습니다.

두세 단락이 시간 순서에 따라 나열되거나 일반 특징-세부 특징으로 나열되기도 하므로, **시점과 고유명사 등을 키워드로 잡고 동사와 형용사 패러프레이징에 유의해야** 합니다.

① 소재에 대한 역사적 세부 사항 ①

명칭의 발생, 발견 시기, 계기, 기원 등을 묻는 경우

Example

K-pop first appeared in the late 1990s, starting with the music of first-generation idols, whose addictive sound combined electronic and hip-hop music of the time. **In the mid-2000s, the second generation of idol boy groups and girl groups in Korea achieved great success in Korea and abroad, and there was a tendency to define the word K-pop only by the music of boy groups and girl groups.**	케이팝은 1990년대 후반 당시 일렉트로닉과 힙합 음악이 어우러진 중독성 있는 사운드를 가진 1세대 아이돌들의 음악을 시작으로 처음 등장했다. 2000년대 중반, 한국의 2세대 아이돌 보이그룹과 걸그룹이 한국과 외국에서 큰 성공을 거두었고, 케이팝이라는 단어를 오직 보이그룹과 걸그룹의 음악으로만 정의하는 경향이 있었다.

Q. **Why** did K-pop **tend to be limited** to idol music?

   (a) Because the first generation of idol groups appeared in the 1990s
   (b) Because it presents unfamiliar and addictive songs
   (c) Because idol groups in the 2000s were very successful
   (d) Because the idol fandom culture was unique

Q. 왜 케이팝이 아이돌 음악으로 **한정되는 경향**이 생겼는가?

   (a) 1990년대 1세대 아이돌 그룹들이 등장했기 때문에
   (b) 낯설고 중독성 있는 노래를 선보이기 때문에
   (c) 2000년대 아이돌 그룹들이 크게 성공했기 때문에
   (d) 아이돌 팬덤 문화가 독특했기 때문에

 **Tip!** 문제의 tend to be limited에 해당하는 본문의 해당 내용 tendency to define을 찾아 읽는다.

2000년대 중반 아이돌 세대의 성공 이후, 케이팝 음악이 보이그룹과 걸그룹 음악으로 한정되어 정의하는 경향이 있다는 언급을 통해 (c) Because idol groups in the 2000s were very successful가 정답임을 알 수 있다.

▶ paraphrasing point

achieved great success → were very successful
tendency to define → tend to be limited to

단어
- **appear** v. 나타나다, 생기다, 발생하다, 등장하다
- **generation** n. 세대
- **tendency** n. 성향, 경향, 추세
- **addictive** adj. 중독성 있는
- **achieve** v. 달성하다
- **define** v. 정의하다

② 소재에 대한 세부 사항 ②

명칭의 발생, 발견 시기, 계기, 기원 등을 묻는 경우

Example

There are usually two sources of an oasis. One is water that has collected underground, and the other is water that flows to the surface from a spring. When the desert was once lush and water was plentiful, water flowed deep underground. Later, the stored water comes out, and the Sahara oasis is a representative example. The other is the case where the water from melting snow and glaciers in nearby high mountains seeps into the ground. When it rains in the desert, some of the water is absorbed deep into the ground. **Water that has entered the ground through this process sometimes erupts from a low point**, an example of which is the **Turpan Basin** in the Uighur Autonomous Region in China.

오아시스의 원천은 대개 두 가지이다. 하나는 지하에 고인 물이고, 다른 하나는 샘에서 수면으로 흘러 드는 물이다. 사막이 한때 무성하고 물이 풍부했을 때, 지하 깊은 곳에서 물이 흘러내렸다. 나중에는, 저장된 물이 흘러나오는데, 사하라 오아시스가 대표적인 예다. 또 다른 경우는 인근 높은 산의 눈과 빙하가 녹은 물이 땅 속으로 스며드는 경우이다. 사막에 비가 오면, 물의 일부는 땅 속 깊숙이 흡수된다. 이 과정을 통해 땅으로 유입된 물은 때때로 낮은 지점에서 분출되는데, 중국 위구르 자치구의 투르판 분지가 그 예이다.

Q. How was the **Turpan Basin** created?

(a) The water stored in the past flows out
(b) Rainwater absorbed into the ground is ejected from a low place
(c) Water from frequent rain is stored in the form of a well
(d) Rainwater is stored and accumulated deep underground

Q. 투르판 분지는 어떻게 생성 되었나?

(a) 과거에 저장된 물이 밖으로 흘러나와서
(b) 땅속에 흡수된 빗물이 낮은 곳에서 분출 되어서
(c) 잦은 비로 인한 물이 우물의 형태로 저장 되어서
(d) 깊은 지하에 물이 저장되고 축적되어서

 Turpan Basin을 찾아 주변부를 읽는다.

지문에서 사막의 특징으로 비가 오면 물의 일부가 땅 속 깊은 곳까지 흡수되며, 이 과정을 통해 땅으로 유입된 물은 낮은 지점에서 분출되는 경우가 있는데, 중국 위구르 자치구의 투르판 분지가 그 예시라고 하는 내용을 통해 정답이 **(b) Rainwater absorbed into the ground is ejected from a low place**임을 알 수 있다.

paraphrasing point

has entered the ground → absorbed into the ground
erupts → ejected
a low point → a low place

단어

source n. 원천, 근원
flow v. 흐르다
underground adj. 지하의
melt v. 녹다, 녹이다
seep v. 스미다, 배다
basin n. 웅덩이, 분지

store v. 저장하다
erupt v. 분출하다
representative adj. 대표적인, 대표하는
glacier n. 빙하
absorb v. 흡수하다
region n. 지방, 지역

③ 현황, 해결책, 전망 등

약간의 추론&종합 능력이 필요한 문제로, 대부분 본문의 마지막 부분에 제시되어 있습니다.

Example

Although electronic money has many advantages such as convenience, privacy, and reduced transaction costs, there remains a problem of how to impose taxes and how to prevent it from being used for crime. **In order to solve this problem**, legal regulations can be strengthened, but **in the long run**, **it is desirable to strengthen security by using a decentralized free and open source system**.	비록 전자화폐가 편리성, 프라이버시, 거래 비용 절감과 같은 많은 장점들을 가지고 있음에도 불구하고, 어떻게 세금을 부과하고 어떻게 그것이 범죄에 이용되는 것을 막을지에 대한 문제가 남아있다. 이 문제를 해결하기 위해서는 법적 규제를 강화할 수 있지만, (앞으로 길게 보았을 때) 결국에는 분산형 자유 및 오픈 소스 시스템을 사용하여 보안을 강화하는 것이 바람직하다.
Q. What most likely is **the long-term plan to solve the problem** of electronic money? (a) to find a way to impose taxes (b) to educate users on ethics **(c) to strengthen security** (d) to combat internet crime	Q. 전자화폐의 문제를 해결하기 위한 장기 방안은 무엇일까? (a) 세금 부과 방안을 찾는 것 (b) 사용자에게 윤리 교육을 하는 것 **(c) 보안을 강화하는 것** (d) 인터넷 범죄를 소탕하는 것

 문제에서 문제 해결을 위한 장기적 계획을 묻고 있으므로 본문에서 '문제 해결'과 '장기적' 키워드를 찾아 읽는다.

이 문제를 해결하기 위해 (앞으로 길게 보았을 때) 결국에는 분산형 자유 및 오픈 소스 시스템을 사용하여 보안을 강화해야 한다고 언급하고 있으므로 **(c) to strengthen security**가 정답이다.

▸ paraphrasing point

in the long run → the long-term plan

단어
- electronic money n. 전자화폐
- convenience n. 편리, 편의, 편리함
- transaction cost n. 거래비용
- prevent v. 막다
- regulation n. 규제
- desirable adj. 바람직한, 가치 있는
- advantage n. 이점, 장점
- reduce v. 줄이다, 낮추다
- impose v. 부과하다
- legal adj. 법적인, 합법의, 법률과 관련된
- in the long run ad. (앞으로 길게 보았을 때) 결국에는
- decentralize v. 분산하다, 분권화하다

Exercise

GREAT PACIFIC GARBAGE PATCH

The Great Pacific Garbage Patch (GPGP) is an area in the North Pacific Ocean where human-produced waste floats and gathers together due to ocean currents. Also known as the "Pacific trash vortex," the GPGP is the largest accumulation of waste, mostly plastics, among the five offshore garbage patches in the world's oceans.

In 1988, the National Oceanic and Atmospheric Administration (NOAA) published a paper predicting the presence of a garbage patch in the North Pacific Ocean. The GPGP was confirmed nine years later when marine researcher Charles Moore sailed in a transpacific yacht race. Upon returning from his voyage, he reported seeing large stretches of floating waste debris in the Pacific Ocean between California and Hawaii.

According to studies, all waste in garbage patches is primarily <u>conveyed</u> there by ocean currents. Both land-based and water-based activities produce human and natural waste that ends up in the oceans. The currents then send the waste to certain points in the oceans.

The collected waste debris gets mostly stuck in "ocean gyres," huge systems of <u>circulating</u> ocean currents found in the middle of each of the five major oceans. The continuous circular motion of the ocean gyres prevents waste from leaving. Meanwhile, various factors, such as sunlight and ocean waves, break them down into smaller pieces. Plastic garbage, which comprises the majority of the waste, lasts for decades and fragments into microplastics.

The most extensive garbage patch in the world's oceans can be found in the North Pacific Gyre. Most of the debris there is generated in the North American and Asian continents, while the rest come from direct deposits from ocean vessels. A study by The Ocean Cleanup project estimates that as of 2018, the GPGP covers 1.6 million square kilometers, or three times the area of France. Moreover, the garbage patch contains nearly 80,000 metric tons of plastic materials. These, alongside other waste and debris, continue to accumulate in the ocean.

Although efforts have been instituted to address this environmental hazard, the garbage patches continue to pose threats to marine life and humans.

69. How do the ocean currents contribute to the formation of garbage patches?

    (a) They extract the plastic debris of watercraft.
    (b) They produce natural marine garbage.
    (c) They scatter debris in the middle of the ocean.
    (d) They bring together land and marine waste.

70. When does debris probably become a permanent part of the GPGP?

    (a) once it gets trapped in the North Pacific Gyre
    (b) once it travels across two continents
    (c) once it is exposed to sunlight
    (d) once it starts mixing with plastics

71. Which aspect of the GPGP is constantly growing?

    (a) the amount of litter it contains
    (b) the land area of a country it covers
    (c) the variety of waste materials it traps
    (d) the water volume it displaces

72. In the context of the passage, conveyed means _____.

    (a) retained
    (b) allocated
    (c) reclaimed
    (d) carried

73. In the context of the passage, circulating means _____.

    (a) flooding
    (b) spinning
    (c) inactive
    (d) violent

 단서

GREAT PACIFIC GARBAGE PATCH

태평양 거대 쓰레기 지대

67) The Great Pacific Garbage Patch (GPGP) is an area in the North Pacific Ocean where human-produced waste floats and gathers together due to ocean currents. Also known as the "Pacific trash vortex," the GPGP is the largest accumulation of waste, mostly plastics, among the five offshore garbage patches in the world's oceans.

67) 태평양 거대 쓰레기 지대(GPGP)는 해류로 인해 인간이 생산한 폐기물이 떠다니고 모이는 북태평양 지역이다. "태평양 쓰레기 소용돌이"라고도 알려진 GPGP는 전 세계 바다의 5대 쓰레기 지대 중 가장 큰 폐기물 축적물로, 대부분 플라스틱이다.

In 1988, the National Oceanic and Atmospheric Administration (NOAA) published a paper predicting the presence of a garbage patch in the North Pacific Ocean. 68) The GPGP was confirmed nine years later when marine researcher Charles Moore sailed in a transpacific yacht race. Upon returning from his voyage, he reported seeing large stretches of floating waste debris in the Pacific Ocean between California and Hawaii.

1988년, 국립해양대기국(NOAA)은 북태평양에 쓰레기 지대가 존재한다는 것을 예측하는 논문을 발표했다. 68) GPGP는 9년 후 해양연구원 찰스 무어가 태평양 횡단 요트 경주에서 항해했을 때 확인되었다. 항해에서 돌아오자마자, 그는 캘리포니아와 하와이 사이의 태평양에 광범위하게 뻗은 떠 있는 폐기물 잔해들을 보았다고 보고했다.

According to studies, 69) all waste in garbage patches is primarily 72) conveyed there by ocean currents. Both land-based and water-based activities produce human and natural waste that ends up in the oceans. 69) The currents then send the waste to certain points in the oceans.

연구에 따르면 69) 쓰레기 지대의 모든 폐기물은 주로 해류에 의해 그곳으로 72) 운반된다. 육상 기반 및 수중 기반 활동 모두 인간 및 자연에 의한 폐기물을 생산하며 결국 바다로 가게 된다. 69) 그런 다음 해류는 폐기물을 바다의 특정 지점으로 보낸다.

The collected waste debris gets mostly stuck in "ocean gyres," huge systems of 73) circulating ocean currents found in the middle of each of the five major oceans. 70) The continuous circular motion of the ocean gyres prevents waste from leaving. Meanwhile, various factors, such as sunlight and ocean waves, break them down into smaller pieces. Plastic garbage, which comprises the majority of the waste, lasts for decades and fragments into microplastics.

쌓인 폐기물 잔해는 오대양의 각 중심부에서 발견되는 해류를 73) 순환시키는 거대 시스템인 "대양 환류"에 대부분 갇히게 된다. 70) 바다 환류의 연속적인 원형 운동은 폐기물이 떠나는 것을 막는다. 한편, 햇빛과 파도와 같은 다양한 요인들은 그것들을 더 작은 조각으로 분해한다. 폐기물의 대부분을 구성하는 플라스틱 쓰레기는 수십 년 동안 지속되며 미세 플라스틱으로 조각난다.

The most extensive garbage patch in the world's oceans can be found in the North Pacific Gyre. Most of the debris there is generated in the North American and Asian continents, while the rest come from direct deposits from ocean vessels. A study by The Ocean Cleanup project estimates that as of 2018, the GPGP covers 1.6 million square kilometers, or three times the area of France. [71] **Moreover, the garbage patch contains nearly 80,000 metric tons of plastic materials. These, alongside other waste and debris, continue to accumulate in the ocean.**

Although efforts have been instituted to address this environmental hazard, the garbage patches continue to pose threats to marine life and humans.

세계 해양에서 가장 규모가 큰 쓰레기 더미는 북태평양 환류에서 찾을 수 있다. 잔해의 대부분은 북미와 아시아 대륙에서 생성되며, 나머지는 해양 선박에서 바로 나와 쌓인 것들이다. 오션 클린업 프로젝트의 한 연구에서는 2018년 기준으로 GPGP가 프랑스 면적의 3배에 달하는 160만 제곱킬로미터에 이르는 것으로 추정한다. [71] 게다가, 쓰레기 지대에는 거의 80,000미터 톤의 플라스틱 물질이 포함되어 있다. 이것들은 다른 폐기물 및 잔해와 함께 바다에 계속 축적된다.

비록 이러한 환경적 위험을 해결하기 위한 노력이 시작되었지만, 쓰레기 지대는 계속해서 해양 생물과 인간에게 위협을 가하고 있다.

단어

garbage patch n. 쓰레기 지대 (잔뜩 모여 섬 같은 형상을 이룬 해양 쓰레기 더미)
primarily ad. 주로, 주요한
current n. 해류
certain ad. 특정한, 확실한, 틀림없는
be stuck in v. ~에 끼이다, 갇히다
circulating adj. 순환하는, 순회하는
circular adj. 원형의, 둥근, 순회하는
comprise v. 구성하다, 포함하다
fragment v. 조각나다, 부서지다 n. 조각, 파편
extensive adj. 확장된, 광범위의
continent n. 대륙
vessel n. 선박
square adj. 평방의
accumulate v. 축적하다, 모으다, 늘어나다
address v. (문제를) 해결하다, 다루다
threat n. 위협

convey v. 나르다, 운반하다
produce v. 생산하다
debris n. 쓰레기, 잔해
gyre n. 환류, 선회 운동
continuous adj. 연속적인, 지속적인
motion n. 운동, 움직임
decade n. 10년
microplastic n. 미세플라스틱
generate v. 생성하다
deposit v. 퇴적하다 n. 보증금
estimate v. 추정하다, 추산하다
nearly ad. 거의
institute v. 시행하다, 시작하다
hazard n. 위험

 문제풀이

69. **How** do the ocean **currents** contribute to the **formation** of garbage patches?

(a) They extract the plastic debris of watercraft.
(b) They produce natural marine garbage.
(c) They scatter debris in the middle of the ocean.
(d) They bring together land and marine waste.

69. 해류는 쓰레기 지대의 **형성**에 **어떻게** 기여하는가?
(a) 해류는 선박의 플라스틱 파편을 추출한다.
(b) 해류는 천연 해양 잔해를 생산한다.
(c) 해류는 바다 한가운데에 잔해를 흩뿌린다.
(d) 해류는 육지와 해양 쓰레기를 모은다.

 해류(currents)가 언급된 곳을 찾아 읽는다.

육지 활동과 수자원 활동 모두 인간 및 자연에 의한 폐기물을 생산하며 결국 바다로 가게 되고, 그런 다음 해류는 폐기물을 바다의 특정 지점으로 보낸다는 본문의 언급을 통해 해류가 육지와 해양 쓰레기를 모으는 역할을 함을 알 수 있다. 따라서 **(d) They bring together land and marine waste**가 정답이다.

▶ paraphrasing point

send the waste to certain points → bring together land and marine waste.

단어 formation n. 형성   extract v. 추출하다   scatter v. ~을 뿌리다, 분산시키다

70. When does debris probably become a permanent part of the GPGP?

    (a) once it gets trapped in the North Pacific Gyre
    (b) once it travels across two continents
    (c) once it is exposed to sunlight
    (d) once it starts mixing with plastics

70. 언제 잔해가 GPGP의 영속적인 부분이 될 수 있을까?

    (a) 북태평양 환류에 갇히게 될 때
    (b) 두 대륙을 여행 할 때
    (c) 햇빛에 노출될 때
    (d) 플라스틱과 혼합되기 시작할 때

바다 환류의 연속적인 원운동은 폐기물이 떠나는 것을 막는다는 내용을 통해 북태평양 환류에 갇히게 되면 폐기물이 GPGP에 영속된다는 것을 알 수 있다. 따라서 **(a) once it gets trapped in the North Pacific Gyre**가 정답이다.

> **paraphrasing point**

prevents waste from leaving → gets trapped

단어	**permanent** adj. 영속적인, 영구적인	**trap** v. 가두다
	continent n. 대륙	**be expose to** v. ~에 노출되다

71. Which aspect of the GPGP is constantly growing?

    (a) the amount of litter it contains
    (b) the land area of a country it covers
    (c) the variety of waste materials it traps
    (d) the water volume it displaces

71. GPGP의 어떤 측면이 지속적으로 성장하는가?

    (a) 포함된 쓰레기의 양
    (b) 해당 국가의 토지 면적
    (c) 그것이 가두어두는 다양한 폐기물
    (d) 그것이 대체하는 물의 양

GPGP의 미세플라스틱 물질이 다른 폐기물 및 잔해와 함꺼 바다에 계속 축적된다는 본문의 내용을 통해 포함된 쓰레기의 양이 GPGP를 계속 커지게 만든다는 것을 확인할 수 있다. 따라서 **(a) the amount of litter it contains**가 정답이다.

> **paraphrasing point**

waste → litter
accumulate → growing

| 단어 | **litter** n. 쓰레기 | **water volume** n. 수량(물의 양) | **displace** v. 내보내다, 쫓아내다, 대체하다 |

72. In the context of the passage, conveyed means _____.

   (a) retained
   (b) allocated
   (c) reclaimed
   (d) carried

72. 글의 문맥에 따르면, conveyed는 _____를 의미한다.

   (a) 보유
   (b) 할당
   (c) 매립
   (d) 운반

모든 쓰레기들이 처음에 해류에 의해 그곳으로 convey된다는 내용을 통해 convey가 '**운반하다**'의 의미라는 것을 알 수 있다. 따라서 **(d) carried**가 정답이다.

73. In the context of the passage, circulating means _____.

   (a) flooding
   (b) spinning
   (c) inactive
   (d) violent

73. 글의 문맥에 따르면, circulating은 _____를 의미한다.

   (a) 침수시키는
   (b) 회전하는
   (c) 움직이지 않는
   (d) 폭력적인

"대양 환류"가 연속적인 원운동(continuous circular motion)으로 해류를 순환시킨다는 내용이 나오고 있으므로, '**회전하는**'이라는 비슷한 의미의 **(b) spinning**이 정답이다.

MINI TEST

PART 3. Read the following encyclopedia article and answer the questions. The underlined word in the article is for a vocabulary question.

PASTEURIZATION

Pasteurization is the process of heating and then rapidly cooling liquids and food items in order to kill disease-causing microorganisms. Pasteurization does not make a substance sterile; rather than destroying bacteria completely, the process makes them harmless. Pasteurization has the added benefit of extending the period during which a substance is safe to consume before it spoils. This method does not affect the flavor of the substance.

The process is named after Louis Pasteur, a French scientist who began experimenting with the method in 1864. Although pasteurization has become most closely associated with milk, it was originally used to stop fermentation in beer and wine. The process was later applied to dairy products when it was discovered that consumption of raw milk could spread serious illnesses, such as tuberculosis.

Pasteurization generally uses mild heat, at temperatures lower than 100 degrees Celsius. The length of time a substance is pasteurized is dependent on the temperature. Milk is pasteurized at a lower temperature of 63 degrees Celsius, which is maintained for 30 minutes. For faster pasteurization, higher temperatures are used. The substance is then cooled quickly to <u>keep</u> the remaining bacteria from multiplying.

01 Based on the article, what mostly likely is the effect of making something sterile?

(a) It eliminates all types of bacteria.
(b) It improves the food's flavor.
(c) It causes food to rot more quickly.
(d) It is ineffective on dangerous bacteria.

02 What was pasteurization first used to do?

(a) to stop dairy products from fermenting
(b) to preserve alcoholic beverages
(c) to provide a cure for deadly diseases
(d) to ensure accuracy in science experiments

03 In the context of the passage, keep means _____.

(a) maintain
(b) save
(c) protect
(d) prevent

DAGUERREOTYPE

Daguerreotype was a form of photography invented in the late 1830s by French artist Louis Daguerre. The process rapidly grew in popularity since a daguerreotype could be created with just a few minutes of light exposure, unlike earlier methods of photography that took hours, or even days, to create an image. The daguerreotype was used in 1839 to capture the first photographic image of a living human.

The daguerreotype was the primary form of photography from the early 1840s until the late 1850s. It was most often used to make portraits, but despite the relatively shorter exposure time, subjects still had to sit motionless for several minutes to avoid appearing out of focus. Daguerreotypes did not use film, making each picture unique and difficult to duplicate.

The creation of a daguerreotype followed a specific process. First, a thin sheet of silver-plated cooper was polished until the surface resembled a mirror. Then a light-sensitive chemical like iodine was sprayed onto the surface. This enabled an image to imprint upon the sheet when exposed to light. At last, the sheet was sprayed with mercury vapor to make the image <u>fixed</u> so that it would not be further affected by light.

04 What is probably true about photography before the daguerreotype was invented?

(a) It could perfectly capture living things.
(b) It was popularized by a French painter.
(c) It could create better images with low light.
(d) It was not used to photograph people.

05 Based on the article, why might a daguerreotype portrait become unfocused?

(a) because the subject moved around too much
(b) because the exposure time was not long enough
(c) because the photographer was inexperienced
(d) because the use of film was unstable

06 In the context of the passage, <u>fixed</u> means _____.

(a) repaired
(b) fastened
(c) permanent
(d) certain

FRANKENSTEIN

Frankenstein; or, The Modern Prometheus is a novel by English author Mary Shelley that was first published in 1818. The story follows a young scientist named Victor Frankenstein who makes a terrifying "creature" by stitching together the body parts of several dead men and then using electricity to give it life.

The story of how the novel was <u>conceived</u> is nearly as famous as the novel itself; English poet Lord Byron invited Shelley and several other writers to spend the summer of 1816 together in Geneva, Switzerland. While in Geneva, Byron challenged them all to a competition to see who could write the best horror story. A few days later, Shelley's winning idea appeared to her in a dream about a scientist who was horrified by the results of his experiment.

Reception of the novel was positive and has had a lasting impact on literature—and on popular culture as a whole. *Frankenstein* is considered to be a landmark in the science fiction genre, and has been adapted and imitated countless times across all media. Furthermore, the novel raised important questions about ethical concerns in science and medicine that are still being discussed today.

07 What most likely was the outcome of Shelley's summer vacation in Geneva?

(a) She was haunted by bad dreams afterwards.
(b) She published her novel immediately.
(c) She was the winner of the story contest.
(d) She gained recognition for her poetry.

08 Based on the article, how has the story of *Frankenstein* maintained its relevance?

(a) by examining issues of morality in science
(b) by encouraging women to write science fiction
(c) by inspiring the creation of new literary genres
(d) by introducing science into popular culture

09 In the context of the passage, conceived means _____.

(a) produced
(b) believed
(c) assumed
(d) accepted

Vocabulary

한눈에 보는 Part 3 보카

absorb v. 흡수하다	accumulate v. 축적하다, 모으다, 늘어나다
accumulation n. 축적물	accuracy n. 정확, 정확도
achieve v. 달성하다	addictive adj. 중독성 있는
address v. (문제를) 해결하다, 다루다	advantage n. 이점, 장점
appear v. 나타나다, 생기다, 발생하다, 등장하다	apply v. 적용하다, 쓰다, 신청하다, 지원하다
be associated with v. ~와 관련되다	author n. 작가
basin n. 웅덩이, 분지	be expose to v. ~에 노출되다
capture v. 포착하다	certain adj. 특정한, 확실한, 틀림없는
challenge v. (경쟁, 도전을) 요구하다, 도전하다	chemical n. 화학 물질
circular adj. 원형의, 둥근, 순회하는	circulating adj. 순환하는, 순회하는
competition n. 경쟁	comprise v. 구성하다, 포함하다
concern n. 문제, 염려, 우려	confirm v. 확인하다
consumption n. 섭취, 소비	continent n. 대륙
continuous adj. 연속적인, 지속적인	convenience n. 편리, 편의, 편리함
reduce v. 줄이다, 낮추다	convey v. 나르다, 운반하다
cooper n. 구리	countless adj. 무수히 많은, 셀 수 없는
current n. 해류	daguerreotype n. 은판 사진(술)
debris n. 쓰레기, 잔해	decade n. 10년
define v. 정의하다	deposit v. 퇴적하다 n. 보증금

desirable adj. 바람직한, 가치 있는	**decentralize** v. 분산하다, 분권화하다
disappear v. 사라지다, 없어지다	**disease** n. 질병, 질환
displace v. 내보내다, 쫓아내다, 대체하다	**dump** v. 버리다, ~을 떠넘기다
duplicate v. 복제하다	**electronic money** n. 전자화폐
eliminate v. 제거하다, 없애다, 삭제하다	**ineffective** adj. 효과 없는
erupt v. 분출하다	**estimate** v. 추정하다, 추산하다
ethical adj. 윤리적인	**existence** n. 존재, 실재
experiment n. 실험 v. 실험하다	**exploration** n. 탐사
exposure n. 노출, 폭로, 알려짐	**extend** v. 연장하다
extensive adj. 확장된, 광범위의	**extract** v. 추출하다
eyewitness n. 목격자, 증인	**fermentation** n. 발효
fermenting n. 발효	**flavor** n. 풍미
float v. 떠다니다, 표류하다, 부유하다	**flow** v. 흐르다
formation n. 형성	**fragment** v. 조각나다, 부서지다 n. 조각, 파편
garbage patch n. 쓰레기 지대(잔뜩 모여 섬 같은 형상을 이룬 해양 쓰레기 더미)	**gather** v. 모이다, 모으다
generate v. 생성하다	**generation** n. 세대
genre n. 장르	**glacier** n. 빙하
gyre n. 환류, 선회 운동	**haunted** adj 귀신이 나오는, 겁에 질린
recognition n. 인정, 인식, 표창	**hazard** n. 위험
horrify v. 소름 끼치게 하다	**imitate** v. 모방하다
impact (on) v. (~에) 영향을 미치다 n. 영향, 충격	**impose** v. 부과하다
in the long run ad. (앞으로 길게 보았을 때) 결국에는	**institute** v. 시행하다, 시작하다

invent v. 발명하다, 지어내다	**landmark** n. 이정표
lasting adj. 지속적인	**legal** adj. 법적인, 합법의, 법률과 관련된
regulation n. 규제	**literature** n. 문학
litter n. 쓰레기	**maintain** v. 유지하다, 지키다
marine adj. 바다의, 해양의	**mercury** n. 수은
microorganism n. 미생물, 박테리아	**microplastic** n. 미세플라스틱
motion n. 운동, 움직임	**motionless** adj. 움직이지 않는, 움직임이 없는
multiply v. 번식시키다	**name after** v. ~의 이름을 따서 명명하다

National Oceanic and Atmospheric Administration n. 국립해양대기청

nearly ad. 거의	**offshore** adj. 앞바다의
Pacific adj. 태평양의 n. 태평양	**pasteurization** n. 저온 살균(법)
permanent adj. 영속적인, 영구적인	**pile up** v. 쌓다
polish v. 광택을 내다, 다듬다, 연마하다	**popularize** v. 대중화하다, 많은 사람들에게 알리다
portrait n. 인물 사진, 초상화	**predict** v. 예측하다
presence n. 존재	**prevent** v. 막다
primarily ad. 주로, 주요한	**produce** v. 생산하다
publication n. 발표, 공개	**publish** v. 발표하다, 출판하다, 게재하다
rapidly ad. 급속히, 신속히	**reception** n. 반응
region n. 지방, 지역	**relatively** ad. 상대적으로
relevance n. 정당성, 타당성, 관련성	**representative** adj. 대표적인, 대표하는
melt v. 녹다, 녹이다	**resemble** v. 닮다, 유사하다
scatter v. ~을 뿌리다, 분산시키다	**seep** v. 스미다, 배다

source n. 원천, 근원	**spray** v. 뿌리다
square adj. 평방의	**sterile** adj. 무균의, 세균이 없는
stitch v. 꿰매다	**store** v. 저장하다
stretch n. 구간, 지역	**be stuck in** v. ~에 끼이다, 갇히다
substance n. 물질	**surface** n. 표면
temperature n. 온도	**tendency** n. 성향, 경향, 추세
terrifying adj. 무서운, 끔찍한	**threat** n. 위협
toxic adj. 독성의	**transaction cost** n. 거래비용
transpacific adj. 태평양 횡단의, 태평양 저편의	**trap** v. 가두다
tuberculosis n. 결핵	**underground** adj. 지하의
unstable adj. 불안정한	**vapor** n. 증기
vessel n. 선박	**vortex** n. 소용돌이
voyage n. 항해	**waste** n. 쓰레기
water volume n. 수량 (물의 양)	

 Quiz

빈칸에 각 단어의 뜻을 적으시오.

① primarily _____   ⑥ store _____

② extensive _____   ⑦ exposure _____

③ imitate _____   ⑧ tendency _____

④ portrait _____   ⑨ relatively _____

⑤ convenience _____   ⑩ duplicate _____

> **정답** ① 주로, 주요한 ② 확장된, 광범위의 ③ 모방하다 ④ 인물 사진, 초상화 ⑤ 편리, 편의, 편리함
> ⑥ 저장하다 ⑦ 노출, 폭로, 알려짐 ⑧ 성향, 경향, 추세 ⑨ 상대적으로 ⑩ 복제하다

PART 4

지텔프 독해 스타터

General Tests of English Language Proficiency

Business or Formal Letter

PART 04 Business or Formal Letter

- **Part4는 비즈니스 서신을 다루며, 명확한 목적을 가지고 쓰인 편지글 입니다.**
- 신제품이나 신규 개업/이벤트에 대한 홍보, 소비자의 불만/이의제기, 기업의 인적 관리 통보(신규채용, 사임, 사원 복지제도 등), 자선사업 관련 요청 또는 안내 등과 같은 다양한 비즈니스 상황이 묘사됩니다.
- 수신인과 발신인을 체크한 뒤 주요 쟁점과 세부사항에 주목해야 합니다.

 ## 필수 공략 포인트

Part 4는 비즈니스 서신을 다루기 때문에, 주 단락의 문제 패턴을 잘 익혀야 합니다.

지문의 흐름 (단락 구성)

 **문제 패턴**

단락 구성 순서	단락별 대표 유형	대표 문제 패턴
수신인	(문제를 풀기 위해 수/발신인 이름과 직책 확인)	
편지의 주제/목적	편지를 쓴 이유 주요 쟁점	Why did S write a letter? Why is S writing to~? What is the purpose of the letter? What is the main reason~?
주쟁점	요구 사항 답변 내용 주요 사항 메인 이벤트 편지를 쓴 배경	What does the writer say about~? Why ~made the decision? What does S want? How will it happen?
세부사항	요구 사항에 대한 조건 부가 정보 예외 사항 주의할 점 서비스 또는 사업 전망	What is true about~? How most likely to~? What will S do when~? How would S do~? When~?
끝인사	문의사항 발생 시 연락처 첨부 파일 안내 수신인이 할 일 발신인의 바람	What will S do when~? What should S do if~? What ~ attached? What ~ enclosed~?
발신인	(문제를 풀기 위해 수/발신인 이름과 직책 확인)	

 **기초 공략 포인트**

① Part 4의 첫 번째 문제는 항상 이 편지의 목적이나 글쓴이가 편지를 쓴 이유 또는 주제를 묻습니다.

➡ 첫 단락에서 편지의 목적을 확인할 수 있지만, 전체 내용을 통해 파악이 가능한 경우도 있습니다.

이 편지는 왜 쓰였는가?
이 편지의 목적은 무엇인가?
이 편지에서 주목하는 문제점이 무엇인가?

② 편지를 쓰게 된 배경 상황, 주요 요구 사항, 발신인이 결정 또는 확신을 하는 이유 등 상황의 쟁점을 묻는 문제가 출제 됩니다.

글쓴이는 무엇을 원하는가?
글쓴이는 어떤 결정을 내렸는가?
글쓴이는 무슨 일을 겪었는가?

 패러프레이징 패턴

1. 편지의 이유/목적/주제

I am writing on~	I am writing to~
I was alarmed~,	I would like to~
Please V~	I'm pleased to~
Be sure to~	Thank you for~
I determined to~	I decided to~

- **We are pleased to** announce your special promotion in honor of your hard work.
  귀하의 노고에 경의를 표하며 특별 승진을 알리게 되어 기쁩니다.

- **I am writing to** extend my thanks for everything you helped me with on my wedding day.
  제 결혼식 날 귀하께서 저를 도와 주신 모든 것에 대해 감사를 표하고자 편지를 씁니다.

- <u>I would like to</u> invite you to be a speaker at our annual conference on wildlife preservation.

  당사의 연례 야생동물 보호 컨퍼런스에 귀하를 연사로 초대하고 싶습니다.

- <u>I am pleased to</u> inform you that your novel, *Quiet Morning*, has been nominated for Most Outstanding Debut.

  귀하의 소설, 「Quiet Morning」이 가장 뛰어난 데뷔작에 지명되었음을 알려드리게 되어 기쁩니다.

- After careful consideration, <u>I decided to</u> decline the offer.

  신중한 고려 끝에, 저는 그 제안을 거절하기로 결정했습니다.

2. 편지를 쓴 배경, 주요 요구/답변 사항

> **have to ~**
> **represent that ~**
> **suspect that ~**
> **decide to ~**
> **made a decision to ~**
> **I am pleased to announce that ~**

- As you know, due to the rising real estate rental rates and our recent business difficulties, our company's management <u>made a decision to</u> move the branch to a new location after careful consideration.

  아시다시피, 부동산 임대료의 상승과 최근 당사의 경영난으로 인해, 당사의 경영진은 신중한 고려 끝에 지점을 새로운 장소로 이전하기로 결정했습니다.

- Experts <u>suspect that</u> unauthorized ingredients in your children's toy cosmetics have caused serious allergies in some children.

  전문가들은 귀사의 어린이 장난감 화장품에 들어있는 승인되지 않은 성분이 일부 어린이들에게 심각한 알레르기 일으킨 것으로 추정합니다.

 **Exercise**

Richard Thompson
Branch Manager
Mysterium Restaurant Inc.
85 Ridgeway Drive
Reedsport, OR

Dear Mr. Thompson:

I am writing on behalf of my client, Ms. Alisson Kane. She and her fiancé held an engagement dinner with their family and friends in your restaurant last August 6.

However, three hours after the event, Ms. Kane began to experience severe gastric distress. She and some of the attendees were eventually hospitalized and had to recover from food poisoning for almost a week.

The doctors have determined that their illness was caused by salmonella bacteria. Those who experienced similar symptoms claim to have eaten your chicken curry dish, while those who did not, remained okay.

We suspect that the food poisoning was caused by undercooked chicken in the curry. Therefore, Mysterium Restaurant is liable for these damages.

⋮

Sincerely,

Atty. Rebecca Andrews
1389 Bridge Street
Portland, OR

74. Why did Andrews write Thompson a letter?

   (a) to learn the details of the dinner
   (b) to check on the guests' health
   (c) to express satisfaction with his restaurant
   (d) to complain about food safety violations

75. What is probably the reason why the chicken curry caused food poisoning?

   (a) It had unwanted body fluids.
   (b) It was prepared with unclean chicken.
   (c) It was improperly cooked.
   (d) It triggered the guests' allergies.

 단서

Richard Thompson
Branch Manager
Mysterium Restaurant Inc.
85 Ridgeway Drive
Reedsport, OR

Dear Mr. Thompson:

74) **I am writing on behalf of my client, Ms. Alisson Kane.** She and her fiancé held an engagement dinner with their family and friends in your restaurant last August 6.

74) **However, three hours after the event, Ms. Kane began to experience severe gastric distress.** She and some of the attendees were eventually hospitalized and had to recover from food poisoning for almost a week.

The doctors have determined that their illness was caused by salmonella bacteria. Those who experienced similar symptoms claim to have eaten your chicken curry dish, while those who did not, remained okay.

75) **We suspect that the food poisoning was caused by undercooked chicken in the curry.** Therefore, Mysterium Restaurant is liable for these damages.

⋮

Sincerely,

Atty. Rebecca Andrews
1389 Bridge Street
Portland, OR

 단어

on behalf of prep. ~을 대신하여, ~을 대표하여
fiancé n. 약혼자
experience n. 경험 v. 겪다, 경험하다
gastric adj. 위(胃)의
attendee n. 참석자
food poisoning n. 식중독
illness n. 병, 아픔
experience v. 겪다, 경험하다 n. 경험
remain v. 계속 ~이다, 남아 있다
suspect v. 의심하다, 추측하다
liable adj. 법적 책임이 있는

client n. 의뢰인, 고객
engagement n. 약혼
severe adj. 심각한, 극심한
distress n. 고통
recover v. 회복하다
determine v. 밝히다, 알아내다
salmonella bacteria n. 살모넬라균
symptom n. 증상
dish v. 요리
undercooked adj. 덜 조리된, 덜 익힌, 설익은

 문제풀이

74. Why did Andrews write Thompson a letter?

   (a) to learn the details of the dinner
   (b) to check on the guests' health
   (c) to express satisfaction with his restaurant
   (d) to complain about food safety violations

74. Andrews는 왜 Thompson에게 편지를 썼는가?

   (a) 저녁 식사의 세부 사항을 배우기 위해
   (b) 손님의 건강을 확인하기 위해
   (c) 그의 식당에 대한 만족을 표현하기 위해
   (d) 식품 안전 위반에 대한 불평을 하기 위해

 편지의 목적을 묻는 문제이므로 첫 단락에서 목적을 찾는다.

자신의 의뢰인을 대신하여 글을 쓰고 있으며 의뢰인이 식당에서 식사 후 식중독으로 입원했으므로 식품 안전 위반에 대한 불평을 하기 위해 편지를 썼음을 알 수 있다. 따라서 **(d) to complain about food safety violations**가 정답이다.

단어 detail n. 세부 사항
express satisfaction with v. ~에 만족감을 표시하다
violation n. 위반, 위법

health n. 건강, 보건, 의료
complain v. 불만을 제기하다, 불평하다, 항의하다

75. What is probably the reason why the chicken curry caused food poisoning?

(a) It had unwanted body fluids.
(b) It was prepared with unclean chicken.
(c) It was improperly cooked.
(d) It triggered the guests' allergies.

74. 치킨 카레가 식중독을 일으킨 이유는 무엇인가?

(a) 원치 않는 체액이 있었다.
(b) 비위생적인 닭으로 준비되었다.
(c) 부적절하게 조리 되었다.
(d) 손님의 알레르기를 유발했다.

식중독의 원인이 덜 익힌 닭고기로 인한 것으로 의심된다는 내용을 통해 정답이 (c) It was improperly cooked임을 확인할 수 있다.

paraphrasing point

undercooked → improperly cooked

단어 body fluid n. 체액   improperly ad. 부적절하게   trigger v. 유발하다, 촉발시키다

심화 공략 포인트

Part 4에서는 편지의 내용을 통해 유추하거나 세부 사항을 확인하는 문제가 출제되므로, **scanning(찾아 읽기)** 을 통해 주어진 정보를 찾는 것이 중요합니다.

① 조건/정보/주의점 세부 사항 문제

> **What is true about~?**
> **How most likely to~?**
> **What will S do when~?**
> **How would S do~? When~?**
>
> ➡ 특정 사실이나 세부 사항에 대한 단락은 글의 중반부터 시작됩니다.
>   문제를 확인하고 관련 내용을 찾아 소거해 나갑니다

Example

After the internship is over, interns who show great achievements on this project **will be given the opportunity to be hired as full-time employees** at the headquarters.	인턴십이 끝나면, 이번 프로젝트에서 훌륭한 성과를 보여주는 인턴들은 본사 **정규직 채용의 기회를 받을 것입니다**.
Q. What opportunities are available to interns with good results? (a) Overseas travel **(b) Hired as the head office** (c) Bonus payment (d) Immediate promotion	Q. 좋은 결과를 내는 인턴에게는 어떤 기회가 주어지는가? (a) 해외 여행 **(b) 본사로 채용됨** (c) 보너스 지급 (d) 즉시 승진

해설

훌륭한 성과를 보여주는 인턴들에게는 본사 정규직 채용 기회가 주어진다는 언급을 통해 **(b) Hired as the head office** 가 정답임을 알 수 있다.

단어
achievement n. 성과, 성취, 달성, 업적
headquater n. 본사
hire v. 고용하다
opportunity n. 기회
overseas adj. 해외의
immediate adj. 즉시, 즉각적인

② 연락처/첨부파일/수신인이 할 일 등 관련 문제 패턴

What will S do when~?
What should S do if~?
What ~ attached?
What ~ enclosed~?

→ 주로 편지의 내용을 통해 간단히 추론할 수 있는 문제를 출제하는 편입니다.

Example

If you find any defects in the delivered product, please contact the Customer Service Center at 555-0182 immediately and we will exchange it for a new product.	배송된 제품에 결함을 발견할 경우, 즉시 고객 서비스 센터에 555-0182로 연락 주시면 새 제품으로 교환해 드릴 것입니다.
Q. What should I do if a product defect is found? (a) Send a dedicated email. (b) Take it to the customer service center. **(c) Make a phone call.** (d) Call a repair engineer.	**Q.** 제품의 하자가 발견된다면 어떻게 해야 하는가? (a) 전용 이메일을 보낸다. (b) 고객 서비스 센터에 가져간다. **(c) 전화를 한다.** (d) 수리 기사를 부른다.

해설
하자가 발견되면 즉시 고객 서비스 센터로 연락하라는 언급과 전화번호를 통해 (c) Make a phone call이 정답임을 알 수 있다.

단어
defect n. 이상, 결함, 부족
exchange n. 교환, 맞바꿈
customer service center n. 고객 서비스 센터
deliver v. 배달하다
dedicated adj. 헌신적인, 전용의
repair v. 수리하다, 보수하다 n. 수리, 보수, 수선

 **Exercise**

Richard Thompson
Branch Manager
Mysterium Restaurant Inc.
85 Ridgeway Drive
Reedsport, OR

Dear Mr. Thompson:

I am writing on behalf of my client, Ms. Alisson Kane. She and her fiancé held an engagement dinner with their family and friends in your restaurant last August 6.

However, three hours after the event, Ms. Kane began to experience severe gastric distress. She and some of the attendees were eventually hospitalized and had to recover from food poisoning for almost a week.

The doctors have determined that their illness was caused by salmonella bacteria. Those who experienced similar symptoms claim to have eaten your chicken curry dish, while those who did not, remained okay.

We suspect that the food poisoning was caused by undercooked chicken in the curry. Therefore, Mysterium Restaurant is liable for these damages.

On behalf of Ms. Kane and other affected parties, we demand:

1. that you provide monetary compensation for the costs of the guests' medical treatment
2. that the restaurant go through a mandatory health inspection
3. that the employee/s found responsible be punished accordingly based on the restaurant's disciplinary measures

The total costs to be covered, including the <u>breakdown</u> of hospital fees and photocopies of their respective receipts, are attached to this letter.

It is not our intention for the restaurant to be closed. We merely ask for the management to be responsible enough to <u>address</u> the inconvenience it has caused its customers. If this issue is left ignored, please be informed that my client, along with other guests who were affected by the incident, will take necessary legal actions.

Sincerely,
<u>Atty. Rebecca Andrews</u>
1389 Bridge Street
Portland, OR

76. How can the restaurant satisfy the affected parties?

    (a) by complying with the list of demands
    (b) by undergoing health inspection procedures
    (c) by disciplining their staff
    (d) by providing monetary compensation

77. Why most likely did Andrews attach photocopies of the hospital bills in the letter?

    (a) so Thompson will know what medicines to buy
    (b) so Thompson knows which hospital to visit the guests
    (c) so Andrews has proof that the guests were hospitalized
    (d) so Thompson knows the total amount to pay

78. According to the letter, what would Andrews client do if Thompson ignored the letter?

    (a) ask for the restaurant to close
    (b) press charges against the management
    (c) invite more people to join her case
    (d) warn the restaurant's other customers

79. In the context of the passage, breakdown means _____.

    (a) separation
    (b) assembly
    (c) summary
    (d) collapse

80. In the context of the passage, address means _____.

    (a) meet
    (b) explain
    (c) speak
    (d) resolve

 단서

Richard Thompson
Branch Manager
Mysterium Restaurant Inc.
85 Ridgeway Drive
Reedsport, OR

Dear Mr. Thompson:

74) **I am writing on behalf of my client, Ms. Alisson Kane.** She and her fiancé held an engagement dinner with their family and friends in your restaurant last August 6.

74) **However, three hours after the event, Ms. Kane began to experience severe gastric distress.** She and some of the attendees were eventually hospitalized and had to recover from food poisoning for almost a week.

The doctors have determined that their illness was caused by salmonella bacteria. Those who experienced similar symptoms claim to have eaten your chicken curry dish, while those who did not, remained okay.

75) **We suspect that the food poisoning was caused by undercooked chicken in the curry.** Therefore, Mysterium Restaurant is liable for these damages.

On behalf of Ms. Kane and other affected parties, 76) **we demand:**

1. that you provide monetary compensation for the costs of the guests' medical treatment

2. that the restaurant go through a mandatory health inspection

---

Richard Thompson
지점 관리자
미스테리움 레스토랑 주식회사
오리건 주 리즈포트
리지웨이 드라이브 85번지

Thompson씨께:

74) 저는 제 의뢰인인 Alisson Kane씨를 대신하여 편지를 씁니다. 그녀와 그녀의 약혼자는 지난 8월 6일 당신의 식당에서 가족 및 친구들과 약혼 만찬을 가졌습니다.

74) 그러나 3시간 후 Kane씨는 심각한 위통을 경험하기 시작했습니다. 그녀와 참석자들 중 일부는 결국 입원했고, 거의 일주일 동안 식중독에서 회복해야 했습니다.

의사들은 그들의 병이 살모넬라균에 의한 것이라고 밝혔습니다. 비슷한 증상을 경험한 사람들은 당신의 치킨 카레 요리를 먹었다고 주장하는 반면, 그렇지 않은 사람들은 멀쩡했습니다.

75) 우리는 식중독이 카레에 덜 익은 닭고기로 인한 것으로 의심됩니다. 따라서 미스테리움 레스토랑은 이러한 손해에 대해 책임이 있습니다.

Kane씨 및 다른 피해 당사자들을 대신하여, 76) 다음을 요구합니다:

1. 손님들의 치료 비용에 대한 금전적 보상을 제공할 것

2. 식당은 의무 건강 검사를 받을 것

3. that the employee/s found responsible be punished accordingly based on the restaurant's disciplinary measures

77) **The total costs to be covered, including the** 79) **breakdown of hospital fees and photocopies of their respective receipts, are attached to this letter.**

It is not our intention for the restaurant to be closed. 76) **We merely ask for the management to be responsible enough to** 80) **address the inconvenience it has caused its customers.** 78) **If this issue is left ignored, please be informed that my client, along with other guests who were affected by the incident, will take necessary legal actions.**

Sincerely,

Atty. Rebecca Andrews
1389 Bridge Street
Portland, OR

3. 식당의 징계 조치에 따라 책임이 있다고 여겨진 직원이 처벌 받도록 하는 것

77) 이 편지에는 병원비 79) 명세서 및 각각의 영수증 사본을 포함하여 처리 되어야 할 총 비용이 첨부되어 있습니다.

식당이 문을 닫는 것은 우리의 의도가 아닙니다. 76) 우리는 단지 경영진이 식당이 고객들에게 끼친 불편을 80) 해결할 수 있을 만큼 충분히 책임질 것을 요구합니다. 78) 이 문제가 무시된다면, 제 의뢰인은 이 사건에 영향을 받은 다른 손님들과 함께 필요한 법적 조치를 취할 것임을 알아두시기 바랍니다.

Rebecca Andrews 변호사
오리건 주 포틀랜드
브릿지 도로 1389번지

단어

affect v. 영향을 미치다
compensation n. 보상, 보상금
mandatory adj. 의무적인
responsible adj. 책임이 있는, 책임지고 있는
disciplinary measure n. 징계 조치, 제재 조치
breakdown n. 명세서
photocopy n. 복사
merely ad. 단지, 그저
ignore v. 무시하다

monetary adj. 금전의
treatment n. 치료, 처치, 대우
inspection n. 검사, 점검
accordingly ad. ~에 따라서, 부응해서, 그에 맞춰
intention n. 의도, 목적, 의사
fee n. 요금, 청구서
attach v. 첨부하다
inconvenience n. 불편함
legal adj. 법적인, 합법의, 법률과 관련된

 **문제풀이**

76. How can the restaurant satisfy the affected parties?

   (a) by complying with the list of demands
   (b) by undergoing health inspection procedures
   (c) by disciplining their staff
   (d) by providing monetary compensation

76. 어떻게 식당은 피해 당사자들을 만족시킬 수 있을까?

   (a) 요구 목록을 준수함으로써
   (b) 건강 검진 절차를 밟음으로써
   (c) 직원을 징계함으로써
   (d) 금전적 보상을 제공함으로써

해설

구체적인 요구 사항 세 개를 나열했으며, 식당이 고객들에게 끼친 불편을 해결할 수 있을 만큼 충분히 책임질 것을 요구한다는 언급을 통해 요구사항을 들어 달라는 것임을 알 수 있다. 따라서 **(a) by complying with the list of demands**가 정답이다.

단어 satisfy v. 만족시키다, 충족시키다   comply (with) v. (~을) 준수하다, 지키다
undergo v. 겪다, 받다   discipline n. 규율, 훈육
compensation n. 보상, 보상금

77. Why most likely did Andrews **attach** photocopies of the hospital **bills** in the letter?

   (a) so Thompson will know what medicines to buy
   (b) so Thompson knows which hospital to visit the guests
   (c) so Andrews has proof that the guests were hospitalized
   (d) so Thompson knows the total amount to pay

77. 앤드류는 왜 편지에 병원 **청구서** 사본을 **첨부했**을 것 같은가?

   (a) 톰슨이 어떤 약을 사야 하는지 알기 위해서
   (b) 톰슨이 어떤 병원을 방문해야 할지 알기 위해서
   (c) 앤드류가 손님들이 병원에 입원했다는 증거를 가지기 위해서
   (d) 톰슨이 지불해야 할 총액을 알기 위해서

138   CHAPTER 1

손해 배상을 위해 청구서를 첨부한 것이므로 Thompson이 지불해야 할 총 금액을 알게 하기 위해서 사본을 첨부한 것임을 알 수 있다. 따라서 **(d) so Thompson knows the total amount to pay**가 정답이다.

> paraphrasing point

fees → bills

단어　bill n. 청구서, 고지서, 계산서　　　proof n. 증거, 증명　　　amount n. 총액, 총계

---

78. According to the letter, what would Andrew's client do if Thompson ignored the letter?

    (a) ask for the restaurant to close
    (b) **press charges against the management**
    (c) invite more people to join her case
    (d) warn the restaurant's other customers

78. 편지에 따르면, 톰슨이 편지를 무시한다면 앤드류의 의뢰인은 무엇을 할 것인가?

    (a) 식당 문을 닫으라고 요청한다
    (b) 경영진을 고발한다
    (c) 그녀의 사건에 더 많은 사람들을 참여시킨다
    (d) 그 식당의 다른 고객에게 경고한다

이 문제가 무시당할 경우 법적 조치를 취할 것이라는 내용이 언급되어 있으므로 식당에 맞서 고소를 하겠다고 보는 것이 가장 적절하다. 따라서 **(b) press charges against the management**가 정답이다.

> paraphrasing point

take legal actions → press charges

단어　ignore v. 무시하다　　　press charges (against) v. (~을 상대로) 고소하다, 기소하다

79. In the context of the passage, breakdown means _____.

(a) separation
(b) assembly
(c) **summary**
(d) collapse

79. 글의 문맥에 따르면, breakdown은 _____을 의미한다.

(a) 분리
(b) 조립
(c) **요약**
(d) 붕괴

> 해설

병원비와 영수증 사본 등의 breakdown을 포함한다는 맥락을 통해 breakdown이 '내역'의 일종이라는 것을 알 수 있다. 따라서 **요약**이라는 의미로 가장 비슷한 어휘인 **(c) summary**가 정답이다.

80. In the context of the passage, address means _____.

(a) meet
(b) explain
(c) speak
(d) **resolve**

80. 글의 문맥에 따르면, address는 _____을 의미한다.

(a) 만나다
(b) 설명하다
(c) 말하다
(d) **해결하다**

> 해설

우리는 단지 고객에게 불편을 초래하는 데 따른 책임을 경영진에게 요구하는 것이라는 내용을 통해 address가 '**(문제를) 해결하다**'의 뜻이라는 것을 유추할 수 있다. 따라서 **(d) resolve**가 정답이다.

MINI TEST

PART 4. Read the following business letter and answer the questions. The underlined word in the letter is for a vocabulary question.

David Akerman

Senior Editor

The Pinewood Daily Herald

Dear Mr. Akerman,

    First of all, I would like to begin this letter by expressing how much I appreciate the write-up on our family event in Sunday's edition of *The Pinewood Daily Herald*. Ms. Jones is a terrific writer so I was very excited to read her article, "The Robinson Family Reunion." I was especially pleased when I saw the photos of our family members having a picnic and playing games together in the park. If possible, I would like to get copies of the photographs as a keepsake of that wonderful day.

    However, as much as I enjoyed the article, there are a few corrections that I would like to make. First of all, the caption under the family group photo misidentified the man on the right as my brother Harold, when in fact he is my cousin Danny. Additionally, while we were happy that Grandpa John's military service in World War II was acknowledged, we were a little disappointed that the article referred to him as an army medic. Being an army medic is a noble position, but Grandpa John actually served as a fighter pilot. I'm not sure how this <u>erroneous</u> information came to be printed.

01 What is the main reason why the writer sent a letter to the editor?

(a) to respond to an article about her family
(b) to request extra copies of the newspaper
(c) to ask them to write about an event
(d) to appreciate the work of their writers

02 Why does the writer say the photo caption is incorrect?

(a) Her cousin was not present at the reunion.
(b) Her family member is wrongly identified.
(c) The photo shows a different family.
(d) The caption misspells her brother's name.

03 In the context of the passage, erroneous means _____.

(a) various
(b) unsafe
(c) delicate
(d) false

George Hoffman

Executive Director

Great Health Pharmaceuticals

Dear Mr. Hoffman,

First of all, thank you so much for offering me the Account Manager position at Great Health Pharmaceuticals. I feel honored that you think I would be a great fit for the team and an integral part of your company's future successes. Thinking back on our interview last week, I was struck by the warmth and respect you showed towards your employees. As a potential worker, that is the kind of environment that I really value.

That said, I would like to take more time to think about the offer before accepting, if possible. At the moment, I have competing offers from a few other companies. I feel that I need to consider all possible angles when making such an important commitment. I apologize for any delay this may cause you in the hiring process, and I understand if you are not able to give me more time for the decision.

I just want to <u>emphasize</u> again how much I enjoyed meeting you and how excited I am at the prospect of working for Great Health. Please let me know if you can wait until next week for my response to the job offer.

Yours truly,

Amy Baker

04 Why did Amy Baker write a letter to George Hoffman?

(a) to tell him that she accepts the job offer
(b) to ask him to give her more time to think
(c) to inform him that she will decline the position
(d) to thank him for the opportunity to interview

05 Why is Amy Baker hesitating about her decision?

(a) She has other options to contemplate.
(b) She wants to learn more about the company.
(c) She cannot start working right away.
(d) She has several interviews to attend.

06 In the context of the passage, <u>emphasize</u> means _____.

(a) sympathize
(b) comprehend
(c) imagine
(d) repeat

Cecile Johnson

Regional Manager

Movers and Shakers Moving Company

Dear Mrs. Johnson,

    I am writing to express how deeply unsatisfied I was with the service from Movers and Shakers. I hired movers from the local branch of your company to help me move into a new house on October 12th of this year, and I would like to make several complaints about the job that the workers did.

    On that morning, the movers were supposed to arrive at 10 a.m., but they didn't show up until well after lunchtime. As a result, it was very late at night when they finally finished unloading my belongings at the new house. They were also quite <u>reckless</u> when moving fragile items. In fact, my television screen was noticeably cracked when two of the movers dropped it on the steps outside.

    As one might expect, I was extremely upset about my ruined TV, as well as the lack of respect toward my time. The next day I contacted the local branch of Movers and Shakers, but the manager refused to acknowledge any mistakes. That's why I am writing to you, in the hopes that the company will take responsibility for these problems by financially compensating me for the damage.

    Awaiting your response,

    Joseph Cutler

07 Why is Mr. Cutler writing the letter to the moving company?

(a) He needs to hire people to help him move.
(b) He wants to praise workers at the local branch.
(c) He has to reschedule his moving date.
(d) He intends to criticize their poor service.

08 What does Mr. Cutler probably want the moving company to do?

(a) to give him money for his broken television
(b) to acknowledge their mistakes frankly
(c) to send him a sincere apology in writing
(d) to have the manager call him personally

09 In the context of the passage, reckless means _____.

(a) mindless
(b) careless
(c) adventurous
(d) impulsive

Vocabulary

한눈에 보는 Part 4 보카

accept v. 수락하다, 받아들이다	accordingly ad. ~에 따라서, 부응해서, 그에 맞춰
achievement n. 성과, 성취, 달성, 업적	opportunity n. 기회
acknowledge v. 인정하다	affect v. 영향을 미치다
amount n. 총액, 총계	apology n. 사과 v. 사과하다
appreciate v. 감사하다, 고마워하다	army medic n. 의무병, 군의관
attach v. 첨부하다	attend v. 참석하다, 다니다
attendee n. 참석자	be supposed to v v. ~하기로 되어있다
belonging n. 물건들, 소지품	bill n. 청구서, 고지서, 계산서
body fluid n. 체액	branch n. 분점, 지사
breakdown n. 명세서	caption n. 설명, 캡션 (사진, 삽화 등에 붙인 설명)
client n. 의뢰인, 고객	commitment n. 책무, 책임, 공약
compensate v. 보상하다	compensation n. 보상, 보상금
competing offer n. (다른 기업으로부터 받은) 비슷한 제안	complain v. 불만을 제기하다, 불평하다, 항의하다
comply (with) v. (~을) 준수하다, 지키다	contact v. ~에게 연락하다
contemplate v. 심사숙고하다, 고려하다, 생각하다	correction n. 수정
crack v. 깨뜨리다	criticize v. 비판하다, 비난하다
customer service center n. 고객 서비스 센터	decline n. 감소 v. 감소하다, 거절하다
dedicated adj. 헌신적인, 전용의	defect n. 이상, 결함, 부족
deliver v. 배달하다	detail n. 세부 사항

148 CHAPTER 1

determine v. 밝히다, 알아내다	disappointed adj. 실망한, 낙담한
disciplinary measure n. 징계 조치, 제재 조치	discipline n. 규율, 훈육
dish n. 요리	distress n. 고통
editor n. 편집자	engagement n. 약혼
exchange n. 교환, 맞바꿈	expect v. 예상하다
experience n. 경험 v. 겪다, 경험하다	express satisfaction with v. 만족감을 표시하다
express v. 표현하다	fee n. 요금, 청구서
fiancé n. 약혼자	fighter pilot n. 전투기 조종사
financially ad. 금전적으로, 재정적으로	food poisoning n. 식중독
fragile adj. 깨지기 쉬운	frankly ad. 솔직히
gastric adj. 위의	headquater n. 본사
health n. 건강, 보건, 의료	hire v. 고용하다
hire v. 고용하다	honor n. 영광
ignore v. 무시하다	ignore v. 무시하다
illness n. 병, 아픔	immediate adj. 즉시, 즉각적인
improperly ad. 부적절하게	inconvenience n. 불편함
inspection n. 검사, 점검	integral adj. 필수적인, 필수의
intend v. 의도하다, 작정하다	intention n. 의도, 목적, 의사
keepsake n. 기념품, 유품	legal adj. 법적인, 합법의, 법률과 관련된
liable adj. 법적 책임이 있는	local adj. 지역의
mandatory adj. 의무적인	merely ad. 단지, 그저
misidentify v. 오인하다, 잘못 확인하다	monetary adj. 금전의
noble adj. 고귀한	noticeably ad. 눈에 띄게

PART 04 _ Business or Formal Letter

offer n. 제안 (v. 제안하다)	**on behalf of** prep. ~을 대신하여, ~을 대표하여
opportunity n. 기회	**overseas** adj. 해외의
photocopy n. 복사	**potential** adj. 향후의, 잠재의
praise n. 칭찬, 찬사 (v. 칭찬하다)	**press charges (against)** v. (~을 상대로) 고소하다, 기소하다
proof n. 증거, 증명	**prospect** n. 전망
recover v. 회복하다	**refer to A as B** v. A를 B로 언급하다
remain v. 계속 ~이다, 남아 있다	**repair** v. 수리하다, 보수하다 n. 수리, 보수, 수선
respond v. 응답하다, 대답하다	**responsibility** n. 책임
responsible adj. 책임이 있는, 책임지고 있는	**reunion** n. 모임
ruin v. 망가뜨리다, 폐허로 만들다	**salmonella bacteria** n. 살모넬라균
satisfy v. 만족시키다, 충족시키다	**severe** adj. 심각한, 극심한
show up v. 나타나다	**sincere** adj. 진실된, 진정한
suspect v. 의심하다, 추측하다	**symptom** n. 증상
treatment n. 치료, 처치, 대우	**trigger** v. 유발하다, 촉발시키다
undercooked adj. 덜 조리된, 덜 익힌, 설익은	**undergo** v. 겪다, 받다
unload v. 짐을 내리다	**unsatisfied** adj. 불만족의
upset v. 속상하게 하다, 잘못되게 만들다 adj. 속상한, 화가 난	**violation** n. 위반, 위법
well after adj. 훨씬 후의	

 Quiz

빈칸에 각 단어의 뜻을 적으시오.

① compensate　_____　⑥ suspect　_____

② commitment　_____　⑦ severe　_____

③ mandatory　_____　⑧ attendee　_____

④ potential　_____　⑨ fragile　_____

⑤ appreciate　_____　⑩ acknowledge　_____

정답　① 보상하다　② 책무, 책임, 공약　③ 의무적인　④ 향후의, 잠재의　⑤ 감사하다, 고마워하다
⑥ 의심하다, 추측하다　⑦ 심각한, 극심한　⑧ 참석자　⑨ 깨지기 쉬운　⑩ 인정하다

CHAPHER 2

지텔프 독해 스타터

General Tests of English Language Proficiency

실전 모의고사

실전 모의고사 1회
실전 모의고사 2회

▶ <정답 및 해설> 해설집 40~87Page

GENERAL TESTS OF ENGLISH LANGUAGE PROFICIENCY

G-TELP™

LEVEL 2

1회

READING AND VOCABULARY SECTION

40 min

시작 시각		시	분	초
목표 종료 시각		시	분	초
종료 시각		시	분	초
총 소요 시간(종료 시각 - 시작 시각)			분	초
초과 시간(총 소요 시간 - 목표 시각)			분	초

DIRECTIONS:

You will now read four different passages. Each passage is followed by comprehension and vocabulary questions. From the four choices for each item, choose the best answer. Then blacken in the correct circle on your answer sheet.

Read the following example and example question.

Example:

> Bill Johnson lives in New York. He is 25 years old. He has four brothers and two sisters.
> How many brothers does Bill Johnson have?
>
> (a) one
> (b) two
> (c) three
> (d) four

The correct answer is (d), so the circle with the letter (d) has been blackened.

NOW TURN THE PAGE AND BEGIN

Part 1. Read the following biography article and answer the questions. The underlined words in the article are for vocabulary questions.

VALENTINA TERESHKOVA

Valentina Tereshkova is a Soviet cosmonaut who became the first woman to travel into space during the U.S.S.R. space program in the 1950s and 1960s. In less than three days, she was able to orbit the Earth 48 times aboard the spacecraft Vostok 6.

Valentina Vladimirovna Tereshkova was born on March 6, 1937 in Maslennikovo, Russia. Her father was a tractor driver, while her mother worked in a textile mill. When Tereshkova's father died, she and her siblings were single-handedly raised by their mother.

Tereshkova did not attend school until she was about ten years old due to their family's financial struggle. Six years later, she left school and began working at the textile mill with her mother to support her siblings. She continued her education by taking lessons from her instructors through the mail.

While balancing her job and studies, Tereshkova joined the Yaroslavl Air Sports Club, and became a parachutist. She completed at least a hundred parachute jumps as an amateur. During this time, the Soviet Union was in a competition against the United States for space travel supremacy—both were eager to send humans into space.

Following the first Soviet spaceflight piloted by a man in 1961, the U.S.S.R. started recruiting women into the Soviet space program. Tereshkova volunteered, even though she had no prior education in piloting. It was, however, her parachuting record and experience that led to her acceptance, since cosmonauts back then were required to parachute from their capsules upon their return to Earth.

For 18 months, Tereshkova trained as a cosmonaut along with four other women. They went through tests to determine if they could handle long periods of being alone, as well as extreme and zero gravity conditions. Of the five trainees, only Tereshkova traveled into space, piloting the spacecraft Vostok 6 on June 16, 1963. She circled the Earth 48 times in just 70.8 hours.

After her voyage, Tereshkova was awarded the title of the Hero of the Soviet Union. She also received various forms of recognition including the Order of Lenin, the highest award given by the Soviet Union to a civilian.

Tereshkova never flew again but she continued working in the Soviet space program. At present, Tereshkova's legacy is widely celebrated in books, museums, and stage productions.

53. What is Valentina Tereshkova most recognized for?

    (a) being the first female to travel in space around the Earth
    (b) having stayed in space for more than three days
    (c) having commanded the first Russian spacecraft
    (d) being the first woman member of the Soviet Union

54. How did Tereshkova keep up with her studies despite her job?

    (a) by accepting jobs only during the night
    (b) by attending classes before going to the mill
    (c) by using mailed lectures to school herself
    (d) by listening to her mother's lessons

55. When did Tereshkova learn how to parachute?

    (a) when she worked as a fabric miller
    (b) when she signed up for an air sports club
    (c) when she joined a Soviet space exploration
    (d) when she enrolled at a pilot school

56. Why most likely was Tereshkova accepted into the space program?

    (a) because she excelled at commanding aircraft
    (b) because she was used to extreme conditions
    (c) because she trained as a cosmonaut beforehand
    (d) because she could land on the Earth by parachuting

57. What did Tereshkova do after the spaceflight?

    (a) She gave a speech during her award ceremony.
    (b) She helped with the later Soviet space programs.
    (c) She wrote a book about her space travel.
    (d) She accepted a position at a space museum.

58. In the context of the passage, record means _____.

    (a) history
    (b) journal
    (c) transaction
    (d) album

59. In the context of the passage, handle means _____.

    (a) operate
    (b) hold
    (c) survive
    (d) govern

Part 2. Read the following megazine article and answer the questions. The underlined words in the article are for vocabulary questions.

DOGS MOVE QUICKLY TO HELP THEIR OWNERS

A study published in *Learning and Behavior* has found that dogs are more likely to come up to a person who is crying than to a person who hums a tune. Additionally, dogs display quicker actions when assisting people in distress.

The recent study was conducted to determine the dogs' capacity for pro-social behavior. Researchers examined how the dogs delivered comfort and attention, and if they were capable of providing substantive help to humans in need. For the experiment, the researchers observed 34 dogs of various ages, sizes, and breeds, along with their respective owners.

The members of the first group were asked to make crying sounds and say "help" in a distressed tone every 15 seconds. Meanwhile, the members of the second group were told to hum the tune of Twinkle, Twinkle, Little Star and say "help" using a normal tone at the same interval. Researchers chose humming among other actions because it is a sound that the dog participants usually had not been exposed to.

One by one, the dog owners were asked to sit behind a clear plastic door that could be easily opened by a dog's nose or paw. The dogs, on the other hand, were positioned in a room where they could see and hear their owners cry or hum. The dog owners had been classified into two groups. After the experiment, it was found that although the number of dogs that opened the door was quite similar in both groups, there was a significant difference in how quickly the dogs in each group "rescued" their owners in the other room.

The dogs in the crying group opened the door and rushed to their owners within 23.43 seconds, while the dogs whose owners hummed took three times longer—95.89 seconds on average. It was also noted that the dogs' ages, sizes, and breeds did not affect how they responded in the experiment.

Overall, the *Learning and Behavior* study reinforced the idea that dogs are capable of detecting human emotions. It also advanced the notion that dogs can be an even greater help to humankind, particularly during therapy.

60. What is the article all about?

    (a) the effects of receiving comfort from dogs
    (b) how dogs react when someone needs help
    (c) the differences between crying and humming sounds
    (d) why people prefer dogs for emotional support

61. Why did the researchers conduct the study?

    (a) to determine whether dogs have emotions
    (b) to estimate how much comfort dogs provide to humans
    (c) to prove that dogs are incapable of ignoring their owners
    (d) to know whether dogs would actually help people in need

62. How was the second group of owners prepared for observation?

    (a) They were asked to hum a lullaby.
    (b) They were instructed to cry for help.
    (c) They were told to ignore their pets.
    (d) They were advised to calm the dogs.

63. Why most likely did dogs respond faster with the first group?

    (a) because the dogs are racing with other dogs
    (b) because dogs take the time to enjoy tunes
    (c) because dogs want to save their owners
    (d) because dogs are irritated by the crying sounds

64. What could be the study's significance in the field of medicine?

    (a) The study will encourage using dogs in treatment programs.
    (b) The study will foster better understanding of pet ownership.
    (c) The study will urge further research on dogs' emotions.
    (d) The study will promote training dogs as house helpers.

65. In the context of the passage, normal means _____.

    (a) healthy
    (b) ordinary
    (c) accepted
    (d) right

66. In the context of the passage, rushed means _____.

    (a) pushed
    (b) delayed
    (c) hurried
    (d) flowed

Part 3. Read the following encyclopedia article and answer the questions. The underlined words in the article are for vocabulary questions.

THE ELIZABETH TOWER

The Elizabeth Tower is a clock tower in London famous for being the most accurate chiming clock in the world. The tower is commonly referred to as "Big Ben," a nickname that pertains to the tower's main bell.

After the old Palace of Westminster had burned down in 1834, architects in England were invited to submit a design for a new palace. After careful selection, the British government chose English architect Charles Barry's proposal, which initially did not include a clock tower. It was only after two years that the clock tower was added to his design with the help of architect Augustus Pugin, who also designed its Gothic interior.

The tower's construction began in September 1843, but it rapidly fell behind the original schedule of completion. The tower was only completed after 15 years, and there was no ribbon-cutting ceremony to celebrate its opening. In 1858, the tower chimed for the first time, and it has become a daily time signal since 1924.

The tower was branded as the "Clock Tower" or "St. Stephen's Tower" during Queen Victoria's reign, and was later renamed the "Elizabeth Tower" to mark Queen Elizabeth II's 60th year on the British throne in 2012.

The Elizabeth Tower stands over 315 feet high and is composed of stone walls and iron frames. It houses the largest bell in the tower, Big Ben, which weighs at least 13 tons and chimes every hour. It also features a public clock with faces that can be seen from all four sides of the tower.

The Elizabeth Tower's reliable timekeeping depends on weight and gravity. Engineers use a stack of old pennies to adjust the clock. If they add a penny on the pendulum, the clock will tick faster. If the penny is removed, then the clock will slow down.

The clock has been stopped by heavy snow, German bombing raids during WWII, and the breakdown of mechanical components used for more than a hundred years. But it has become a point of national pride to keep the clock running dependably. To date, the Elizabeth Tower remains a British cultural icon, an enduring symbol of the United Kingdom and parliamentary democracy.

67. What is most remarkable about the Elizabeth Tower?

    (a) its precision in telling the time
    (b) having a wrong nickname
    (c) its very large bells
    (d) being the world's first clock tower

68. When did the need to build a palace arise?

    (a) after British officials had ordered renovations
    (b) after the edifice was destroyed by fire
    (c) after the original construction plan took so long
    (d) after architects proposed new building designs

69. Why was the clock tower renamed as Elizabeth Tower in 2012?

    (a) to remember the British queen's birthday
    (b) to proclaim the tower's first-ever chime
    (c) to celebrate the clock's 15 years of completion
    (d) to honor a ruler's 60-year reign in England

70. What most likely are the pennies used for?

    (a) to control the clock tower's gravity
    (b) to serve as tokens to keep the clock going
    (c) to adjust the mechanism with their weight
    (d) to set its time with British history

71. Why most likely are British people proud of the clock tower?

    (a) It went undamaged during WWII.
    (b) It has stood tall for almost a hundred years.
    (c) It can be trusted to display the time.
    (d) It never stops working.

72. In the context of the passage, proposal means _____.

    (a) program
    (b) policy
    (c) petition
    (d) plan

73. In the context of the passage, houses means _____.

    (a) conceals
    (b) limits
    (c) contains
    (d) guards

Part 4. Read the following business letter and answer the questions. The underlined words in the letter are for vocabulary questions.

ATTENTION

To: ALL RESIDENTS OF SOUTHWOODS ESTATES
From: HOMEOWNERS ASSOCIATION BOARD (HOA)
Re: PREVENTIVE MEASURE AGAINST MEASLES

We are alarmed by the ongoing measles outbreak in the country. In our state alone, the number of measles cases has tripled from only five during the last month. While no case of the disease has been reported in Northville yet, we believe that keeping our neighborhood measles-free should still be our priority. Therefore, we should work together to prevent the disease before it <u>strikes</u>, rather than cure it once it affects our families.

In line with this, the HOA will be conducting a medical mission with the aid of volunteer doctors from the Iowa Medical Center. The mission will include an orientation regarding the infection, covering its causes, symptoms, and treatment. All residents, especially parents, must attend the event to better understand measles and the risks it entails.

Apart from the briefing, residents will also be accommodated for medical consultations and physical examinations. Doctors will evaluate general health and check for symptoms of measles. Anyone found positive to the virus will be prescribed antiviral medicines and recommended for vaccination.

While the consultations and assessments are free, the measles <u>shot</u> will cost $75 and will be available at the pharmacist's table. Have it administered by the attending doctor after the diagnoses.

The schedule and venues for the medical mission are as follows:
- **Briefing:** March 7, from 9:00 a.m. to 12:00 p.m. at the Club House
- **General Consultation:** March 7-8, from 8:00 a.m. to 5:00 p.m. at the Sports Complex

We are hoping for your full cooperation.

Anna Sue Bennett
HOA Chairperson

74. What is the purpose of the letter?

    (a) to warn homeowners against a contagious disease
    (b) to call for participation in a medical program
    (c) to remind residents about vaccination schedules
    (d) to propose a campaign on ending an outbreak

75. How most likely can the community ensure they are measles-free?

    (a) by treating measles cases immediately
    (b) by kicking out affected families from the area
    (c) by avoiding the infection before it spreads
    (d) by transferring everyone to another neighborhood

76. Why should homeowners go to the orientation?

    (a) so they can get used to the new facility
    (b) so they can volunteer as doctors' assistants
    (c) so they can study medical procedures
    (d) so they can familiarize themselves with the infection

77. When will a patient probably NOT receive prescription drugs?

    (a) if one is found to have zero symptoms
    (b) if one is currently on prescription medication
    (c) if one has immediately caught the virus
    (d) if one has already been vaccinated

78. What most likely should one do to get the measles shot?

    (a) purchase a vaccine from the pharmacist
    (b) finish the briefing given on the first day
    (c) consult with their private physician
    (d) visit both days of the medical mission

79. In the context of the letter, strikes means _____.

    (a) collides
    (b) arrives
    (c) punches
    (d) misses

80. In the context of the letter, shot means _____.

    (a) picture
    (b) explosion
    (c) attempt
    (d) injection

GENERAL TESTS OF ENGLISH LANGUAGE PROFICIENCY

G-TELP™

LEVEL 2

READING AND VOCABULARY SECTION

40 min

시작 시각		시	분	초
목표 종료 시각		시	분	초
종료 시각		시	분	초
총 소요 시간(종료 시각 - 시작 시각)			분	초
초과 시간(총 소요 시간 - 목표 시각)			분	초

DIRECTIONS:

You will now read four different passages. Each passage is followed by comprehension and vocabulary questions. From the four choices for each item, choose the best answer. Then blacken in the correct circle on your answer sheet.

Read the following example and example question.

Example:

> Bill Johnson lives in New York. He is 25 years old. He has four brothers and two sisters.
>
> How many brothers does Bill Johnson have?
>
> (a) one
> (b) two
> (c) three
> (d) four

The correct answer is (d), so the circle with the letter (d) has been blackened.

NOW TURN THE PAGE AND BEGIN

Part 1. Read the following biography article and answer the questions. The underlined words in the article are for vocabulary questions.

L. FRANK BAUM

L. Frank Baum was an American author best known for writing *The Wonderful Wizard of Oz*. He is considered the "Father of the American Fairy Tale" for creating the Oz series, which ranks among the most famous and widely translated works of American literature.

Baum was born in Chittenango, New York, on May 15, 1856. Young Baum was homeschooled during his early years. Due to health issues, he was unable to continue his formal education and earn a high school degree. At the age of 15, Baum took to writing stories. He later began self-publishing his own journals when his father brought home a printing press.

While writing short stories for various magazines in his 20s, Baum ventured into acting in stage plays. Baum's father owned a theater company during that time and in 1880, his father delegated the management of the company to him. Two years later, he would write and stage his first play, which became a modest success.

Unfortunately, Baum's theater burned down in 1882 along with all of his costumes, props, and many of his manuscripts. Baum, disheartened, would search for a more stable job to support his family. For the next two decades, he worked as a traveling salesman and then as a journalist for various magazines and newspapers.

In 1897, Baum wrote a collection of stories based on famous nursery rhymes entitled *Mother Goose in Prose*. The book's reception allowed Baum to quit being a salesman and become a full-time writer. Two years later, he followed it up with a poetry book, *Father Goose, His Book*, which became the best-selling children's book of the year.

Baum's next work, *The Wonderful Wizard of Oz*, was the first major American fairy tale during a time when most fairy tales were written by Europeans. Following the fantastical adventures of his characters, the novel features a real American setting and a fictional world filled with talking trees and everlasting rainbows: the mystical Land of Oz. Many children were captivated by the story, a fairy tale that was bright and playful when so many others were dark and grim, and they wrote letters to Baum requesting a sequel. Baum satisfied his fans by writing 13 sequels throughout the following years.

Baum continued writing stories in the Land of Oz until he passed away on May 6, 1919. After Baum's death, the Oz series remained so popular that it was continued by other authors, who produced an additional 26 books.

53. What is L. Frank Baum most recognized for?

    (a) creating the fairy tale genre
    (b) authoring a popular work of fiction
    (c) being the Wizard of Oz
    (d) translating American literature

54. When did Baum start writing?

    (a) after he began acting on stage
    (b) as soon as his health improved
    (c) when he published his father's journals
    (d) before he received the printing press

55. Why did Baum decide to leave the theater and find a new profession?

    (a) because he wanted to become like his father
    (b) because his workplace was ruined
    (c) because his first play wasn't liked by people
    (d) because theater management was unprofitable

56. Why was Baum able to work as a full-time writer?

    (a) because he wrote the best-selling children's book
    (b) because he was good at selling his stories
    (c) because his first book was successful
    (d) because there was a big market for poetry

57. Based on the text, what probably made *The Wonderful Wizard of Oz* successful?

    (a) The adventures are fun and colorful.
    (b) The author was not European.
    (c) It is the original American fairy tale.
    (d) It has many interesting sequels.

58. In the context of the passage, delegated means _____.

    (a) moved
    (b) delivered
    (c) assigned
    (d) brought

59. In the context of the passage, stable means _____.

    (a) secure
    (b) even
    (c) balanced
    (d) healthy

Part 2. Read the following magazine article and answer the questions. The underlined words in the article are for vocabulary questions.

FAR-UVC LIGHT HAS POTENTIAL TO CONTROL THE SPREAD OF DEADLY DISEASES

Scientists have identified that some wavelengths of ultraviolet C light, or UVC light, can safely limit the spread of diseases. UVC light is a certain range within the ultraviolet (UV) light spectrum. A specific range of UVC light, which is called "far-UVC light," does not harm human skin and has shown potential to be effective against all microbes.

UV light has long been used to disinfect water, food, instruments, and other items by killing harmful bacteria. However, UV light is not recommended to kill airborne viruses in areas with people. It penetrates the outer layer of the skin and can cause skin-related illnesses such as premature aging and skin cancer. This is why public spaces have to be cleared of people first before being sterilized with UV light.

Researchers at the Center for Radiological Research at Columbia University Irving Medical Center have studied the possibility of using UV light to eliminate microbes safely and effectively. They discovered that a low dose of far-UVC light, which measures 207 to 222 nanometers in wavelength, can safely kill germs on the human skin. Far-UVC light is safe because it does not break through the skin's outer layer.

Far-UVC light works by rendering bacteria and viruses inactive, notably "superbugs," which are bacteria that have gained resistance to antibiotics over time. Because superbugs are expected to kill an estimated 10 million people by 2050, far-UVC light is poised to be used in different applications to fight the bacteria. These include cleaning surgical wounds and sanitizing vulnerable body parts prior to medical procedures to avoid infection.

In particular, the researchers believe that far-UVC light may be ideal for sterilizing indoor public spaces. People interact the most in public locations such as airports and schools, making diseases easy to transmit through coughing and sneezing. However, far-UVC light could be applied in these spaces without inconveniencing people.

For almost a decade, the researchers have been testing the safety of far-UVC light on humans as well as on the environment. Experiments continue to be conducted to confirm that far-UVC light is indeed efficient, and that it will not have short- or long-term undesirable effects on skin.

60. What makes far-UVC light ideal for controlling the spread of diseases?

    (a) It is harmless to the skin of people.
    (b) It cures most human diseases.
    (c) It has a wide range of wavelengths.
    (d) It can reach bacteria located deep down the skin.

61. How can far-UVC light be used for medical treatment?

    (a) by curing patients with skin cancer
    (b) by preventing the skin from aging too early
    (c) by letting patients endure high doses of UV treatment
    (d) by getting rid of germs on the skin surface

62. What makes "superbugs" stand out among microbes?

    (a) being able to spread in the air more easily
    (b) having immunity to the effects of ultraviolet light
    (c) having higher tolerance to anti-bacterial drugs
    (d) being able to pass through human tissue

63. Based on the article, why most likely is it ideal to use far-UVC light to sterilize public locations?

    (a) It doesn't come into contact with people in these spaces.
    (b) It doesn't require clearing these spaces of people first.
    (c) These spaces attract all sorts of bacteria and viruses.
    (d) These spaces can easily be rid of people first.

64. When will experiments on far-UVC light probably conclude?

    (a) if it proves effective against the most common microbes
    (b) if its use shows no harm on the skin for any duration
    (c) if regular UV light is no longer harmful on the skin
    (d) if safer methods are found to kill superbugs

65. In the context of the passage, disinfect means _____.

    (a) cure
    (b) wash
    (c) clean
    (d) pollute

66. In the context of the passage, transmit means _____.

    (a) transfer
    (b) control
    (c) broadcast
    (d) bring

Part 3. Read the following encyclopedia article and answer the questions. The underlined words in the article are for vocabulary questions.

FLEUR-DE-LIS

The fleur-de-lis is an ancient symbol resembling a lily flower composed of three petals bound together at their bases. Widely used as a religious, political, and artistic symbol, the fleur-de-lis has long been associated with the French crown, and has been used by French kings as an emblem of their sovereignty.

The fleur-de-lis's <u>association</u> with the French monarchs may be rooted in the era of Clovis I, King of the Franks. Legend has it that the fleur-de-lis is the baptismal lily presented by an angel to Clovis as a symbol of his purity. The lily is believed to have sprung from the tears of Eve, the first woman in the Bible, as she left Eden.

King Philip I has been depicted on his throne holding a short cane with fleur-de-lis on one end. A similar cane was seen in the Great Seal of Louis VII during the 12th century. At the time, Louis VII also had little golden fleur-de-lis scattered on his blue shield. Since then, kings have used the scattered fleur-de-lis on their shields, armors, and coats of arms to emphasize their divine right to the throne.

The symbol has had different meanings throughout history. Some historians believe that the three petals represent the three social classes of medieval social hierarchy: the commoners, the clergy, and the nobility. The modern fleur-de-lis has been said to stand for life, light, and perfection. Over time, the versatile symbol has retained a number of values, and has proven itself capable of evoking different feelings from different people.

Between the classical and the modern periods, artists began to adopt the shape of the fleur-de-lis and stylize it according to their patrons' <u>tastes</u>. As the symbol's popularity increased, it began to appear in market stalls and shop windows. It has been used in architecture to adorn the tops of fences and roofs, and even in the military as a badge of honor. Versions of the fleur-de-lis have also become logos for many sports teams and universities.

67. What is the fleur-de-lis?

    (a) a plant that is frequently used for decoration
    (b) an ancient symbol that represents royalty
    (c) a flower-like gem that is attached to crowns
    (d) an old symbol for France's independence

68. Why was Clovis given a lily during his baptism?

    (a) because he resembled an angel from the heavens
    (b) because he was a son of the first woman in the Bible
    (c) because he was the first king of the Franks
    (d) because he was purified by the event

69. How was the fleur-de-lis used around the 12th century?

    (a) It was placed on kings' canes.
    (b) It was scattered on royal seals.
    (c) It was sewn on blue coats.
    (d) It was printed on the king's throne.

70. What did the fleur-de-lis represent during the medieval period?

    (a) the spread of power throughout France
    (b) the religious beliefs of the people
    (c) the social structure of that time
    (d) the reign of fashionable nobility

71. Why most likely has the fleur-de-lis become a popular symbol?

    (a) because artists can easily copy it
    (b) because it was promoted by the military
    (c) because its meaning is so consistent
    (d) because it can be viewed in many ways

72. In the context of the passage, association means _____.

    (a) society
    (b) connection
    (c) alliance
    (d) friendship

73. In the context of the passage, tastes means _____.

    (a) likings
    (b) flavors
    (c) experiences
    (d) samples

Part 4. Read the following business letter and answer the questions. The underlined words in the letter are for vocabulary questions.

Mr. Barry Carney

Accounting Manager

Falcon Industries

Dear Mr. Carney:

Please accept this letter as a notice of my resignation from my position as an accounting associate at Falcon Industries. My last day of employment at the company will be on the 7th of January.

I recently received an offer from the company that I have always dreamt of joining. After careful <u>consideration</u>, I have decided to accept the offer.

Falcon Industries is the first company I have ever worked for, so my three years of work with you have been truly memorable. I am grateful for having been part of the then newly formed digital accounting department, which was entrusted with the responsibility of digitizing the company's financial records.

I am proud of my tenure at the department because we have successfully improved the accuracy of the company's accounting system. As a result, the company's credit rating increased, which attracted new investors.

I am confident that the accounting team can handle the transition with ease. Nonetheless, I would still like to help with the turnover of work to my replacement. As such, I am <u>willing</u> to train the new employee on my responsibilities. I will also ensure that all of my pending reports are completed immediately to make the transition as smooth as possible.

Thank you again for the opportunity to work for Falcon Industries. I wish for more success for the company, and I look forward to keeping in touch with you. You can email me anytime at sharmainelance@gmail.com or call me at my personal number, 317-573-9250.

Sincerely,

Sharmaine Lance

Accounting Associate

74. Why is Sharmaine Lance writing to Barry Carney?

   (a) to negotiate the terms of her resignation
   (b) to notify him of her departure from the company
   (c) to accept a job offer in her dream department
   (d) to request an interview with his accounting firm

75. Why does Lance consider her stay in Falcon Industries unforgettable?

   (a) She had the chance to form a new department.
   (b) Falcon Industries is her dream company.
   (c) She received her first job opportunity there.
   (d) Falcon Industries developed digital accounting.

76. What is probably one of Lance's greatest contributions to the company?

   (a) helping the company gain more business
   (b) creating a new fiscal system from scratch
   (c) assessing the credit rating of the business
   (d) locating investors for the company

77. How does Lance plan to aid with the turnover?

   (a) by suggesting applicants for her replacement
   (b) by allocating her pending tasks to her teammates
   (c) by creating a timetable of her report deadlines
   (d) by providing guidance to her replacement

78. What is Lance's wish for Falcon Industries?

   (a) for it to finally gain success
   (b) for it to keep contacting former employees
   (c) for it to achieve further success
   (d) for it to succeed without her services

79. In the context of the passage, consideration means _____.

   (a) attention
   (b) sympathy
   (c) thinking
   (d) doubting

80. In the context of the passage, willing means _____.

   (a) hesitant
   (b) prepared
   (c) fortunate
   (d) satisfied

CHAPHER 3

지텔프 독해 스타터

General Tests of English Language Proficiency

부 록

핵심 보카 500
시크릿 노트 G

CHAPTER 3 핵심 보카 500

명사 (Noun)

- 001 **accuracy** [ǽkjurəsi] 정확, 정확도
- 002 **achievement** [ətʃíːvmənt] 성과, 성취, 달성, 업적
- 003 **adaptation** [ædəptéiʃən] 각색, 적용
- 004 **advantage** [ædvǽntidʒ] 이점, 장점
- 005 **allergy** [ǽlərdʒi] 알레르기
- 006 **amount** [əmáunt] 총액, 총계
- 007 **antiseptic** [æntəséptik] 소독제, 살균제
- 008 **apology** [əpálədʒi] 사과
- 009 **apprentice** [əpréntis] 견습생
- 010 **arrangement** [əréindʒmənt] 편곡, 배열
- 011 **association** [əsòusiéiʃən] 협회, 단체, 관련, 연관
- 012 **attendee** [ətèndíː] 참석자
- 013 **attention** [əténʃən] 집중, 주의, 주목, 관심
- 014 **attitude** [ǽtitjùːd] 태도, 자세, 사고방식
- 015 **audience** [ɔ́ːdiəns] 관객, 청중
- 016 **author** [ɔ́ːθər] 작가
- 017 **award** [əwɔ́ːrd] 상
- 018 **basin** [béisn] 웅덩이, 분지
- 019 **behavior** [bihéivjər] 행동, 행실, 태도
- 020 **belongings** [bɪˈlɔːŋɪŋz] 물건들, 소지품
- 021 **beverage** [bévəridʒ] 음료
- 022 **bill** [bil] 청구서, 고지서, 계산서
- 023 **branch** [bræntʃ] 분점, 지사
- 024 **breakdown** [breiˈkdauˌn] 명세서
- 025 **capacity** [kəpǽsəti] 능력, 용량, 수용력
- 026 **caption** [kǽpʃən] 설명, 캡션(사진, 삽화 등에 붙인 설명)
- 027 **career** [kəríər] 경력, 직업
- 028 **cell** [sel] 세포
- 029 **chemical** [kémikəl] 화학 물질
- 030 **childhood** [tʃáildhùd] 어린 시절
- 031 **client** [kláiənt] 의뢰인, 고객
- 032 **college** [kálidʒ] 대학
- 033 **combination** [kàmbənéiʃən] 조합, 결합, 연합
- 034 **commercial** [kəmə́ːrʃəl] (상업)광고
- 035 **commitment** [kəmítmənt] 책무, 책임, 공약

036 **compensation** [kàmpənséiʃən] 보상, 보상금

037 **competing offer** (다른 기업으로부터 받은) 비슷한 제안

038 **competition** [kàmpətíʃən] 경쟁

039 **completion** [kəmplíːʃən] 완성

040 **concern** [kənsə́ːrn] 문제, 염려, 우려

041 **consideration** [kənsìdəréiʃən] 고려, 생각

042 **consumption** [kənsʌ́mpʃən] 섭취, 소비, 소비량, 소모

043 **continent** [kántənənt] 대륙

044 **contract** [kəntrækt] 계약

045 **convenience** [kənvíːnjəns] 편리, 편의, 편리함

046 **convent** [kánvent] 수녀원

047 **cooper** [kúːpər] 구리

048 **correction** [kərékʃən] 수정

049 **course** [kɔːrs] 과목, 강의, 강좌

050 **current** [kə́ːrənt] 해류

051 **debris** [dəbríː] 쓰레기, 잔해

052 **decade** [dékeid, dikéid] 10년

053 **decision** [disíʒən] 결정, 판단

054 **decline** [dikláin] 감소 (v. 감소하다, 거절하다)

055 **defect** [díːfekt] 이상, 결함, 부족

056 **degree** [digríː] 학위

057 **department** [dipáːrtmənt] 부서

058 **detail** [díːteil] 세부 사항

059 **development** [divéləpmənt] 발달, 성장, 개발

060 **diet** [dáiət] 식단, 식사

061 **discipline** [dísəplin] 규율, 훈육

062 **discovery** [diskʌ́vəri] 발견

063 **disease** [dizíːz] 질병, 질환

064 **dish** [diʃ] 요리

065 **distress** [distrés] 고통

066 **downfall** [daunˈfɔl] 몰락, 몰락의 원인

067 **duration** [djuréiʃən] 지속되는 시간, 기간

068 **editor** [édətər] 편집자

069 **effect** [ifékt] 영향, 효과

070 **elation** [iléiʃən] (큰)행복감, 기쁨, 의기양양

071 **electricity** [ilektrísəti] 전기

072 **employee** [implóiiː] 고용인, 종업원

073 **engagement** [ingéidʒmənt] 약혼

074 **evidence** [évədəns] 증거

075 **exchange** [ikstʃéindʒ] 교환, 맞바꿈

076 **existence** [igzístəns] 존재, 실재

077 **experience** [ikspíəriəns] 경험 (v. 겪다, 경험하다)

078 **experiment** [ikspérəmənt] 실험 (v. 실험하다)

079 **exploration** [èkspləréiʃən] 탐사

080	**exposure** [ikspóuʒər] 노출, 폭로, 알려짐	105	**honor** [ánər] 영광
081	**eyewitness** [aiwítnis] 목격자, 증인	106	**hyperactivity** [haiֽpərækti'viti] 과잉 행동
082	**factor** [fæktər] 요인, 요소	107	**illness** [ílnis] 병, 아픔
083	**fatality** [feitǽləti] 사망률	108	**illustrator** [íləstrèitər] 일러스트레이터, 삽화가
084	**fee** [fi:] 요금, 청구서	109	**inconvenience** [inkənví:njəns] 불편함
085	**fermentation** [fə̀:rmentéiʃən] 발효	110	**infection** [infékʃən] 감염
086	**fermenting** [fə́:rment] 발효	111	**ingredient** [ingrí:diənt] (특히 요리 등의) 재료
087	**fiancé** [fi:ɑ:nˈseɪ] 약혼자	112	**innovation** [inəvéiʃən] 혁신
088	**fighter pilot** 전투기 조종사	113	**inspection** [inspékʃən] 검사, 점검
089	**figure** [fígjər] 인물 (v. 중요하다)	114	**instruction** [instrʌ́kʃən] 설명 (=directions)
090	**film director** 영화감독	115	**intention** [inténʃən] 의도, 목적, 의사
091	**flavor** [fléivər] 풍미	116	**inventor** [invéntər] 발명가
092	**footprint** [ˈfʊtprɪnt] 발자국	117	**journalism** [dʒə́:rnəlìzm] 저널리즘, 신문학
093	**formation** [fɔ:rméiʃən] 형성	118	**journalist** [dʒə́:rnəlist] 언론인, 저널리스트, (신문·방송·잡지사의) 기자
094	**gathering** [gæðəriŋ] 모임		
095	**generation** [dʒènəréiʃən] 세대	119	**keepsake** [kiˈpseik] 기념품, 유품
096	**genre** [ʒá:nrə] 장르	120	**lack** [læk] 부족, 결핍
097	**geography** [dʒiágrəfi] 지리학	121	**landmark** [lǽndmà:rk] 이정표
098	**germ** [dʒə:rm] 세균, 미생물	122	**literature** [lítərətʃər] 문학
099	**glacier** [gléiʃər] 빙하	123	**litter** [lítər] 쓰레기
100	**gourmet meal** 고급 음식, 고급 식료품	124	**mainstream** [méinstrì:m] 주류
101	**grocery** [gróusəri] 식료품점	125	**microscope** [máikrəskòup] 현미경
102	**hazard** [hǽzərd] 위험	126	**motion** [móuʃən] 운동, 움직임
103	**headquarters** [heˈdkwɔˌrtərz] 본사	127	**myth** [miθ] 근거 없는 믿음, 신화
104	**health** [helθ] 건강, 보건, 의료	123	**nomination** [nàmənéiʃən] 추천, 지명

129	**observation** [àbzərvéiʃən] 관찰		154	**recognition** [rèkəgníʃən] 인정, 인식, 표창
130	**occasion** [əkéiʒən] 경우, 때		155	**record** [rikɔ́ːrd] 기록, 이력 (v. 기록하다)
131	**offer** [ɔ́ːfər] 제안 (v. 제안하다)		156	**region** [ríːdʒən] 지방, 지역
132	**operation** [àpəréiʃən] 운영, 가동, 수술		157	**regulation** [règjuléiʃən] 규제
133	**opportunity** [àpərtjúːnəti] 기회		158	**relevance** [réləvəns] 정당성, 타당성, 관련성
134	**patriot** [péitriət] 애국자		159	**responsibility** [rispànsəbíləti] 책임
135	**peak** [piːk] 최고조, 꼭대기		160	**retreat** [ritríːt] 피정, 수행
136	**performance** [pərfɔ́ːrməns] 성능, 성과, 실적		161	**reunion** [rijúːnjən] 모임
137	**period** [píːəriəd] 기간		162	**salmonella bacteria** 살모넬라균
138	**photocopy** [fouˈtoukəˌpi] 복사		163	**screenplay** [skriˈnpleiˌ] 시나리오
139	**portrait** [pɔ́ːrtrit] 인물 사진, 초상화		164	**sequel** [síːkwəl] (책·영화·연극 등의) 속편
140	**praise** [preiz] 칭찬, 찬사 (v. 칭찬하다)		165	**shelter** [ʃéltər] 대피, 피신 (v. (비·바람으로부터) ~을 보호하다)
141	**precaution** [prikɔ́ːʃən] 예방조치			
142	**preference** [préfərəns] 선호		166	**shop owner** 점주
143	**presence** [prézns] 존재		167	**shot** [ʃat] 촬영, 시도, 주사
144	**procedure** [prəsíːdʒər] 수술, 절차		168	**signature** [sígnətʃər] 특징
145	**process** [práses] 과정, 진행, 방법		169	**source** [sɔːrs] 원천, 근원
146	**processing** [prásesiŋ] 과정, 절차		170	**span** [spæn] 범위, 기간
147	**producer** [prədjúːsər] 제작자		171	**species** [spíːʃiːz] 종
148	**production company** 제작사		172	**startup company** 스타트업 회사
149	**proof** [pruːf] 증거, 증명		173	**sterilization** [stèrəlizéiʃən] 소독, 살균
150	**proposal** [prəpóuzəl] 계획, 제안		174	**strategy** [strǽtədʒi] 전략
151	**prospect** [práspekt] 전망		175	**stretch** [stretʃ] 구간, 지역
152	**publication** [pʌbləkéiʃən] 발표, 공개		176	**structure** [strʌ́ktʃər] 구조
153	**reception** [risépʃən] 반응		177	**substance** [sʌ́bstəns] 물질

178	**success** [səksés] 성공, 성과
179	**suicide** [sjúːəsàid] 자살
180	**supply** [səplái] 공급량, 비축량
181	**surface** [sə́ːrfis] 표면
182	**surgeon** [sə́ːrdʒən] 외과의사
183	**symptom** [símptəm] 증상
184	**taste** [teist] 입맛, 맛
185	**temperature** [témpərətʃər] 온도
186	**tendency** [téndənsi] 성향, 경향, 추세
187	**threat** [θret] 위협
188	**trait** [treit] 특성
189	**transaction cost** 거래비용
190	**traveling salesman** 외판원
191	**treatment** [tríːtmənt] 치료, 처치, 대우
192	**tuberculosis** [tjubə̀ːrkjulóusis] 결핵
193	**vapor** [véipər] 증기
194	**vegan** [víːgən] 엄격한 채식주의, 채식주의자
195	**vegetarian** [vèdʒətɛ́əriən] 채식주의자
196	**vessel** [vésəl] 선박
197	**violation** [vàiəléiʃən] 위반, 위법
198	**vortex** [vɔ́ːrteks] 소용돌이
199	**voyage** [vɔ́iidʒ] 항해
200	**waste** [weist] 쓰레기
201	**weight** [weit] 무게, 체중
202	**wound** [wuːnd] 상처

동사 (Verb)

203	**absorb** [æbzɔ́ːrb] 흡수하다
204	**accept** [æksépt] 수락하다, 받아들이다
205	**accumulate** [əkjúːmjulèit] 축적하다, 모으다, 늘어나다
206	**achieve** [ətʃíːv] 달성하다
207	**acknowledge** [əknálidʒ] 인정하다
208	**acquire** [əkwáiər] 습득하다
209	**address** [ǽdres] (문제를) 해결하다, 다루다
210	**affect** [əfékt] 영향을 미치다
211	**allow** [əláu] 허락하다, 허용하다
212	**amuse** [əmjúːz] 즐겁게 하다, 재미있게 하다
213	**appear** [əpíər] 나타나다, 생기다, 발생하다, 등장하다
214	**apply** [əplái] 적용하다, 쓰다, 신청하다, 지원하다
215	**appreciate** [əpríːʃièit] 감사하다, 고마워하다
216	**assist** [əsíst] 돕다, 거들다
217	**assume** [əsúːm] 가정하다, 추정하다
218	**attach** [ətǽtʃ] 첨부하다
219	**attempt** [ətémpt] 시도하다
220	**attend** [əténd] 참석하다, 다니다
221	**avoid** [əvɔ́id] 피하다
222	**behave** [bihéiv] 행동하다
223	**capture** [kǽptʃər] 포착하다

224	**challenge** [tʃǽlindʒ] (경쟁, 도전을) 요구하다, 도전하다	243	**crack** [kræk] 깨뜨리다
225	**collaborate** [kəlǽbərèit] 협력하다	244	**criticize** [krítəsàiz] 비판하다, 비난하다
226	**commission** [kəmíʃən] 맡기다, 위임하다, 주문하다	245	**debunk** [di:bʌ́ŋk] (생각·믿음 등이) 틀렸음을 드러내다, 밝히다
227	**compensate** [kámpənsèit] 보상하다	246	**decentralize** [di:séntrəlàiz] 분산하다, 분권화하다
228	**compete** [kəmpí:t] 출전하다, 참가하다	247	**decide** [disáid] 결정하다
229	**complain** [kəmpléin] 불만을 제기하다, 불평하다, 항의하다	248	**decrease** [dikrí:s] 줄다, 감소하다
230	**comply (with)** [kəmplái] (~을) 준수하다, 지키다	249	**define** [difáin] 정의하다
231	**comprise** [kəmpráiz] 구성하다, 포함하다	250	**delegate** [déligèit] 위임하다
232	**concentrate (on)** [kánsəntrèit] (~에) 집중하다	251	**deliver** [dilívər] 배달하다
233	**conclude** [kənklú:d] 결론짓다	252	**deposit** [dipázit] 퇴적하다 (n. 보증금)
234	**confirm** [kənfə́:rm] 확인하다	253	**determine** [ditə́:rmin] 밝히다, 알아내다
235	**consume** [kənsú:m] 먹다, 소모하다, 섭취하다, 소비하다	254	**develop** [divéləp] 발달하다, 성장하다, 성장시키다
236	**contact** [kántækt] ~에게 연락하다	255	**differ (from)** [dífər] (~와) 다르다
237	**contain** [kəntéin] ~이 들어있다	256	**disappear** [dìsəpíər] 사라지다, 없어지다
238	**contemplate** [kántəmplèit] 심사숙고하다, 고려하다, 생각하다	257	**discover** [diskʌ́vər] 발견하다
239	**continue** [kəntínju:] 계속되다, 계속하다	258	**disinfect** [dìsinfékt] 소독하다
240	**contribute** [kəntríbju:t] 기여하다, 기부하다, ~의 원인이 되다	259	**displace** [displéis] 내보내다, 쫓아내다, 대체하다
241	**convey** [kənvéi] 나르다, 운반하다	260	**display** [displéi] 보여주다, 전시하다
242	**cover** [kʌ́vər] 덮다	261	**divert** [divə́:rt] 다른 데로 돌리다, 전환시키다
		262	**dump** [dʌmp] 버리다, ~을 떠넘기다
		263	**duplicate** [djú:plikət] 복제하다
		264	**earn** [ə:rn] 돈을 벌다, 수익을 올리다

#	단어	뜻
265	**eliminate** [ilímənèit]	제거하다, 없애다, 삭제하다
266	**endure** [indjúər]	지속하다
267	**entrust (A with B)** [intrʌst]	(A에게 B를) 맡기다, 위임하다
268	**erupt** [irʌpt]	분출하다
269	**estimate** [éstəmèit]	추정하다, 추산하다
270	**evoke** [ivóuk]	불러일으키다, 환기시키다
271	**exhibit** [igzíbit]	전시하다
272	**exist** [igzíst]	존재하다, 실존하다
273	**expect** [ikspékt]	예상하다
274	**express** [iksprés]	표현하다
275	**extend** [iksténd]	확대하다, 확장하다, 연장하다
276	**extract** [ikstrǽkt]	추출하다
277	**face** [feis]	직면하다, 직면하게 하다
278	**fit** [fit]	알맞다, 적합하다
279	**float** [flout]	떠다니다, 표류하다, 부유하다
280	**flow** [flou]	흐르다
281	**fold** [fould]	접다
282	**function** [fʌŋkʃən]	기능하다
283	**gather** [gǽðər]	모이다, 모으다
284	**generate** [dʒénərèit]	생성하다
285	**graduate** [grǽdʒuət]	졸업하다, 학위를 받다
286	**handle** [hǽndl]	다루다, 처리하다
287	**heal** [hi:l]	치유되다, 낫다, 상처가 아물다
288	**hire** [haiər]	고용하다
289	**horrify** [hɔ́:rəfài]	소름 끼치게 하다
290	**house** [hauz]	수용하다, 보관하다, 거처를 제공하다
291	**identify** [aidéntəfài]	식별하다, 구별하다
292	**ignore** [ignɔ́:r]	무시하다
293	**imitate** [ímətèit]	모방하다
294	**impact (on)** [ímpækt]	(~에) 영향을 미치다 (n. 영향, 충격)
295	**impose** [impóuz]	부과하다
296	**improve** [imprú:v]	향상시키다, 개선하다
297	**increase** [inkrí:s]	증가하다, 늘다
298	**inspire** [inspáiər]	영감을 주다
299	**institute** [ínstətjù:t]	시행하다, 시작하다
300	**intend** [inténd]	의도하다, 작정하다
301	**invent** [invént]	발명하다, 지어내다
302	**investigate** [invéstəgeit]	조사하다, 수사하다, 살피다
303	**maintain** [meintéin]	유지하다, 지키다
304	**melt** [melt]	녹다, 녹이다
305	**misidentify** [mìsaidéntəfai]	오인하다, 잘못 확인하다
306	**multiply** [mʌ́ltəplài]	번식시키다
307	**penetrate** [pénətrèit]	관통하다, 침입하다
308	**perceive** [pərsí:v]	인식하다

309 **perform** [pərfɔ́:rm] 수행하다
310 **personalize** [pə́:rsənəlàiz] 개인화하다, 개인에 맞추다
311 **polish** [páliʃ] 광택을 내다, 다듬다, 연마하다
312 **popularize** [pápjuləràiz] 대중화하다, 많은 사람들에게 알리다
313 **predict** [pridíkt] 예측하다
314 **prevent** [privént] 막다
315 **produce** [prədjú:s] 생산하다
316 **publish** [pʌ́bliʃ] 발표하다, 출판하다, 게재하다, 출간하다
317 **receive** [risí:v] 받다
318 **recover** [rikʌ́vər] 회복하다
319 **reduce** [ridjú:s] 줄이다, 낮추다
320 **release** [rilí:s] 발표하다, 출시하다
321 **remain** [riméin] 계속 ~이다, 남다 있다
322 **resemble** [rizémbl] 닮다, 유사하다
323 **respond** [rispánd] 응답하다, 대답하다
324 **retain** [ritéin] 유지하다, 보유하다
325 **revolutionize** [rèvəlú:-ʃənàiz] 혁신을 일으키다
326 **ruin** [rú:in] 망가뜨리다, 폐허로 만들다
327 **rush** [rʌʃ] 서두르다
328 **satisfy** [sǽtisfài] 만족시키다, 충족시키다
329 **scatter** [skǽtər] ~을 뿌리다, 분산시키다
330 **seep** [sí:p] 스미다, 배다

331 **shield** [ʃi:ld] 보호하다, 막다
332 **shuffle** [ʃʌfl] 뒤섞다
333 **spark** [spɔ:rk] 불러일으키다, 발화시키다
334 **splash** [splæʃ] 물을 튀기다
335 **spray** [sprei] 뿌리다
336 **store** [stɔ:r] 저장하다, 보관하다
337 **strike** [straik] (재난·질병 등이 갑자기) 발생하다, 덮치다
338 **suffer** [sʌ́fər] (질병·고통·슬픔·결핍 등에) 시달리다, 고통받다
339 **suspect** [səspékt] 의심하다, 추측하다
340 **synthesize** [sínθəsàiz] 합성하다
341 **transmit** [trænsmít] 전송하다, 보내다
342 **trap** [:ræp] 가두다
343 **trigger** [trígər] 유발하다, 촉발시키다
344 **undergo** [ə̀ndərgóu] 겪다, 받다
345 **unload** [ənlóu'd] 짐을 내리다
346 **withstand** [wiðstǽnd] 견디다
347 **be associated with** ~와 관련되다
348 **be best known for** ~로 가장 잘 알려져 있다
349 **be capable of** ~할 수 있다
350 **be connected to** ~와 관련 있다
351 **be exposed to** ~에 노출되다
352 **be regarded as** ~로 여겨지다

353 **be stuck in** ~에 끼이다, 갇히다
354 **be supposed to v** ~하기로 되어있다
355 **be unaware of** ~을 알지 못하다, 모르다
356 **be willing to v** 기꺼이 ~하다
357 **burn down** (화재로) 소실되다, 전소되다
358 **drop out** 중퇴하다
359 **leave A behind** A를 두고 가다, 뒤로 하다
360 **name after** ~의 이름을 따서 명명하다
361 **pile up** 쌓다
362 **press charges (against)** (~을 상대로) 고소하다, 기소하다
363 **refer to A as B** A를 B로 언급하다
364 **show up** 나타나다
365 **take care of** ~을 돌보다, ~의 책임을 지다
366 **tend to v** ~하는 경향이 있다

형용사 (Adjective)

367 **accomplished** [əkámpliʃt] 기량이 뛰어난, 재주가 많은
368 **addictive** [ədíktiv] 중독성 있는
369 **additional** [ədíʃənl] 추가적인
370 **affiliated** [əfílièitid] 부속의, 산하의, 소속된
371 **ancient** [éinʃənt] 고대의
372 **apparent** [əpǽrənt] 명백한, 분명한
373 **burdensome** [bə́:rdnsəm] 부담이 되는
374 **certain** [sə́:rtn] 특정한, 확실한, 틀림없는
375 **common** [kámən] 흔한, 일반적인
376 **comparable** [kámpərəbl] 비교할 수 있는
377 **contemporary** [kəntémpərèri] 동시대의
378 **continuous** [kəntínjuəs] 연속적인, 지속적인
379 **contrary** [kántreri] ~와는 다른, 반대되는
330 **countless** [káuntlis] 무수히 많은, 셀 수 없는
381 **crowded** [kráudid] 붐비는
382 **cultural** [kʌ́ltʃərəl] 문화의, 문화와 관련된
383 **dedicated** [dédikèitid] 헌신적인, 전용의
384 **desirable** [dizáiərəbl] 바람직한, 가치 있는
385 **dire** [daiər] 몹시 나쁜, 심각한, 끔찍한
386 **disappointed** [dìsəpɔ́intid] 실망한, 낙담한
387 **distracted** [distrǽktid] 산만해진
388 **disturbing** [distə́:rbiŋ] 충격적인, 불안감을 주는

389 **divine** [diváin] 신의, 신성의
390 **dubious** [djú:biəs] 의심하는, 미심쩍어 하는
391 **emotional** [imóuʃənl] 감정적인, 정서의
392 **energetic** [ènərdʒétik] 활기찬, 혈기 왕성한
393 **environmental** [invàiərənméntl] 환경의
394 **established** [istǽbliʃt] 인정받는, 존경받는
395 **ethical** [éθikəl] 윤리적인
396 **experienced** [ikspíəriənst] 경험이 있는, 능숙한
397 **extensive** [iksténsiv] 확장된, 광범위의
398 **fatal** [féitl] 치명적인, 죽음을 초래하는
399 **fictional** [fíkʃənl] 가상의, 허구의
400 **former** [fɔ́:rmər] 이전의
401 **fragile** [frǽdʒəl] 깨지기 쉬운
402 **gastric** [gǽstrik] 위(胃)의
403 **genetic** [dʒənétik] 유전의, 유전적인
404 **haunted** [hɔ́:ntid] 귀신이 나오는, 겁에 질린
405 **haunting** [hɔ́:ntiŋ] 잊혀지지 않는
406 **hidden** [hídn] 숨겨진
407 **ideal** [aidí:əl] 이상적인
408 **identical** [aidéntikəl] 동일한, 똑같은
409 **immediate** [imí:diət] 즉시, 즉각적인
410 **impressive** [imprésiv] 인상적인
411 **inappropriate** [inəpróupriət] 부적절한, 부적합한

412 **ineffective** [iniféktiv] 효과 없는
413 **inexperienced** [inspáiərin] 경험이 없는, 미숙한
414 **influential** [influénʃəl] 영향력 있는
415 **insufficient** [insəfíʃənt] 부족한, 불충분한
416 **integral** [íntigrəl] 필수적인, 필수의
417 **lasting** [lǽstiŋ] 지속적인, 영구적인
418 **legal** [líːgəl] 법적인, 합법의. 법률과 관련된
419 **liable** [láiəbl] 법적 책임이 있는
420 **lightweight** [laiˈtweiˈt] 경량의
421 **local** [lóukəl] 지역의
422 **mandatory** [mǽndətɔ̀:ri] 의무적인
423 **marine** [mərí:n] 바다의, 해양의
424 **massive** [mǽsiv] 거대한, 엄청나게 큰
425 **monetary** [mǽnətèri] 금전의
426 **motionless** [móuʃənlis] 움직이지 않는, 움직임이 없는
427 **noble** [nóubl] 고귀한
428 **notable** [nóutəbl] 유명한
429 **odd** [ad] 이상한
430 **offshore** [ɔˈfʃɔˈr] 앞바다의
431 **organic** [ɔ:rgǽnik] 유기농의
432 **original** [ərídʒənl] 원래의, 본래의
433 **outstanding** [auˌtstæˈndiŋ] 뛰어난, 탁월한
434 **overseas** [loʊvər | si:z] 해외의

#	Word		#	Word	
435	**permanent** [pə́ːrmənənt]	영속적인, 영구적인	457	**suitable** [súːtəbl]	적합한, 알맞은
436	**persistent** [pərsístənt]	지속적인	458	**surgical** [sə́ːrdʒikəl]	외과의, 수술의
437	**phenomenal** [finámənl]	경이로운	459	**terrifying** [térəfàin]	무서운, 끔찍한
438	**post-operation**	수술 후의	460	**touching** [tʌtʃin]	감동적인
439	**potential** [pəténʃəl]	향후의, 잠재의	461	**toxic** [táksik]	독성의
440	**present** [préznt]	현재의	462	**traditional** [trədíʃənl]	전통적인, 전통의
441	**prestigious** [prestídʒəs]	권위 있는, 명망 있는, 일류의	463	**transpacific** [trænspəsífik]	태평양 횡단의, 태평양 저편의
442	**prolific** [prəlífik]	다작의, 다작하는	464	**undercooked** [əndərkúˑkt]	덜 조리된, 덜 익힌, 설익은
443	**quirky** [kwə́ːrki]	기이한, 별난	465	**underground** [əˈndərgraùnd]	지하의
444	**recognized** [rékəgnàizd]	인정된, 알려진	466	**underside** [əˈndərsaid]	밑면의
445	**record-breaking**	기록을 깨는	467	**unexciting** [əniksaiˈtin]	흥미롭지 않은, 재미있지 않은, 따분한
446	**representative** [rèprizéntətiv]	대표적인, 대표하는	468	**unique** [juːníːk]	독특한, 특이한, 특별한
447	**resistant** [rizístənt]	저항하는, 저항의	469	**unreleased** [ənriliˈst]	미개봉의, 공개되지 않은
448	**responsible** [rispánsəbl]	책임이 있는, 책임지고 있는	470	**unsatisfied** [ʌnsǽtisfàid]	불만족의
449	**severe** [sivíər]	심각한, 극심한	471	**unstable** [ənsteiˈbəl]	불안정한
450	**significant** [signífikənt]	큰, 상당한	472	**upset** [ʌpset]	속상한, 화가 난 (v. 속상하게 하다, 잘못되게 만들다)
451	**similar** [símələr]	비슷한, 유사한, 닮은	473	**versatile** [və́ːrsətl]	다변하는, 다재다능한
452	**sincere** [sinsíər]	진실된, 진정한	474	**vulnerable** [vʌlnərəbl]	취약한
453	**square** [skwɛər]	평방의	475	**weak** [wiːk]	약한, 힘이 없는
454	**stable** [stéibl]	안정적인	476	**wet** [wet]	젖은
455	**sterile** [stéril]	무균의, 세균이 없는	477	**widespread** [waiˈdspreˈd]	널리 퍼진, 광범위한
456	**successful** [səksésfəl]	(어떤 일에) 성공한, 성공적인			

부사 (Adverb)

478 **abroad** [əbrɔ́ːd] 해외에, 해외로
479 **accordingly** [əkɔ́ːrdiŋli] ~에 따라서, 부응해서, 그에 맞춰
480 **biologically** [bàiəládʒikəli] 생물학적으로
481 **continuously** [kəntínjuəsli] 연달아, 끊임없이
482 **financially** [fainǽnʃəli] 금전적으로, 재정적으로
483 **frankly** [frǽŋkli] 솔직히
484 **frequently** [fríːkwəntli] 자주, 흔히
485 **improperly** [imprápərli] 부적절하게
486 **in the long run** (앞으로 길게 보았을 때) 결국에는
487 **merely** [míərli] 단지, 그저
488 **nearly** [níərli] 거의
489 **noticeably** [nóutisəbli] 눈에 띄게
490 **primarily** [praimérəli] 주로, 주요한
491 **randomly** [rǽndəmli] 무작위로, 임의로
492 **rapidly** [rǽpidli] 급속히, 신속히
493 **recently** [ríːsntli] 최근에
494 **relatively** [rélətivli] 상대적으로
495 **single-handedly** 단독으로, 혼자의 힘으로
496 **tragically** [trǽdʒikəli] 비극적으로

전치사 (Preposition)

497 **among** [əmʌ́ŋ] ~에 둘러싸인, ~의 가운데에
498 **apart from** ~와는 별개로, ~외에도
499 **despite** [dispáit] ~에도 불구하고
500 **on behalf of** ~을 대신하여, ~을 대표하여

G-TELP 공식주관사

**핵심 기본 다지기부터 실전 모의고사 적용까지
한 권으로 완성하는 전략 입문서**

LEVEL 2

빠르고 쉬운 시작~

지텔프 퀵스타터

해설집
정답·해석·해설

G-TELP KOREA 출판사업본부

LEVEL 2

빠르고 쉬운 시작~

지텔프 퀵스타터 해설집

정답·해석·해설

지텔프 독해 스타터

General Tests of English Language Proficiency

<정답 및 해설>

MINI TEST | 실전모의고사

Part 01. Biography Article MINI TEST

01 (a)   02 (d)   03 (b)   04 (c)   05 (a)   06 (d)   07 (d)   08 (c)   09 (a)

PART 1. Read the following biography article and answer the questions. The underlined word in the article is for a vocabulary question. (1~3)

NICK DRAKE

Nick Drake was an English folk singer who released three albums before dying tragically at the age of 26. **1) Although his music received little attention during his lifetime, he gradually became regarded as an influential figure to other musicians in the decades following his death.**

Nicholas Rodney Drake was born on June 19, 1948 in Rangoon, Burma. Two years later, his family returned to England. **2) Motivated by his mother, who wrote and recorded songs at home,** he learned to play the piano at a young age. As a teen, he cared more about music than schoolwork and dropped out of college after signing a contract with Island Records to make his first album.

In 1969, he released his debut *Five Leaves Left* to mixed reviews and poor sales. He continued to work on his music until he died by apparent suicide in 1974. He was 3) <u>largely</u> forgotten until the 1980s when a new generation of songwriters started to cite him as an inspiration. Drake's music finally achieved something close to mainstream recognition in 1999 when his song "Pink Moon" was used in a Volkswagen commercial, sparking a new wave of interest. His now much-imitated style is characterized by soft vocals, haunting melodies, and simple arrangements.

닉 드레이크

닉 드레이크는 26세의 나이에 비극적으로 죽기 전 세 장의 앨범을 발표한 영국 포크송 가수였다. 1) 비록 그의 음악은 일생 동안 거의 관심을 받지 못했지만, 그는 그의 죽음 이후 수십 년 뒤 다른 음악가들에게 점차 영향력 있는 인물로 여겨졌다.

니콜라스 로드니 드레이크는 1948년 6월 19일 버마 랑군에서 태어났다. 2년 후, 그의 가족은 영국으로 돌아왔다. 2) 집에서 곡을 쓰고 녹음을 했던 어머니에게 동기 부여를 얻은 그는 어린 나이에 피아노 연주를 배웠다. 10대 때, 그는 학업보다 음악에 더 신경을 썼고, 아일랜드 레코드와 그의 첫 앨범을 만들기 위해 계약을 맺은 후 대학을 중퇴했다.

1969년, 그는 그의 데뷔작 「Five Leaves Left」를 발매하여 평이 엇갈렸고 판매가 부진했다. 그는 1974년 명백한 자살로 죽을 때까지 그의 음악 작업을 계속했다. 그는 신세대 작곡가들이 그를 영감의 대상으로 언급하기 시작했던 1980년대까지는 3) 거의 잊혀졌었다. 드레이크의 음악은 1999년 그의 노래 "Pink Moon"이 폭스바겐 광고에 사용되면서 마침내 대중의 인기를 끌었고, 새로운 관심의 물결을 불러 일으켰다. 그의 현재는 많이 모방된 스타일은 부드러운 보컬, 잊혀지지 않는 멜로디, 그리고 단순한 편곡으로 특징지어진다.

단어

release v. 발표하다, 출시하다
attention n. 관심
influential adj. 영향력 있는
drop out v. 중퇴하다
apparent adj. 명백한, 분명한
mainstream n. 주류
commercial n. (상업)광고
new wave n. 새 물결
haunting adj. 잊혀지지 않는

tragically ad. 비극적으로
be regarded as v. ~로 여겨지다
figure n. 인물
decade n. 10년
suicide n. 자살
recognition n. 인정, 인식
spark v. 불러일으키다, 발화시키다
imitate v. 모방하다
arrangement n. 편곡, 배열

 **문제풀이**

1. Based on the text, what is **notable** about Nick Drake's musical career?

   (a) He became more famous after death.
   (b) He became successful at a young age.
   (c) He influenced musicians during his lifetime.
   (d) He received much attention after his first album.

1. 본문에 따르면, 닉 드레이크의 음악 경력에서 주목할 만한 점은 무엇인가?

   (a) 그는 죽음 후에 더 유명해졌다.
   (b) 그는 어린 나이에 성공했다.
   (c) 그는 그의 일생 동안 음악가들에게 영향을 미쳤다.
   (d) 그는 첫 앨범 이후 많은 관심을 받았다.

Tip! 문제의 Based on~은 추론 문제임을, notable ~ musical career은 음악적으로 유명해진 이유를 묻는 것임을 알 수 있다. 지문에서 그의 음악적 경력에서 주목할 만한 특이한 점이 있는지를 찾아 읽는다.

해설
그는 생전에 주목받지 못했지만, 그가 죽고 나서 다른 음악가 들에 의해 영향력 있는 인물로 여겨지며 점차 유명해졌다는 것을 단락에서 확인할 수 있다. 따라서 (a) He became more famous after death가 정답이다.

paraphrasing point

gradually became regarded → became more famous
following his death → after death

 career n. 경력, 직업   lifetime n. 일생, 생애

2. What most likely **inspired** Drake to become a musician?

(a) learning to play piano at school
(b) living abroad at a young age
(c) receiving an album contract offer
(d) listening to his mother's songs

2. 무엇이 드레이크가 뮤지션이 되도록 **영감을 주었을** 것 같은가?

(a) 학교에서 피아노 연주 배우기
(b) 어린 나이에 해외 생활하기
(c) 앨범 계약 제안 받기
(d) 어머니의 노래 듣기

 문제의 inspire은 인물의 어린 시절, 그 분야에 계기가 되므로 해당 단락에서 동의 표현인 motivate를 찾아 읽는다.
문제의 보기에는 단락에서 언급된 사실들을 제시하므로 '경험적 사실'이 아니라 '직접적 계기'를 찾아야 한다는 것을 잊지 말아야 한다.

드레이크가 집에서 곡을 쓰고 녹음을 했던 그의 어머니로부터 동기 부여를 받았다는 내용을 통해 그가 어머니의 노래를 듣고 자랐음을 추론할 수 있다. 따라서 **(d) listening to his mother's songs**가 정답이다.

단어 abroad ad. 해외에, 해외로   contract n. 계약

---

3. In the context of the passage, <u>largely</u> means _____.

(a) massively
(b) mostly
(c) grandly
(d) generously

3. 글의 문맥에 따르면, <u>largely</u>는 _____를 의미한다.

(a) 대규모
(b) 대부분
(c) 웅장하게
(d) 아낌없이

 사전적 의미가 아닌 문맥적 의미를 찾아야 한다.

글의 문맥을 보면, 앞서 그의 데뷔작은 엇갈린 평가와 판매 부진을 겪었으며, 신세대 작곡가들이 그를 언급하기 전까지 잊혀졌다는 내용과 이후 광고 음악으로 사용되며 주류 인식에 가까운 것이 되었다는 내용을 통해 largely는 '거의' 잊혀졌다는 의미로 쓰이고 있음을 알 수 있다. 따라서 **(b) mostly**가 정답이다.

PART 1. Read the following biography article and answer the questions. The underlined word in the article is for a vocabulary question. (4~6)

RICHARD MATHESON

Richard Matheson was a prolific American writer of novels, short stories, and screenplays who published most of his works in the mid-to late-20th century. His writing style was notable for ⁶⁾ **synthesizing** elements of science fiction, fantasy, and horror.

Matheson was born on February 20, 1926, in Allendale, New Jersey. ⁴⁾ **He developed an interest in writing at a young age, publishing his first short story in the local newspaper when he was only eight years old.** He started writing novels after he graduated from college with a degree in journalism.

He became successful not long after his first novel was published in 1953. The next year, he released the post-apocalyptic vampire novel *I am Legend*, ^(5-b) **which would go on to inspire three film adaptations,** including the 2007 blockbuster of the same name. In total, ^(5-c) **seven of his books were adapted into Hollywood films.** In the late 60's ^(5-d) he started writing screenplays for films and popular television shows even as he continued to write and publish novels. ^(5-a) **The stories that he penned throughout his** career **had a** huge impact **on other contemporary writers, especially the legendary horror writer Stephen King, who has frequently praised Matheson's work.**

리처드 매티슨

리처드 매티슨은 20세기 중후반에 그의 작품 대부분을 출판한 소설, 단편 소설 시나리오를 다루는 미국의 다작 작가였다. 그의 글쓰기 스타일은 공상 과학, 판타지 및 공포의 요소를 ⁶⁾합성하는 것으로 유명했다.

매티슨은 1926년 2월 20일 뉴저지 주의 앨런데일에서 태어났다. ⁴⁾그는 어린 나이에 글쓰기에 관심을 갖게 되었고, 8살 밖에 안 됐을 때 처음으로 지역 신문에 단편 소설을 실었다. 그는 저널리즘 분야의 학위를 받고 대학을 졸업한 후 소설을 쓰기 시작했다.

그는 1953년 그의 첫 소설이 출판된 지 얼마 지나지 않아 성공을 거두었다. 이듬해, 그는 포스트 아포칼립스 뱀파이어 소설인 「나는 전설이다」를 발표했고, 이 소설은 더 나아가 같은 이름의 2007년 블록버스터 영화를 포함하여 ^(5-b)3편의 영화 각색에 영감을 주었다. ^(5-c)그의 책 총 7권이 할리우드 영화로 각색되었다. 60년대 후반, ^(5-d)그는 계속해서 소설을 쓰고 출판하는 그 동안에도 영화와 인기 TV쇼의 각본을 쓰기 시작했다. ^(5-a)그가 그의 경력 내내 쓴 이야기들은 다른 동시대의 작가들, 특히 매티슨의 작품을 자주 찬양해온 전설적인 공포물 작가 스티븐 킹에게 큰 영향을 미쳤다.

 **단어**

prolific adj. 다작의, 다작하는
publish v. 게재하다, 출간하다
synthesize v. 합성하다
college n. 대학
journalism n. 저널리즘, 신문학
pen v. 쓰다
frequently ad. 자주, 흔히

screenplay n. 시나리오
notable adj. 유명한
develop v. 발달하다, 성장하다, 성장시키다
degree n. 학위
adaptation n. 각색, 적용
contemporary adj. 동시대의
praise v. 칭찬하다

 **문제풀이**

4. When did Matheson first start writing?

   (a) when he got a job as a journalist
   (b) after he graduated from college
   (c) when he was a very young boy
   (d) after he joined the school newspaper

4. 매티슨은 언제 처음 글을 쓰기 시작했는가?

   (a) 그가 기자로 취직했을 때
   (b) 그가 대학을 졸업한 후
   (c) 그가 아주 어린 소년이었을 때
   (d) 그가 학교 신문에 가입한 후

해설

그가 어렸을 때 글쓰기에 관심을 가졌고, 8살 밖에 안 된 나이에 첫 소설을 신문에 게재했으므로 그가 글을 쓰기 시작한 것은 그가 아주 어린 소년이었을 때임을 알 수 있다. 따라서 **(c) when he was a very young boy**가 정답이다.

단어 graduate v. 졸업하다, 학위를 받다

5. According to the article, what is most likely true about Matheson's career?

(a) **He had a lasting influence in the world of horror fiction.**
(b) He had several failed film adaptations of his books.
(c) He achieved his lifelong goal of working in Hollywood.
(d) He quit writing novels in favor of screenplays.

5. 기사에 따르면, 매티슨의 경력에 관해서 무엇이 가장 사실인 것 같은가?

(a) **그는 공포 소설의 세계에 지속적인 영향을 미쳤다.**
(b) 그는 그의 책의 영화 각색을 여러 번 실패했다.
(c) 그는 할리우드에서 일한다는 일생의 목표를 달성했다.
(d) 그는 시나리오를 위해 소설 쓰기를 그만 두었다.

해설

(a) 그가 경력 내내 쓴 이야기들이 전설적인 공포물 작가인 스티븐 킹에게 큰 영향을 미쳤으므로 그가 공포 소설의 세계에 영향을 미쳤음을 알 수 있다.
(b) 그의 소설이 동명의 2007년 블록버스터 영화 뿐만 아니라 3편의 영화 각색에 영감을 주었으므로 영화로 바꾸는 데 실패하지 않았다.
(c) 그의 책이 할리우드에서 각색된 것이지 그가 할리우드에서 일한다는 목표를 가지지 않았다.
(d) 그는 소설을 계속 쓰고 출판하면서 영화와 TV 프로그램의 각본을 썼으므로 시나리오를 위해 소설 쓰기를 그만두지 않았다.

paraphrasing point
huge impact → lasting influence

단어 lasting adj. 지속적인, 영구적인

---

6. In the context of the passage, synthesizing _____.

(a) arranging
(b) cooperating
(c) inventing
(d) **mixing**

6. 글의 문맥에 따르면, synthesizing는 _____를 의미한다.

(a) 배열하는 것
(b) 협력하는 것
(c) 발명하는 것
(d) **혼합하는 것**

해설

문맥상 공상 과학, 판타지, 공포의 요소들을 언급하고 있으므로 여러 요소를 '혼합하는 것'이라는 의미로 쓰이고 있음을 알 수 있다. 따라서 **(d) mixing**이 정답이다.

PART 1. Read the following biography article and answer the questions. The underlined word in the article is for a vocabulary question. (7~9)

JOSEPH LISTER

Joseph Lister was a British surgeon and professor whose research led to a reduction in post-operation fatalities. He is now known as the "father of modern surgery" due to his use of antiseptics, which revolutionized surgical sterilization.

Lister was born in Upton, England on April 5, 1827. **7) His father, who was interested in plant and animal cells, designed a new kind of lens that improved the performance of microscopes. Joseph Lister developed an early passion for science and medicine, owing in part to his father.** He attended medical school and in 1860 became a professor of surgery at the University of Glasgow.

At the time, most doctors were unaware of the existence of germs and believed that illnesses were caused by "bad air." Surgeons rarely took precautions such as handwashing or sterilizing surgical tools, which frequently led to severe or fatal infections in patients. After learning about bacteria, Lister started to experiment with carbolic acid as a potential antiseptic. **8) He observed that infections decreased and wounds healed more quickly when carbolic acid was applied.** In 1867, **he published his findings, but other medical professionals remained 9) dubious about his ideas. However, 8) as doctors began to see positive results for themselves**, the practice of using antiseptics gradually became more widespread.

조지프 리스터

조지프 리스터는 수술 후 사망자 수 감소를 이끌었던 연구를 한 영국의 외과의사이자 교수였다. 그는 외과 살균에 혁명을 일으킨 소독제의 사용으로 현재 "현대 수술의 아버지"로 알려져 있다.

리스터는 1827년 4월 5일 영국의 업턴에서 태어났다. 7) 식물과 동물 세포에 관심이 있었던 그의 아버지는 현미경의 성능을 향상시키는 새로운 종류의 렌즈를 고안했다. 조지프 리스터는 부분적으로 그의 아버지 덕분에, 일찍이 과학과 의학에 대한 열정을 키웠다. 그는 의과 대학에 다녔고 1860년에 글래스고 대학의 외과 교수가 되었다.

그 당시, 대부분의 의사들은 세균의 존재를 몰랐고, 질병이 "나쁜 공기"로 인해 발생한다고 믿었다. 외과의사들은 손 씻기나 수술도구 살균과 같은 예방조치를 거의 취하지 않았고, 이로 인해 종종 환자들의 심각한 또는 치명적인 감염으로 이어졌다. 박테리아에 대해 알게 된 후, 리스터는 잠재적인 살균제로서 석탄산을 실험하기 시작했다. 8) 그는 석탄산을 발랐을 때 감염이 줄고 상처가 더 빠르게 치유되는 것을 관찰했다. 1867년, 그는 그의 연구 결과를 발표했지만, 다른 의학 전문가들은 그의 생각에 대해 여전히 9) 의심스러워했다. 하지만, 8) 의사들이 스스로 긍정적인 결과를 보기 시작하면서, 살균제를 사용하는 관행이 점차 더 널리 퍼지게 되었다.

단어

surgeon n. 외과의사
fatality n. 사망률
revolutionize v. 혁신을 일으키다
sterilization n. 소독, 살균
microscope n. 현미경
germ n. 세균, 미생물
sterilize v. 살균하다, 소독하다
infection n. 감염
carbolic acid n. 석탄산, 페놀(살균제, 소독제로 쓰는 화학물질)
dubious adj. 의심하는, 미심쩍어 하는

post-operation adj. 수술 후의
antiseptic n. 살균제, 소독제
surgical adj. 외과의, 수술의
improve v. 향상시키다, 개선하다
be unaware of v. ~을 알지 못하다, 모르다
precaution n. 예방조치
fatal adj. 치명적인, 죽음을 초래하는
experiment v. 실험하다 n. 실험
wound n. 상처
widespread adj. 널리 퍼진, 광범위한

문제풀이

---

7. What contributed to Lister's desire to become a medical professional?

(a) a need for better microscopes
(b) his classes in medical school
(c) new discoveries about animal cells
(d) his father's scientific work

7. 무엇이 의학 전문가가 되고자 하는 리스터의 바람에 기여했는가?

(a) 더 나은 현미경의 필요성
(b) 의과대학에서의 그의 수업
(c) 동물 세포에 대한 새로운 발견들
(d) 아버지의 과학적 업적

해설

현미경의 성능을 향상시키는 새로운 종류의 렌즈를 고안했던 아버지 덕에 과학과 의학에 대한 열정을 키웠다는 설명을 통해 아버지의 과학적 업적이 리스터의 바람에 기여했음을 알 수 있다. 따라서 **(d) his father's scientific work**가 정답이다.

단어 | contribute v. 기여하다 | discovery n. 발견 | cell n. 세포

8. What mostly likely happened when other doctors used antiseptics during their surgical procedures?

(a) Carbolic acid supplies at hospitals ran low.
(b) Wounds healed at the same rate as before.
(c) Fewer patients died following operations.
(d) They published articles about their findings.

8. 다른 의사들이 수술 과정 동안 소독약을 사용했을 때 무슨 일이 일어났을 것인가?

(a) 병원에 석탄산 비축량이 떨어져갔다.
(b) 상처가 전과 같은 속도로 아물었다.
(c) 수술 후 더 적은 환자들이 사망했다.
(d) 그들의 발견에 대한 기사들을 게재했다.

> **해설**

소독약을 사용하지 않았을 때에는 환자들이 치명적인 감염에 자주 노출되었지만, 소독약을 사용한 이후부터는 감염이 줄고 상처가 빨리 낫는 등의 긍정적인 결과를 보게 되었다는 부분을 통해 사망하는 환자의 수가 감소했음을 추측할 수 있다. 따라서 **(c) Fewer patients died following operations**가 정답이다.

단어 procedure n. 수술, 절차 supply n. 공급량, 비축량
heal v. 치유되다, 낫다, 상처가 아물다   operation n. 수술

---

9. In the context of the passage, <u>dubious</u> means _____.

(a) doubtful
(b) problematic
(c) unreliable
(d) ambiguous

9. 글의 문맥에 따르면, <u>dubious</u>은 _____을 의미한다.

(a) 의심스러운
(b) 문제가 있는
(c) 믿을 수 없는, 신뢰할 수 없는
(d) 애매한, 모호한

> **해설**

문맥상 '리스터의 발견에 대해 다른 의학 전문가들은 여전히 의심했다'는 내용을 통해 dubious는 '**의심스러운**'이라는 의미로 쓰이고 있음을 알 수 있다. 따라서 **(a) doubtful**이 정답이다.

Part 02. Magazine Article MINI TEST

01 (a) 02 (b) 03 (c) 04 (b) 05 (c) 06 (a) 07 (c) 08 (a) 09 (c)

PART 2. Read the following magazine article and answer the questions. The underlined word in the article is for a vocabulary question. (1~3)

THE RISE AND FALL OF MEAL KIT DELIVERY SERVICES

In 2012, startup company Blue Apron **popularized** a new kind of service: the delivery of high-quality meal kits directly to customers each week. [1] People using the service could make a home-cooked meal in 30 minutes or less, using fresh ingredients that had already been measured and chopped. The kits even included simple instructions for cooking and assembling the meal. People could say goodbye to the hassle of meal-planning and grocery shopping.

Following Blue Apron's success, dozens of similar businesses sprang up around the country. A meal kit service now exists for any consumer's taste preferences or **dietary restrictions**. [2] **Many of these services can provide food that is organic, vegetarian, or vegan. People with food allergies and people who want to lose weight can now find plans that cater to their needs.**

However, the meal kit delivery industry is now in [3] **dire** condition. Many companies are already bankrupt and the survivors have been losing money for years. A key factor in this downfall is the massive cost of such an operation. The companies need to purchase premium ingredients and hire large staffs to prepare and deliver the kits.

밀키트 배송 서비스의 상승과 하락

2012년, 스타트업 회사인 블루 에이프런은 매주 고객들에게 고품질 식사 키트를 직접 배달하는 새로운 종류의 서비스를 대중화했다. [1] 이 서비스를 이용하는 사람들은 이미 계량되고 다져진 신선한 재료를 사용하여 30분 혹은 그보다 더 짧은 시간으로 집에서 요리한 식사를 만들 수 있었다. 심지어 그 키트에는 식사 요리 및 조리에 대한 간단한 설명도 포함시켰다. 사람들은 식사 계획 그리고 식료품점 쇼핑의 번거로움과 작별 인사를 할 수 있었다.

블루 에이프런의 성공에 뒤이어, 수십 개의 유사 업체들이 전국적으로 생겨났다. 이제 소비자의 입맛 선호도나 식단 제한을 위한 밀키트 서비스가 존재한다. [2] 이러한 서비스 중 다수는 유기농, 채식주의 또는 비건 식품을 제공할 수 있다. 음식 알레르기가 있는 사람과 체중 감량을 원하는 사람은 이제 그들의 요구에 적합한 계획을 찾을 수 있다.

그러나 밀키트 배달 산업은 현재 [3] 몹시 나쁜 상황에 처해있다. 많은 회사들이 이미 파산했고 생존 회사들도 수년간 금전 손실을 입고 있다. 이러한 몰락의 핵심 요인은 그러한 운영에 드는 막대한 비용이다. 업체들은 프리미엄 식재료를 구입하고 키트를 준비하고 납품하기 위해 대규모 인력을 고용할 필요가 있다.

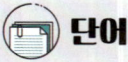 단어

startup company n. 스타트업 회사
ingredient n. (특히 요리 등의) 재료
instruction n. 설명 (=directions)
spring up v. 갑자기 생겨나다, 나타나다
taste n. 입맛, 맛
dietary restriction n. 식단 제한
vegetarian n. 채식주의자
allergy n. 알레르기
cater to v. (~의 요구에) 맞추다, 응하다
factor n. 요인, 요소
massive adj. 거대한, 엄청나게 큰

popularize v. 대중화하다, 많은 사람들에게 알리다
chop v. 다지다, 썰다
grocery n. 식료품점
exist v. 존재하다, 실존하다
preference n. 선호
organic adj. 유기농의
vegan n. 엄격한 채식주의, 채식주의자
weight n. 무게, 체중
dire adj. 몹시 나쁜, 심각한, 끔찍한
downfall n. 몰락, 몰락의 원인
operation n. 운영, 가동, 수술

 문제풀이

1. According to the article, why most likely did meal kit services become **popular**?

   (a) because of the convenience
   (b) because of their low prices
   (c) because of the daily deliveries
   (d) because of their gourmet meals

1. 기사에 따르면, 왜 밀키트 서비스가 인기를 끌었을까?

   (a) 편리함 때문에
   (b) 저렴한 가격 때문에
   (c) 일일 배송 때문에
   (d) 고급 음식 때문에

Tip! 문제에서 묻는 popular에 해당하는 곳(popularized)을 찾아 읽는다.

 해설

이미 계량되고 다져진 신선한 재료를 사용하여 30분 혹은 그보다 더 적은 시간으로 집에서 요리한 식사를 만들어 먹을 수 있다는 내용을 통해 편리함이 인기를 끌게 했음을 유추할 수 있다. 따라서 **(a) because of the convenience**가 정답이다.

단어   gourmet meal n. 고급 음식, 고급 식료품

2. How can meal kits be useful for people who have **dietary restrictions**?

(a) Customers can order fewer meals per week.
(b) Customers can personalize the contents of a kit.
(c) All of the kits are made from organic produce.
(d) All of the plans are good for people on a diet.

2. 어떻게 **식단 제한**이 있는 사람들에게 밀키트가 유용할 수 있는가?

(a) 고객들은 주당 더 적은 식사를 주문할 수 있다.
(b) 고객들은 키트의 내용물을 개인화할 수 있다.
(c) 모든 키트는 유기농 농산물로 만들어진다.
(d) 모든 계획은 다이어트 중인 사람들에게 좋다.

 Tip! 문제의 키워드인 dietary restrictions를 본문에서 찾아 읽는다.

해설

소비자의 취향이나 **식단 제한**을 위한 밀키트 서비스가 제공되며, **자신의 요구에 맞는 방안을 찾을 수 있다**는 내용을 통해 고객이 키트의 내용을 개인화할 수 있다는 사실을 유추할 수 있다. 따라서 **(b) Customers can personalize the contents of a kit**가 정답이다.

단어 personalize v. 개인화하다, 개인에 맞추다   produce v. 생산하다

---

3. In the context of the passage, <u>dire</u> means _____.

(a) gruesome
(b) cruel
(c) poor
(d) vital

3. 글의 문맥에 따르면, <u>dire</u>는 _____(을)를 의미한다.

(a) 섬뜩한
(b) 잔인한
(c) 빈약한
(d) 필수의

해설

문맥상 많은 회사가 이미 파산했고, 생존 회사들도 금전적 손실을 입었다는 내용을 통해 dire이 밀키트 배달 산업이 현재 '**매우 나쁜**' 상황임을 의미한다는 것을 알 수 있다. 따라서 **(c) poor**가 정답이다.

PART 2. Read the following magazine article and answer the questions. The underlined word in the article is for a vocabulary question. (4~6)

THE MYTH OF THE SUGAR HIGH

Parents have long believed that their children become more energetic and harder to control when they consume more sugar. They call the effect a "sugar high." However, the sugar high is largely a myth that was [6] **debunked** by a series of scientific studies in the mid-1990s.

A study **in 1994** tested three groups of children. One group was given a diet that included real sugar, and the other two groups were each given a different artificial sweetener. Parents were not told which type of diet their children were consuming during the observation period. [4] **At the end of the study, parents and researchers did not record any significant differences in behavior among the three groups.**

So why has the sugar high remained such a persistent myth despite evidence to the contrary? [5] **One possible explanation is that children tend to consume more sugar on special occasions, such as birthday parties and holiday gatherings, when feelings of elation are already at their peak.** In that case, the rise in energy levels is caused by the situation and not by sugar. Because of the parents' belief in the sugar high, [5] **they perceive their children's hyperactivity to be connected to the consumption of cakes, candy, and sugary beverages.**

슈거 하이의 근거 없는 믿음

부모들은 오랫동안 그들의 자녀들이 더 많은 설탕을 섭취할 때 더 활기차지고 통제하기가 어려워진다고 믿어왔다. 그들은 그 효과를 "슈거 하이"라고 부른다. 하지만, 슈거 하이는 대체로 1990년대 중반 일련의 과학적 연구에 의해 [6] **틀렸음이 밝혀진** 근거 없는 믿음이다.

1994년 한 연구에서 세 그룹의 어린이를 테스트했다. 한 그룹에는 실제 설탕을 포함한 식단이 제공되었고, 다른 두 그룹에는 각각 다른 인공 감미료가 제공되었다. 부모는 관찰 기간 동안 자녀가 어떤 종류의 식단을 먹었는지 듣지 못했다. [4] **연구가 종료되었을 때**, 부모와 연구자들은 세 그룹 간의 행동에서 어떠한 큰 차이를 보지 못했다.

그렇다면 슈거 하이*는 반대되는 증거에도 불구하고 왜 그토록 끈질기게 근거 없는 믿음으로 남아 있는가? [5] **한 가지 가능한 설명은 아이들의 행복감이 이미 최고조에 달했을 때, 생일 파티나 휴일 모임과 같은 특별한 경우에 더 많은 설탕을 섭취하는 경향이 있다는 것이다.** 이 경우, 에너지 레벨의 상승은 설탕이 아닌 상황에 의해 발생한다. 슈거 하이에 대한 부모의 믿음 때문에, [5] **그들은 그들의 자녀의 과잉 행동이 케이크, 사탕, 설탕 음료의 섭취와 관련이 있다고 인식한다.**

*슈거 하이: 과도한 당 섭취에 의한 일시적 흥분 상태

단어

energetic adj. 활기찬, 혈기 왕성한
myth n. 근거 없는 믿음, 신화
artificial sweetener n. 인공 감미료
observation n. 관찰
significant adj. 큰, 상당한
persistent adj. 지속적인
evidence n. 증거
tend to v v. ~하는 경향이 있다
gathering n. 모임
peak n. 최고조, 꼭대기
hyperactivity n. 과잉 행동
consumption n. 소비, 소비량, 소모

consume v. 섭취하다, 소비하다
debunk v. (생각·믿음 등이) 틀렸음을 드러내다, 밝히다
diet n. 식단, 식사
period n. 기간
behavior n. 행동, 행실, 태도
despite prep. ~에도 불구하고
contrary n. 반대, 반대되는 것 adj. 반대되는
occasion n. 경우, 때
elation n. (큰)행복감, 기쁨, 의기양양
perceive v. 인식하다
be connected to v. ~와 관련 있다
beverage n. 음료

 문제풀이

4. What most likely did scientists **conclude** about sugar at the end of the 1994 study?

(a) It is superior to artificial sweeteners.
(b) It has little or no effect on behavior.
(c) It has a greater effect on the parents.
(d) It is not suitable for most children.

4. 1994년 연구가 종료되었을 때 과학자들은 설탕에 대해 뭐라고 **결론을 내렸을까**?

(a) 인공 감미료보다 우수하다.
(b) 행동에 거의 또는 전혀 영향을 미치지 않는다.
(c) 부모에게 더 큰 영향을 미친다.
(d) 대부분의 어린이에게 적합하지 않다.

Tip! 문제에서 특정 연도(1994년)에 관한 질문을 한다면, 본문에서 해당 연도가 있는 문단으로 가서 근거를 찾도록 한다.

해설

연구가 끝날 무렵 부모와 연구자들은 세 그룹 사이에서 행동의 차이점을 기록하지 않았다는 내용을 통해 과학자들이 설탕이 행동에 거의 또는 전혀 영향을 미치지 못한다고 결론 내렸다는 것을 유추할 수 있다. 따라서 **(b) It has little or no effect on behavior**이 정답이다.

단어 effect n. 영향, 효과   suitable adj. 적합한, 알맞은

5. According to the article, **why** would children **behave** differently if they go to a **party**?

(a) because of their parents' attitudes
(b) because they consume more food
(c) because of increased excitement
(d) because they have too much sugar

5. 기사에 따르면, 아이들이 파티에 가게 되면 왜 다르게 행동하는가?

(a) 부모의 태도 때문에
(b) 그들이 더 많은 음식을 소비하기 때문에
(c) 증가된 흥분 때문에
(d) 그들이 너무 많은 설탕을 갖기 때문에

 Tip! 문제에서 party에 갈 때 행동이 달라지는 이유를 묻고 있으므로 본문에서 party관련 부분을 찾아 읽는다.

해설

아이들의 행복감이 최고치에 달하는 생일 파티와 같은 특별한 경우에 더 많은 설탕을 섭취하게 되며, 과잉 행동이 발생하기 때문이라는 내용을 통해 (c) because of increased excitement가 정답임을 알 수 있다.

단어 behave v. 행동하다   attitude n. 태도, 자세, 사고방식

---

6. In the context of the passage, <u>debunked</u> means _____.

(a) disproved
(b) insulted
(c) confirmed
(d) disliked

6. 글의 문맥에 따르면, <u>debunked</u>는 _____를 의미한다.

(a) 반증이 된
(b) 모욕을 당한
(c) 확인된
(d) 미움을 받는

Tip! debunked 문장의 앞 뒤 문맥으로 유추한다. 해당 문장이 however로 시작하므로 앞 문장의 반대어임을 유추할 수 있다.

해설

문맥상 부모는 자녀가 설탕을 많이 섭취하면 더 활기차고 통제가 어렵다고 믿어왔다는 내용 뒤에 '그러나 그 믿음은 연구에 의해 debunked되었다'는 내용이 나온다. 즉, debunked가 앞서 언급된 부모의 믿음이 '반박' 또는 '반증'이 되었다는 것임을 알 수 있다. 따라서 (a) disproved가 정답이다.

PART 2. Read the following magazine article and answer the questions. The underlined word in the article is for a vocabulary question. (7~9)

NO SUCH THING AS A PERFECT UMBRELLA

Devices made to shield us from the rain have existed in some form since the ancient times. The lightweight folding model that is most familiar to us first appeared in the early 1700s, but it seems we haven't been able to improve on it much since then. The perfectly circular umbrella with a collapsible structure on the underside has endured for centuries **but still** 9) <u>**poses**</u> a number of problems for the user.

The wind is a common threat, frequently catching the umbrella from the wrong angle and turning it inside out. **Traditional umbrellas** can also be burdensome as the user tries to avoid hitting other people on crowded streets while carrying bags or attempting to make phone calls with only one hand. An additional concern is the lack of protection from water splashed by passing cars. 7) **An umbrella can keep your hair dry, but what about your legs**?

A number of inventors have tried to offer solutions to these problems. Several products released in the last few years have played with shape to make umbrellas that are wind-resistant. One such innovation is the aerodynamic Senz umbrella that can withstand winds of more than 60 miles per hour. 8) **However, due to the odd shape—with a short, wide front and a long, narrow tail—two people cannot comfortably share the same umbrella.**

완벽한 우산 같은 것은 없다

우리를 비로부터 보호하기 위해 만들어진 장치들은 고대 이래로 어떤 형태로든 존재해 왔다. 우리에게 가장 친숙한 경량 접이식 모델은 1700년대 초에 처음 등장했지만, 그 이후로는 크게 개선되지 못한 것으로 보인다. 밑면이 접이식의 구조로 된 완벽한 원형 우산은 수 세기 동안 지속해 왔지만 여전히 사용자에게 많은 문제를 9) 안겨준다.

바람은 흔한 위협이며, 종종 잘못된 각도에서 우산을 잡고 그것을 안에서 밖으로 뒤집어 놓는다. 전통적인 우산은 또한 사용자가 가방을 들고 붐비는 거리에서 다른 사람을 치는 것을 피하려고 노력하거나 오직 한 손으로 전화를 걸려고 시도하는 것을 피하려 할 때 부담이 될 수 있다. 추가적인 우려는 지나가는 자동차로 인해 튀는 물로부터 보호가 부족하다는 것이다. 7) 우산은 당신의 머리카락을 건조하게 유지할 수 있지만, 당신의 다리는 어떻겠는가?

많은 발명가들이 이러한 문제에 대한 해결책을 제시하기 위해 노력해왔다. 지난 몇 년 안에 출시된 여러 제품들은 바람에 저항하는 우산을 만들기 위해 모양을 조정했다. 그러한 혁신 하나는 시속 60 마일 이상의 바람을 견딜 수 있는 공기 역학적 센즈 우산이다. 8) 그러나, 짧고 넓은 앞면과 길고 좁은 꼬리를 가진 이상한 모양 때문에 두 사람이 같은 우산을 편안하게 공유할 수 없다.

 단어

shield v. 보호하다, 막다
ancient adj. 고대의
fold v. 접다
improve v. 개선하다
collapsible adj. 접이식의
underside adj. 밑면의
common adj. 흔한, 일반적인
turn inside out v. (안에서 밖으로) 뒤집다
burdensome adj. 부담이 되는, 힘겨운
crowded adj. 붐비는
additional adj. 추가적인
lack n. 부족, 결핍
inventor n. 발명가
resistant adj. 저항하는, 저항의
aerodynamic adj. 공기 역학의
odd adj. 이상한

exist v. 존재하다
lightweight adj. 경량의
appear v. 나타나다, 생기다, 발생하다
circular adj. 원형의
structure n. 구조
endure v. 지속하다
threat n. 위협
traditional adj. 전통적인, 전통의
avoid v. 피하다
attempt v. 시도하다
concern n. 우려, 염려
splash v. 물을 튀기다
release v. 출시하다
innovation n. 혁신
withstand v. 견디다

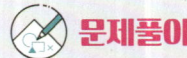 문제풀이

7. What is an **advantage** of the **traditional umbrella**?

(a) keeping one's legs from getting wet
(b) letting one use both hands for certain tasks
(c) protecting one's head from the rain
(d) sheltering one from strong winds

7. 전통적인 우산의 장점은 무엇인가?

(a) 다리가 젖지 않도록 하는 것
(b) 특정 작업에 양손을 사용하게 하는 것
(c) 비로부터 머리를 보호하는 것
(d) 강한 바람으로부터 피하는 것

Tip! 문제에서 언급된 traditional umbrella를 찾아 단락을 읽는다. 또한 문제에서 '장점'을 물었기 때문에 단락에서 단점은 배제하고 장점을 찾아야 한다.

해설

전통 우산이 언급된 단락은 주로 단점을 언급하지만 '머리카락을 건조하게 유지할 수 있다'는 내용은 전통 우산의 능력 또는 장점이라고 볼 수 있다. 따라서 **(c) protecting one's head from the rain**이 정답이다.

paraphrasing point

keep your hair dry → protecting one's head from the rain

 wet adj. 젖은   shelter n. 대피, 피신 v. (바·바람으로부터) ~을 보호하다

8. Based on the article, why is the **Senz** umbrella **not ideal for all situations**?

   (a) **It is unable to shield more than one person.**
   (b) It will not fit comfortably into a bag.
   (c) Its odd shape makes it hard to hold.
   (d) Its water-resistance is weak in heavy rain.

8. 기사에 따르면, 센즈 우산이 모든 상황에 이상적이지 않은 이유는 무엇인가?

   (a) **한 사람보다 많은 사람을 보호할 수 없다.**
   (b) 가방에 수월하게 들어가지 않을 것이다.
   (c) 이상한 모양이 그것을 잡기 어렵게 만든다.
   (d) 폭우 시 내수성이 약하다.

> **해설**

센즈 우산은 짧고 넓은 앞면과 길고 좁은 꼬리를 가진 이상한 모양 때문에 두 사람이 같은 우산을 편안하게 공유할 수 없다는 내용을 통해 (a) It is unable to shield more than one person이 정답임을 알 수 있다.

> **paraphrasing point**

two people cannot comfortably share the same umbrella → unable to shield more than one person

단어 shield v. 보호하다   weak adj. 약한, 힘기 없는

---

9. In the context of the passage, <u>poses</u> means _____.

   (a) pretends
   (b) arranges
   (c) presents
   (d) models

9. 글의 문맥에 따르면, <u>poses</u>는 _____를 의미한다.

   (a) ~인 척하다
   (b) 나열하다
   (c) 주다
   (d) 모방하다

> **해설**

문맥상 밑면이 접이식 구조로 된 완벽한 원형 우산은 수 세기 동안 지속해 왔지만 여전히 사용자에게 많은 문제를 안겨준다는 내용을 통해 pose가 '(문제 등을) 야기하다'의 의미로 쓰였음을 알 수 있다. 따라서 '**보여주다, 제시하다**'의 의미로 문맥상 가장 비슷한 어휘인 (c) presents가 정답이다.

Part 03. Encyclopedia Article MINI TEST

01 (a) 02 (b) 03 (d) 04 (d) 05 (a) 06 (c) 07 (c) 08 (a) 09 (a)

PART 3. Read the following encyclopedia article and answer the questions. The underlined word in the article is for a vocabulary question. (1~3)

PASTEURIZATION

Pasteurization is the process of heating and then rapidly cooling liquids and food items in order to kill disease-causing microorganisms. **1) Pasteurization does not make a substance sterile; rather than destroying bacteria completely, the process makes them harmless.** Pasteurization has the added benefit of extending the period during which a substance is safe to consume before it spoils. This method does not affect the flavor of the substance.

The process is named after Louis Pasteur, a French scientist who began experimenting with the method in 1864. Although pasteurization has become most closely associated with milk, **2) it was originally used to stop fermentation in beer and wine.** The process was later applied to dairy products when it was discovered that consumption of raw milk could spread serious illnesses, such as tuberculosis.

Pasteurization generally uses mild heat, at temperatures lower than 100 degrees Celsius. The length of time a substance is pasteurized is dependent on the temperature. Milk is pasteurized at a lower temperature of 63 degrees Celsius, which is maintained for 30 minutes. For faster pasteurization, higher temperatures are used. **The substance is then cooled quickly to 3) keep the remaining bacteria from multiplying.**

저온 살균

저온 살균은 질병을 일으키는 미생물을 죽이기 위해 액체와 식품을 가열한 다음 급속으로 냉각하는 과정이다. 1) 저온 살균은 물질을 무균 상태로 만들지 않는다; 박테리아를 완전히 파괴하기보다, 그 과정에서 박테리아를 무해하게 만든다. 저온 살균은 물질이 부패하기 전에 섭취하기에 안전한 기간을 연장하는 추가적인 이점을 가진다. 이 방법은 물질의 풍미에 영향을 미치지 않는다.

이 과정은 1864년에 이 방법을 실험하기 시작한 프랑스 과학자 루이 파스퇴르의 이름을 따서 명명되었다. 비록 저온 살균은 우유와 가장 밀접한 관련이 있지만, 2) 원래는 맥주와 와인 내 발효를 막기 위해 사용되었다. 이 과정은 원유 섭취가 결핵과 같은 심각한 질병을 퍼뜨릴 수 있다는 사실이 밝혀지면서 그 이후에 유제품에 적용되었다.

저온 살균은 일반적으로 섭씨 100도 미만의 약한 열을 사용한다. 물질이 저온 살균되는 시간은 온도에 따라 다르다. 우유는 섭씨 63도의 저온에서 저온 살균되며, 30분 동안 유지된다. 더 빠른 저온 살균을 위해, 고온이 사용된다. 그런 다음 물질을 빠르게 냉각시켜 남아있는 박테리아가 번식하는 것을 3) 막는다.

 ## 단어

pasteurization n. 저온 살균(법)
microorganism n. 미생물, 박테리아
sterile adj. 무균의, 세균이 없는
flavor n. 풍미
experiment n. 실험 v. 실험하다
fermentation n. 발효
consumption n. 섭취, 소비
temperature n. 온도
multiply v. 번식시키다

rapidly ad. 급속히, 신속히
substance n. 물질
extend v. 연장하다
name after v. ~의 이름을 따서 명명하다
be associated with v. ~와 관련되다
apply to v. 적용하다
tuberculosis n. 결핵
maintain v. 유지하다, 지키다

 ## 문제풀이

1. Based on the article, what mostly likely is the effect of making something **sterile**?

(a) It eliminates all types of bacteria.
(b) It improves the food's flavor.
(c) It causes food to rot more quickly.
(d) It is ineffective on dangerous bacteria.

1. 기사에 따르면, 무언가를 **무균 상태**로 만드는 효과는 무엇인가?

(a) 모든 종류의 박테리아를 제거한다.
(b) 음식의 풍미를 향상시킨다.
(c) 음식을 더 빨리 썩게 한다.
(d) 위험한 박테리아에는 효과가 없다.

Tip! sterile(살균)의 효과를 유추하는 문제이므로 살균을 언급하는 상단에서 답을 찾는다.

 해설

저온 살균은 물질을 무균 상태로 만드는 것이 아니라 박테리아를 무해하게 한다는 내용을 통해 무언가를 무균 상태로 만드는 효과는 모든 종류의 박테리아를 제거하는 것이라고 볼 수 있다. 따라서 (c) It eliminates all types of bacteria가 정답이다.

▶ paraphrasing point

destroying → eliminates

 sterile adj. 무균의, 살균의　　**eliminate** v. 제거하다, 없애다, 삭제하다　　**ineffective** adj. 효과 없는

2. What was pasteurization **first** used to do?

    (a) to stop dairy products from fermenting
    (b) to preserve alcoholic beverages
    (c) to provide a cure for deadly diseases
    (d) to ensure accuracy in science experiments

2. 저온 살균은 무엇을 하기 위해 처음 사용되었는가?

    (a) 유제품 발효를 막기 위해
    (b) 알코올성 음료를 보존하기 위해
    (c) 치명적인 질병에 대한 치료법을 제공하기 위해
    (d) 과학 실험의 정확성을 보장하기 위해

 저온 살균의 목적을 묻는 문제이다. first used에 해당하는 내용을 찾아 읽는다.

 저온 살균은 원래 맥주와 와인의 발효를 중지하기 위해 사용되었다는 내용을 통해 **(b) to preserve alcoholic beverages**가 정답임을 알 수 있다.

▶ **paraphrasing point**
originally → first

단어   fermenting n. 발효   disease n. 질병, 질환   accuracy n. 정확, 정확도

---

3. In the context of the passage, <u>keep</u> means _____.

    (a) maintain
    (b) save
    (c) protect
    (d) prevent

3. 글의 문맥에 따르면, <u>keep</u>은 _____을 의미한다.

    (a) 유지하다
    (b) 저장하다
    (c) 보호하다
    (d) 방지하다

해설
문맥상 '그런 다음 그 물질을 빠르게 냉각시켜 남은 박테리아가 번식하는 것을 keep한다'는 내용을 통해 keep이 '**막다, 멈추다, 방지하다**'로 쓰였다는 것을 알 수 있다. 또한 keep 목적어 from -ing는 '~을 막다, 방지하다'라는 뜻을 갖는다. 따라서 **(d) prevent**가 정답이다.

PART 3. Read the following encyclopedia article and answer the questions. The underlined word in the article is for a vocabulary question. (4~6)

DAGUERREOTYPE

Daguerreotype was a form of photography **invented** in the late 1830s by French artist Louis Daguerre. The process rapidly grew in popularity since a daguerreotype could be created with just a few minutes of light exposure, unlike earlier methods of photography that took hours, or even days, to create an image. 4) **The daguerreotype was used in 1839 to capture the first photographic image of a living human.**

The daguerreotype was the primary form of photography from the early 1840s until the late 1850s. It was most often used to make portraits, but despite the relatively shorter exposure time, 5) **subjects still had to sit motionless for several minutes to avoid appearing out of focus.** Daguerreotypes did not use film, making each picture unique and difficult to duplicate.

The creation of a daguerreotype followed a specific process. First, a thin sheet of silver-plated cooper was polished until the surface resembled a mirror. Then a light-sensitive chemical like iodine was sprayed onto the surface. This enabled an image to imprint upon the sheet when exposed to light. At last, the sheet was sprayed with mercury vapor to make the image 6) <u>fixed</u> so that it would not be further affected by light.

은판 사진술

은판 사진술은 1830년대 후반 프랑스 예술가 루이 다게르에 의해 발명된 사진의 한 형태였다. 그 과정은 이미지를 만드는 데 몇 시간, 또는 며칠이 걸리는 이전의 사진 방법과 달리 단 몇 분의 빛 노출로 은판 사진을 만들 수 있었기 때문에 빠르게 인기를 얻었다. 4) 은판 사진술은 1839년에 살아있는 인간의 첫 번째 사진 이미지를 포착하는 데 사용되었다.

은판 사진술은 1840년대 초부터 1850년대 후반까지 사진의 주요 형태였다. 그것은 인물 사진을 만들기 위해 가장 많이 사용되었지만, 상대적으로 더 짧은 노출 시간에도 불구하고, 5) 피사체는 초점이 맞지 않게 나타나는 것을 피하기 위해 몇 분 동안 움직이지 않고 앉아 있어야 했다. 은판 사진술은 필름을 사용하지 않아서 각각의 사진을 독특하면서 복제하기 어렵게 만들었다.

은판 사진술의 제작은 특정 과정을 따랐다. 먼저, 은도금 구리의 얇은 시트를 표면이 거울과 비슷해질 때까지 광택을 냈다. 그런 다음 요오드와 같은 빛에 민감한 화학 물질이 표면에 뿌려졌다. 이는 빛에 노출되었을 때 이미지가 시트 위에 각인될 수 있도록 했다. 마지막으로, 시트는 빛에 더 이상 영향을 받지 않도록 이미지를 6) 영구적으로 만들기 위해 수은 증기가 분사되었다.

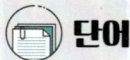 **단어**

daguerreotype n. 은판 사진(술)
portrait n. 인물 사진, 초상화
exposure n. 노출
appear v. 나타나다, 생기다, 발생하다
cooper n. 구리
surface n. 표면
chemical n. 화학 물질
vapor n. 증기

capture v. 포착하다
relatively ad. 상대적으로
motionless adj. 움직이지 않는, 움직임이 없는
duplicate v. 복제하다
polish v. 광택을 내다, 다듬다, 연마하다
resembled v. 닮다, 유사하다
spray v. 뿌리다
mercury n. 수은

 **문제풀이**

4. What is probably **true** about photography **before** the daguerreotype was **invented**?

    (a) It could perfectly capture living things.
    (b) It was popularized by a French painter.
    (c) It could create better images with low light.
    (d) It was not used to photograph people.

4. 은판 사진술이 **발명되기 전** 사진에 대해 **사실**인 것은 무엇인가?

    (a) 생물을 완벽하게 포착할 수 있었다.
    (b) 프랑스 화가에 의해 대중화되었다.
    (c) 저조도에서 더 나은 이미지를 만들 수 있었다.
    (d) 사람을 촬영하는 데 사용되지 않았다.

▶ **해설**

은판 사진술이 발명되고 1839년에 처음으로 살아있는 사람의 이미지를 포착했다는 내용을 통해 은판 사진술이 발명되기 이전에는 사람의 사진을 찍지 않았다는 것을 알 수 있다. 따라서 (d) It was not used to photograph people이 정답이다.

▶ **paraphrasing point**

capture the photographic image of → photograph
a living human → people

단어 **invent** v. 발명하다, 지어내다   **popularize** v. 대중화하다, 많은 사람들에게 알리다

5. Based on the article, why might a daguerreotype portrait become **unfocused**?

(a) because the subject moved around too much
(b) because the exposure time was not long enough
(c) because the photographer was inexperienced
(d) because the use of film was unstable

5. 기사에 따르면, 왜 은판 사진술 초상화가 초점이 맞지 않을 지도 모르는가?

(a) 피사체가 너무 많이 움직였기 때문에
(b) 노출 시간이 충분히 길지 않았기 때문에
(c) 사진 작가가 경험이 없었기 때문에
(d) 필름 사용이 불안정했기 때문에

> 해설

피사체는 초점이 맞지 않는 것을 피하기 위해 몇 분 동안 움직이지 않고 앉아 있어야 했다는 내용을 통해 **(a) because the subject moved around too much**가 정답임을 알 수 있다.

▶ paraphrasing point
out of focus → unfocused

단어 exposure n. 노출, 폭로, 알려짐   unstable adj. 불안정한

---

6. In the context of the passage, <u>fixed</u> means _____.

(a) repaired
(b) fastened
(c) permanent
(d) certain

6. 글의 문맥에 따르면, <u>fixed</u>는 _____를 의미한다.

(a) 수리된
(b) 고정된
(c) 영구적인
(d) 특정적인

> 해설

문맥상 시트는 빛에 더 이상 영향을 받지 않도록 이미지를 영구적으로 만들기 위해 수은 증기가 분사되었다는 내용을 통해 fixed가 '더 이상 영향을 받지 않는 상태'를 의미한다는 것을 알 수 있다. 따라서 **(c) permanent**가 정답이다.

PART 3. Read the following encyclopedia article and answer the questions. The underlined word in the article is for a vocabulary question. (7~9)

FRANKENSTEIN

Frankenstein; or, The Modern Prometheus is a novel by English author Mary Shelley that was first published in 1818. The story follows a young scientist named Victor Frankenstein who makes a terrifying "creature" by stitching together the body parts of several dead men and then using electricity to give it life.

The story of how the novel was 9) conceived is nearly as famous as the novel itself; English poet Lord Byron invited Shelley and several other writers to spend the summer of 1816 together in Geneva, Switzerland. 7) While in Geneva, Byron challenged them all to a competition to see who could write the best horror story. A few days later, Shelley's winning idea appeared to her in a dream about a scientist who was horrified by the results of his experiment.

Reception of the novel was positive and has had a lasting impact on literature—and on popular culture as a whole. *Frankenstein* is considered to be a landmark in the science fiction genre, and has been adapted and imitated countless times across all media. Furthermore, 8) the novel raised important questions about ethical concerns in science and medicine that are still being discussed today.

프랑켄슈타인

「프랑켄슈타인」; 혹은 「현대의 프로메테우스」는 1818년에 처음 출판된 영국 작가 메리 셸리의 소설이다. 이 이야기는 여러 명의 죽은 남성의 신체 부위를 꿰맨 다음 생명을 불어넣기 위해 전기를 사용함으로써 무서운 "생명체"를 만드는 젊은 과학자 빅터 프랑켄슈타인의 이야기를 따른다.

소설이 어떻게 9) 착안되었는지에 대한 이야기는 거의 소설 그 자체만큼이나 유명하다; 영국의 시인 바이런 경은 스위스의 제네바에서 1816년 여름을 함께 보내기 위해 셸리와 다른 여러 작가들을 초대했다. 7) 제네바에 있는 동안, 바이런은 그들 모두에게 최고의 공포 이야기를 쓸 수 있는 사람을 찾기 위한 경쟁을 요구했다. 며칠 후, 셸리에게 승리를 안겨준 아이디어가 꿈 속에서 그녀에게 떠올랐는데, 자신의 실험 결과에 경악을 금치 못한 한 과학자에 대한 것이었다.

소설의 반응은 긍정적이었으며 문학과 대중문화에 전체적으로 지속적인 영향을 미쳤다. 「프랑켄슈타인」은 공상과학 장르에서 이정표로 간주되며, 모든 미디어를 넘나들며 수없이 각색되고 모방되었다. 또한, 8) 이 소설은 여전히 오늘날까지 논의되고 있는 과학과 의학의 윤리적 문제에 대한 중요한 질문을 제기했다.

단어

author n. 작가
terrifying adj. 무서운, 끔찍한
challenge v. (경쟁, 도전을) 요구하다, 도전하다
horrify v. 소름 끼치게 하다
lasting adj. 지속적인
literature n. 문학
genre n. 장르
countless adj. 무수히 많은, 셀 수 없는
concern n. 문제, 염려

publish v. 출판하다
stitch v. 꿰매다
competition n. 경쟁
reception n. 반응
impact n. 영향, 충격
landmark n. 이정표
imitate v. 모방하다
ethical adj. 윤리적인

 문제풀이

7. What most likely was **the outcome of Shelley's summer vacation in Geneva**?

(a) She was haunted by bad dreams afterwards.
(b) She published her novel immediately.
(c) She was the winner of the story contest.
(d) She gained recognition for her poetry.

7. 셜리의 제네바 여름 휴가의 결과는 어땠을 것 같은가?

(a) 그녀는 나중에 나쁜 꿈에 사로잡혔다.
(b) 그녀는 즉시 소설을 출판했다.
(c) 그녀는 스토리 콘테스트의 우승자였다.
(d) 그녀는 시로 인정을 받았다.

 Tip! Geneva는 바꿔 쓸 수 없는 고유 명사이므로 Geneva를 먼저 찾아 주변부를 읽는다.

해설

제네바에서 여름을 보내면서 누가 최고의 공포 이야기를 쓸 수 있는지를 겨루었고, 며칠 후 셜리의 꿈에 그녀의 우승 아이디어가 나타났다는 언급을 통해 그녀의 공포 이야기가 우승했다는 것을 알 수 있다. 따라서 **(c) She was the winner of the story contest**가 정답이다.

▶ **paraphrasing point**

winning idea → winner of the story

단어 haunted adj. 귀신이 나오는, 겁에 질린
recognition n. 인정, 인식

8. Based on the article, how has the story of *Frankenstein* **maintained its relevance**?

(a) by examining issues of morality in science
(b) by encouraging women to write science fiction
(c) by inspiring the creation of new literary genres
(d) by introducing science into popular culture

8. 기사에 따르면, 「프랑켄슈타인」 이야기는 어떻게 정당성을 유지했는가?

(a) 과학의 도덕성 문제를 시험함으로써
(b) 여성이 공상 과학 소설을 쓰도록 장려함으로써
(c) 새로운 문학 장르의 창조를 고무함으로써
(d) 과학을 대중 문화로 도입함으로써

해설

소설 「프랑켄슈타인」의 정당성 유지에 관하여 본문에서 '이 소설은 오늘날까지 논의되고있는 과학과 의학의 윤리적 문제에 대한 중요한 질문을 제기했다'고 설명하고 있으므로 **(a) by examining issues of morality in science**가 정답이다.

paraphrasing point

ethical concerns → issues of morality

단어

relevance n. 정당성, 타당성, 관련성
inspire v. 고무하다, 영감을 주다

---

9. In the context of the passage, <u>conceived</u> means _____.

(a) produced
(b) believed
(c) assumed
(d) accepted

9. 글의 문맥에 따르면, <u>conceived</u>는 _____를 의미한다.

(a) 생산된
(b) 믿어지는
(c) 추정되는
(d) 수락된

해설

해당 단락에서 conceive는 '계획이나 생각이 만들어지거나 지어낸'라는 의미로 쓰이고 있다. 따라서 '**생산된, 만들어진**'라는 의미로 가장 비슷한 어휘인 **(a) produced**가 정답이다.

Part 04. Business Letter MINI TEST

01 (a)　02 (b)　03 (d)　04 (b)　05 (a)　06 (d)　07 (d)　08 (a)　09 (b)

PART 4. Read the following business letter and answer the questions. The underlined word in the letter is for a vocabulary question. (1~3)

David Akerman
Senior Editor
The Pinewood Daily Herald

Dear Mr. Akerman,

1) **First of all, I would like to begin this letter by expressing how much I appreciate the write-up on our family event in Sunday's edition of The Pinewood Daily Herald.** Ms. Jones is a terrific writer so I was very excited to read her article, "The Robinson Family Reunion." I was especially pleased when I saw the photos of our family members having a picnic and playing games together in the park. If possible, I would like to get copies of the photographs as a keepsake of that wonderful day.

However, as much as I enjoyed the article, there are **a few corrections** that I would like to make. First of all, 2) **the caption under the family group photo misidentified the man on the right as my brother Harold, when in fact he is my cousin Danny.** Additionally, while we were happy that Grandpa John's military service in World War II was acknowledged, we were a little disappointed that the article referred to him as an army medic. Being an army medic is a noble position, but Grandpa John actually served as a fighter pilot. I'm not sure how this 3) **erroneous** information came to be printed.

David Akerman
선임 편집자
파인우드 데일리 해럴드

Akerman씨께,

1) 우선, 저는 「파인우드 데일리 해럴드」의 일요일 호에서 우리 가족 행사에 대한 글을 작성해 주셔서 얼마나 감사하게 생각하는지 표현하며 이 편지를 시작하고 싶습니다. Jones씨는 훌륭한 저자이므로 그녀의 기사 "The Robinson Family Reunion"을 읽게 되어 매우 기뻤습니다. 저는 특히 공원에서 함께 피크닉을 하고 놀이를 하는 우리 가족들의 사진을 보고 기뻤습니다. 가능하다면, 그 멋진 날의 기념품으로 사진 복사본을 받고 싶습니다.

하지만, 기사를 즐겼던 만큼, **몇 가지 수정하고 싶은 부분**이 있습니다. 우선, 2) 가족 그룹 사진 아래의 **설명**은 오른쪽에 있는 남자를 내 남동생인 Harold로 오인했는데, 사실 그는 내 사촌 Danny입니다. 게다가, John 할아버지의 2차 세계대전 때 군복무 하셨던 사실이 알려져 기쁘기는 했지만, 기사에서 그를 의무병이라고 일컬었던 것에 약간 실망했습니다. 의무병이 되는 것은 고귀한 직책이지만, John 할아버지는 실제로는 전투기 조종사로 복무했습니다. 어떻게 이 3) **잘못된** 정보가 인쇄되었는지 잘 모르겠습니다.

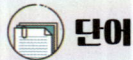 **단어**

express v. 표현하다	**appreciate** v. 감사하다
keepsake n. 기념품	**correction** n. 수정
caption n. 설명, 캡션 (사진, 삽화 등에 붙인 설명)	**misidentify** v. 오인하다, 잘못 확인하다
acknowledge v. 인정하다	**disappointed** adj. 실망한, 낙담한
refer to A as B v. A를 B로 언급하다	**army medic** n. 의무병
noble adj. 고귀한	**fighter pilot** n. 전투기 조종사

 문제풀이

1. What is the main reason why the writer sent a letter to the editor?

(a) to respond to an article about her family
(b) to request extra copies of the newspaper
(c) to ask them to write about an event
(d) to appreciate the work of their writers

1. 작가가 편집자에게 편지를 보낸 주된 이유는 무엇인가?

(a) 가족에 관한 기사에 답하기 위해
(b) 신문의 추가 사본을 요청하기 위해
(c) 이벤트에 대해 글을 쓰도록 요청하기 위해
(d) 작가들의 작품을 감상하기 위해

해설

「파인우드 데일리 헤럴드」에 자신의 가족 행사에 대한 글을 작성해줘서 감사하다고 언급하고 있으므로 가족에 관한 기사에 답하기 위해 작성된 글임을 알 수 있다. 따라서 **(a) to respond to an article about her family**가 정답이다.

▶ **paraphrasing point**
the write-up on our family event → an article about her family

단어 **editor** n. 편집자   **respond** v. 응답하다, 대답하다

2. Why does the writer say **the photo caption is incorrect**?

(a) Her cousin was not present at the reunion.
(b) Her family member is wrongly identified.
(c) The photo shows a different family.
(d) The caption misspells her brother's name.

2. 글쓴이가 사진 설명이 잘못되었다고 말하는 이유는 무엇인가?

(a) 그녀의 사촌은 모임에 참석하지 않았다.
(b) 그녀의 가족 구성원이 잘못 구별되었다.
(c) 사진이 다른 가족을 보여준다.
(d) 설명이 형제의 이름을 잘못 입력했다.

 **Tip!** caption과 incorrect에 대한 부분을 찾아 읽는다.

해설

사진에서 오른쪽 남자를 남동생인 Harold라고 되어 있었는데 사실은 사촌 Danny라고 설명하고 있으므로 그녀의 가족 구성원이 잘못 구별되었다는 것을 알 수 있다. 따라서 **(b) Her family member is wrongly identified**가 정답이다.

▶ **paraphrasing point**
misidentified → wrongly identified

| 단어 | reunion n. 모임 | wrongly ad. 잘못되게, 틀리게 | misspell v. ~의 철자를 잘못 쓰다 |

3. In the context of the passage, <u>erroneous</u> means _____.

(a) various
(b) unsafe
(c) delicate
(d) false

3. 글의 문맥에 따르면, <u>erroneous</u>는 _____를 의미한다.

(a) 다양한
(b) 안전하지 않은
(c) 섬세한
(d) 거짓의

해설

문맥상 몇 가지 수정 사항에 대해 이야기하는 과정에서 '어떻게 이런 erroneous한 정보가 인쇄되었는지 모르겠다'는 내용을 통해 erroneous가 '**고쳐야 할 점, 잘못된 것**'을 의미한다는 것을 알 수 있다. 따라서 (d) false가 정답이다.

PART 4. Read the following business letter and answer the questions. The underlined word in the letter is for a vocabulary question. (4~6)

George Hoffman
Executive Director
Great Health Pharmaceuticals

Dear Mr. Hoffman,

First of all, thank you so much for offering me the Account Manager position at Great Health Pharmaceuticals. I feel honored that you think I would be a great fit for the team and an integral part of your company's future successes. Thinking back on our interview last week, I was struck by the warmth and respect you showed towards your employees. As a potential worker, that is the kind of environment that I really value.

That said, [4)] **I would like to take more time to think about the offer before accepting, if possible.** [5)] **At the moment, I have competing offers from a few other companies.** I feel that I need to consider all possible angles when making such an important commitment. I apologize for any delay this may cause you in the hiring process, and I understand if you are not able to give me more time for the decision.

[6)] **I just want to <u>emphasize</u> again how much I enjoyed meeting you and how excited I am at the prospect of working for Great Health.** Please let me know if you can wait until next week for my response to the job offer.

Yours truly,
Amy Baker

George Hoffman
이사
Great Health 제약회사

Hoffman 씨께,

우선, 저에게 Great Health 제약회사에서 고객 담당 매니저 직책을 제안해 주신 것에 대해 정말 감사합니다. 제가 팀에 매우 적합하고 귀사의 미래 성공에 필수적인 부분이 될 것이라고 생각하신 것을 영광으로 생각합니다. 지난주 인터뷰를 다시 생각해보면, 직원들에게 보여주신 따뜻함과 존경심에 놀랐습니다. 향후 근로자로서, 이것이 제가 정말로 가치를 두는 환경의 종류입니다.

그렇기는 하지만, [4)] 가능하다면, 수락하기 전에 제안에 대해 좀더 생각할 시간을 갖고 싶습니다. [5)] 현재, 저는 다른 몇몇 회사들로부터 비슷한 제안을 받았습니다. 이런 중요한 일에는 가능한 모든 관점을 고려해야 한다고 생각합니다. 채용 과정에 있어 귀사에 야기할지도 모르는 어떠한 지연에 대해 사과드리며, 저에게 결정을 위한 더 많은 시간을 줄 수 없다고 하셔도 이해합니다.

[6)] 제가 당신을 만나서 정말 즐거웠고, 그리고 Great Health에서 근무할 생각에 정말 흥분된다는 것을 다시 <u>강조하고</u> 싶습니다. 일자리 제안에 대한 저의 답변을 다음 주까지 기다려 주실 수 있는지를 저에게 알려주시기 바랍니다.

Amy Baker 드림

 **단어**

offer n. 제안
integral adj. 필수적인, 필수의
accept v. 수락하다
commitment n. 책무, 책임, 공약

honor n. 영광
potential adj. 향후의, 잠재의
competing offer n. (다른 기업으로부터 받은) 비슷한 제안
prospect n. 전망

 **문제풀이**

4. Why did Amy Baker write a letter to George Hoffman?

   (a) to tell him that she accepts the job offer
   (b) to ask him to give her more time to think
   (c) to inform him that she will decline the position
   (d) to thank him for the opportunity to interview

4. Amy Baker는 왜 George Hoffman에게 편지를 썼는가?

   (a) 그녀가 구인 제안을 수락한다고 말하기 위해
   (b) 그녀에게 생각할 시간을 더 줄 것을 요청하기 위해
   (c) 그녀가 그 직책을 거절할 것이라고 알리기 위해
   (d) 인터뷰 기회에 대해 감사하기 위해

 해설

구인 제안을 수락하기 전에 가능하다면 조금 더 생각할 시간을 갖고 싶다는 언급을 통해 (b) to ask him to give her more time to think가 정답임을 알 수 있다.

단어 accept v. 수락하다, 받아들이다   decline v. 거절하다   opportunity n. 기회

5. Why is Amy Baker hesitating about her decision?

(a) She has other options to contemplate.
(b) She wants to learn more about the company.
(c) She cannot start working right away.
(d) She has several interviews to attend.

5. Amy Baker는 왜 그녀의 결정에 주저하는가?

(a) 그녀가 숙고해야 할 다른 선택지들이 있어서
(b) 그녀가 회사에 대해 더 알고 싶어서
(c) 그녀가 즉시 일을 시작할 수 없어서
(d) 그녀가 참석할 몇 개의 다른 면접이 있어서

해설

다른 회사들로부터 비슷한 제안을 받았다는 언급을 통해 그녀가 결정을 주저하는 이유가 숙고해야 할 다른 선택지들이 있기 때문임을 알 수 있다. 따라서 (a) She has other options to contemplate가 정답이다.

paraphrasing point

competing offers → other options to contemplate

단어 contemplate v. 심사숙고하다, 고려하다, 생각하다   attend v. 참석하다, 다니다

---

6. In the context of the passage, <u>emphasize</u> means _____.

(a) sympathize
(b) comprehend
(c) imagine
(d) repeat

6. 글의 문맥에 따르면, <u>emphasize</u>는 _____를 의미한다.

(a) 동정하다
(b) 이해하다
(c) 상상하다
(d) 반복하다

해설

문맥상 만나서 즐거웠고 Great Health에서 근무할 생각에 정말 흥분된다는 것을 '강조하고' 싶다는 내용이므로, 이 경우 '반복하다'라는 의미가 가장 비슷하다는 것을 알 수 있다. 따라서 (d) repeat가 정답이다.

PART 4. Read the business letter article and answer the questions. The underlined word in the letter is for a vocabulary question. (7~9)

Cecile Johnson
Regional Manager
Movers and Shakers Moving Company

7) **I am writing to express how deeply unsatisfied I was with the service from Movers and Shakers.** I hired movers from the local branch of your company to help me move into a new house on October 12th of this year, and I would like to make several complaints about the job that the workers did.

On that morning, the movers were supposed to arrive at 10 a.m., but they didn't show up until well after lunchtime. As a result, it was very late at night when they finally finished unloading my belongings at the new house. They were also quite 9) **reckless** when moving fragile items. In fact, my television screen was noticeably cracked when two of the movers dropped it on the steps outside.

As one might expect, I was extremely upset about my ruined TV, as well as the lack of respect toward my time. The next day I contacted the local branch of Movers and Shakers, but the manager refused to acknowledge any mistakes. 8) **That's why I am writing to you, in the hopes that the company will take responsibility for these problems by financially compensating me for the damage.**

Awaiting your response,

Joseph Cutler

Cecile Johnson
지역 담당자
Movers and Shakers 이삿짐 운송 회사

7) 저는 Movers and Shakers의 서비스에 대해 제가 얼마나 많이 불만족했는지를 표현하기 위해 글을 쓰고 있습니다. 저는 올해 10월 12일에 제가 새 집으로 이사할 수 있도록 귀사의 지점에서 이사 직원들을 고용했고, 저는 직원들이 했던 일에 대해 몇 가지 불만을 제기하고 싶습니다.

그날 아침, 이사 직원들은 오전 10시에 도착하기로 되어 있었지만, 점심 시간이 훨씬 지나도록 나타나지 않았습니다. 그 결과, 그들이 마침내 제 물건들을 새 집에 내리는 것을 끝냈을 때는 매우 늦은 밤이었습니다. 그들은 또한 깨지기 쉬운 물건을 옮길 때에도 상당히 9) **부주의**했습니다. 사실, 제 텔레비전 화면은 두 직원이 밖에 있는 계단 위로 떨어뜨렸을 때 눈에 띄게 금이 갔습니다.

예상할 수 있듯이, 저는 제 시간을 존중하지 않는 것뿐만 아니라 제 망가진 TV에 대해 극도로 화가 났습니다. 다음날 저는 Movers and Shakers의 지역 분점에 연락했지만, 매니저는 어떠한 실수도 인정하지 않았습니다. 8) 그래서 회사가 저에게 피해에 대해 금전적으로 보상함으로써 이러한 문제에 대해 책임을 지기를 바라며 **편지를 씁니다.**

당신의 응답을 기다리며

Joseph Cutler 드림

 단어

unsatisfied adj. 만족하고 있지 않은
complain v. 불만을 제기하다
show up v. 나타나다
unload v. 짐을 내리다
fragile adj. 깨지기 쉬운
crack v. 깨뜨리다
upset v. 속상하게 하다, 잘못되게 만들다 adj. 속상한, 화가 난
contact v. ~에게 연락하다
branch n. 분점, 지사
responsibility n. 책임
compensate v. 보상하다

hire v. 고용하다
be supposed to v v. ~하기로 되어있다
as a result ad. 그 결과, 결과적으로
belongings n. 물건들, 소지품
noticeably ad. 눈에 띄게
expect v. 예상하다
ruin v. 망가뜨리다
local adj. 지역의
acknowledge v. 인정하다
financially ad. 금전적으로, 재정적으로

 문제풀이

7. Why is Mr. Cutler writing the letter to the moving company?

(a) He needs to hire people to help him move.
(b) He wants to praise workers at the local branch.
(c) He has to reschedule his moving date.
(d) He intends to criticize their poor service.

7. Cutler씨는 왜 이삿짐 운송 회사에 편지를 쓰고 있는가?

(a) 그는 그의 이사를 도와줄 사람들을 고용할 필요가 있다.
(b) 그는 지역 분점 직원들을 칭찬하기를 원한다.
(c) 그는 그의 이사 날짜를 변경해야 한다.
(d) 그는 그들의 형편없는 서비스를 비판하려고 한다.

해설

첫 문장에서 이사 회사의 서비스에 대해 얼마나 불만족했는지 표현하기 위해 편지를 쓴다는 언급을 통해 **(d) He intends to criticize their poor service**가 정답임을 알 수 있다.

▶ paraphrasing point
to express how deeply unsatisfied → criticize

단어 **praise** v. 칭찬하다 　　**intend** v. 의도하다, 작정하다 　　**criticize** v. 비판하다, 비난하다

8. What does Mr. Cutler probably want the moving company to do?

   (a) to give him money for his broken television
   (b) to acknowledge their mistakes frankly
   (c) to send him a sincere apology in writing
   (d) to have the manager call him personally

8. Cutler씨가 이삿짐 운송 회사에게 무엇을 해 달라고 원하는 것 같은가?

   (a) 그의 망가진 텔레비전에 대해 그에게 돈을 주는 것
   (b) 그들의 실수를 솔직하게 인정하는 것
   (c) 그에게 서면으로 진심의 사과를 보내는 것
   (d) 매니저가 그에게 직접 연락하라고 하는 것

> 해설

마지막 문단에서 '회사가 피해에 대해 금전적으로 보상하여 이러한 문제에 대한 책임을 지기를 바란다'고 언급 했으므로 (a) to give him money for his broken television이 정답임을 알 수 있다.

> paraphrasing point

financially compensating me for the damage → give him money for his broken television

단어 frankly ad. 솔직히   sincere adj. 진실된, 진정한   apology n. 사과

---

9. In the context of the passage, reckless means _____.

   (a) mindless
   (b) careless
   (c) adventurous
   (d) impulsive

9. 글의 문맥에 따르면, reckless는 _____를 의미한다.

   (a) 아무 생각이 없는
   (b) 부주의한
   (c) 모험심이 강한
   (d) 충동적인

> 해설

문맥상 그들이 물건을 옮길 때 reckless했다고 언급한 두 텔레비전이 깨졌다는 내용을 통해 reckless는 '부주의한'을 뜻한다는 것을 알 수 있다. 따라서 (b) careless가 정답이다.

실전모의고사 <제1회>

53 (a)	54 (c)	55 (b)	56 (d)	57 (b)	58 (a)	59 (c)	60 (b)	61 (d)	62 (a)
63 (c)	64 (a)	65 (b)	66 (c)	67 (a)	68 (b)	69 (d)	70 (c)	71 (c)	72 (d)
73 (c)	74 (b)	75 (c)	76 (d)	77 (a)	78 (a)	79 (b)	80 (d)		

PART 1. Read the following biography article and answer the questions. The underlined words in the article are for vocabulary questions.

53~59

VALENTINA TERESHKOVA

Valentina Tereshkova is 53) **a Soviet cosmonaut who became the first woman to travel into space during the U.S.S.R. space program in the 1950s and 1960s.** In less than three days, she was able to orbit the Earth 48 times aboard the spacecraft Vostok 6.

Valentina Vladimirovna Tereshkova was born on March 6, 1937 in Maslennikovo, Russia. Her father was a tractor driver, while her mother worked in a textile mill. When Tereshkova's father died, she and her siblings were single-handedly raised by their mother.

Tereshkova did not attend school until she was about ten years old due to their family's financial struggle. Six years later, she left school and began working at the textile mill with her mother to support her siblings. 54) **She continued her education by taking lessons from her instructors through the mail.**

발렌티나 테레시코바

발렌티나 테레시코바는 53) 1950년대와 1960년대 U.S.S.R. 우주 프로그램 동안 우주를 여행한 최초의 여성이 된 소련 우주 비행사이다. 3일도 채 되지 않아, 그녀는 우주선 보스토크 6호를 타고 지구의 궤도를 48바퀴 돌 수 있었다.

발렌티나 블라디미로브나 테레시코바는 1937년 3월 6일 러시아의 마슬레니코보에서 태어났다. 그녀의 아버지는 트랙터 운전사였고, 그녀의 어머니는 방직 공장에서 일했다. 테레시코바의 아버지가 죽었을 때, 그녀와 그녀의 형제들은 홀어머니에 의해 길러졌다.

테레시코바는 가족의 재정적 어려움으로 인해 10살 무렵이 될 때까지 학교에 다니지 못했다. 6년 후, 그녀는 학교를 그만두고 그녀의 형제자매들을 지원하기 위해 어머니와 함께 방직 공장에서 일하기 시작했다. 54) 그녀는 우편을 통해 그녀의 교사들로부터 수업을 받음으로써 교육을 계속했다.

55) **While balancing her job and studies, Tereshkova joined the Yaroslavl Air Sports Club, and became a parachutist.** She completed at least a hundred parachute jumps as an amateur. During this time, the Soviet Union was in a competition against the United States for space travel supremacy—both were eager to send humans into space.

Following the first Soviet spaceflight piloted by a man in 1961, the U.S.S.R. started recruiting women into the Soviet space program. Tereshkova volunteered, even though she had no prior education in piloting. It was, however, 56) **her parachuting** 58) **record** and experience that led to her acceptance, since cosmonauts back then were required to parachute from their capsules upon their return to the Earth.

For 18 months, Tereshkova trained as a cosmonaut along with four other women. They went through tests to determine if they could 59) **handle** long periods of being alone, as well as extreme and zero gravity conditions. Of the five trainees, only Tereshkova traveled into space, piloting the spacecraft Vostok 6 on June 16, 1963. She circled the Earth 48 times in just 70.8 hours.

After her voyage, Tereshkova was awarded the title of the Hero of the Soviet Union. She also received various forms of recognition including the Order of Lenin, the highest award given by the Soviet Union to a civilian.

57) **Tereshkova never flew again but she continued working in the Soviet space program.** At present, Tereshkova's legacy is widely celebrated in books, museums, and stage productions.

55) 그녀의 직업과 학업의 균형을 유지하면서, 테레시코바는 야로슬라블 항공스포츠클럽에 가입하여 낙하산 선수가 되었다. 그녀는 아마추어로서 최소 100번의 낙하산 점프를 완료했다. 이 기간 동안, 소련은 우주 여행의 패권을 잡기 위해 미국과 경쟁하고 있었고, 양국 모두 인간을 우주로 보내기를 열망했다.

1961년에 한 남성에 의해 처음으로 조종된 소련 우주 비행에 이어, U.S.S.R.은 소련 우주 프로그램에 여성을 모집하기 시작했다. 테레시코바는 비록 조종에 대한 사전 교육이 없었음에도 불구하고 자원했다. 56) 그러나, 당시 우주 비행사들은 지구로 돌아오자마자 (우주선의) 캡슐로부터 낙하산을 타고 뛰어내리는 것이 요구되었기 때문에, 그녀의 낙하산 타기 58) 기록과 경험이 그녀를 합격으로 이끌었다.

18개월 동안, 테레시코바는 네 명의 다른 여성들과 함께 우주 비행사로 훈련받았다. 그들은 극한의 무중력 상태뿐만 아니라 오랜 시간을 혼자서 59) 견딜 수 있는지를 알아내기 위한 테스트들을 거쳤다. 다섯 명의 훈련생 중, 오로지 테레시코바만이 1963년 6월 16일 우주선 보스토크 6호를 조종하여 우주를 여행했다. 그녀는 불과 70.8시간 만에 지구를 48바퀴 돌았다.

항해 후, 테레시코바는 소련의 영웅이라는 칭호를 부여받았다. 그녀는 또한 소련이 민간인에게 수여하는 최고의 상인 레닌 훈장을 포함하여 다양한 형태의 표창을 받았다.

57) 테레시코바는 다시는 비행하지 않았지만 소련 우주 프로그램에서 계속 일했다. 현재, 테레시코바의 유산은 책, 박물관 및 무대 조품에서 널리 찬양받는다.

 **단어**

cosmonaut n. (과거 러시아의) 우주 비행사	**orbit** n. 궤도, 영향권 v. 궤도를 돌다
aboard prep. ~에 탑승하여	**spacecraft** n. 우주선
textile n. 방직, 직물	**mill** n. 공장, 제재소
single-handedly ad. 단독으로, 혼자의 힘으로	**sibling** n. 형제자매
attend v. ~에 다니다, 참석하다	**not A until B** phr. B가 되어서야 A하다
struggle n. 어려움, 고투	**instructor** n. 교사, 강사
balance n. 균형 v. 균형을 유지하다	**join** v. 가입하다
parachutist n. 낙하산을 타고 뛰어내리는 사람, 낙하산 선수	**competition** n. 경쟁
supremacy n. 패권, 우위	**spaceflight** n. 우주 비행
pilot v. 조종하다 n. 조종사	**recruit** v. 모집하다
volunteer v. 자원하다	**prior** adj. 사전의, 이전의
acceptance n. 허가, 인정, 수락	**go through** v. 거치다, 겪다
determine v. 결정하다, 알아내다	**handle** v. 견디다, 다루다
extreme adj. 극심한	**gravity** n. 중력
trainee n. 훈련생	**circle** v. (원을 그리며) 돌다, 선회하다
voyage n. 항해	**recognition** n. 인정, 인식, 표창
civilian n. 민간인, 시민, 일반인	**legacy** n. 유산
celebrate v. 찬양하다	

 문제풀이

53. What is Valentina Tereshkova most recognized for?

 (a) being the first female to travel in space around the Earth
 (b) having stayed in space for more than three days
 (c) having commanded the first Russian spacecraft
 (d) being the first woman member of the Soviet Union

53. 발렌티나 테레시코바는 무엇으로 가장 잘 알려져 있는가?

 (a) 지구 주위의 우주를 여행한 최초의 여성이 된 것
 (b) 3일 이상 우주에 머무른 것
 (c) 최초의 러시아 우주선을 지휘한 것
 (d) 소련 연방 최초의 여성 의원이 된 것

해설

발렌티나 테레시코바는 1950년대와 1960년대 우주 프로그램 동안 우주를 여행한 최초의 여성이 된 소련 우주 비행사라는 언급을 통해 (a) being the first female to travel in space around the Earth가 정답이다.

paraphrasing point

the first woman → the first female

단어 **command** v. 지시하다, 지휘하다, 명령하다

54. How did Tereshkova **keep up with her studies** despite her job?

(a) by accepting jobs only during the night
(b) by attending classes before going to the mill
(c) by using mailed lectures to school herself
(d) by listening to her mother's lessons

54. 테레시코바는 일이 있음에도 불구하고 어떻게 공부를 계속했는가?

(a) 야간 동안에만 일을 받아들임으로써
(b) 공장에 가기 전에 수업에 참석함으로써
(c) 독학을 위해 우편 강의를 이용함으로써
(d) 어머니의 교습을 들음으로써

해설

그녀가 우편을 통해 교사들로부터 수업을 받음으로써 교육을 계속했다는 언급을 통해 **(c) by using mailed lectures to school herself**가 정답임을 알 수 있다.

paraphrasing point

continued her education → keep up with her studies
taking lessons from her instructors through the mail → using mailed lectures to school herself

단어

keep up with v. (뒤처지지 않게) 계속 ~을 따라가다
lecture n. 강의, 강연

---

55. When did Tereshkova learn how to parachute?

(a) when she worked as a fabric miller
(b) when she signed up for an air sports club
(c) when she joined a Soviet space exploration
(d) when she enrolled at a pilot school

55. 테레시코바는 언제 낙하산 타는 법을 배웠는가?

(a) 그녀가 직물공으로 일했을 때
(b) 그녀가 항공스포츠클럽에 가입했을 때
(c) 그녀가 소련 우주 탐사에 참여했을 때
(d) 그녀가 파일럿 학교에 등록했을 때

해설

야로슬라블 항공스포츠클럽에 들어가 낙하산을 타고 뛰어내리는 사람이 되었다는 내용을 통해 항공스포츠클럽에 가입했을 때 낙하산 타는 법을 배웠음을 알 수 있다. 따라서 **(b) when she signed up for an air sports club**이 정답이다.

paraphrasing point

joined → signed up for

단어

parachute n. 낙하산 v. 낙하산을 타고 낙하하다
enroll v. 등록하다, 입학하다
exploration n. 탐사, 답사, 탐험

56. Why most likely was Tereshkova accepted into the space program?

(a) because she excelled at commanding aircraft
(b) because she was used to extreme conditions
(c) because she trained as a cosmonaut beforehand
(d) because she could land on the Earth by parachuting

56. 왜 테레시코바가 우주 프로그램에 합격한 것 같은가?

(a) 그녀가 항공기 지휘에 탁월했기 때문에
(b) 그녀가 극한 조건에 익숙했기 때문에
(c) 그녀가 이전에 우주 비행사로 훈련했기 때문에
(d) 그녀가 낙하산으로 지구에 착륙할 수 있었기 때문에

> **해설**
> 이유를 나타내는 접속사 since 구문에 주목하면, 당시 우주 비행사들은 지구로 돌아오자마자 (우주선의) 캡슐로부터 낙하산을 타고 뛰어내려야 했기 때문에 그녀의 낙하산 타기 기록과 경험이 그녀를 합격으로 이끌었다는 내용을 통해 **(d) because she could land on the Earth by parachuting**이 정답임을 알 수 있다.

> **단어**
> excel v. 뛰어나다, 탁월하다   cosmonaut n. 우주 비행사   beforehand ad. 미리, 이전에

57. What did Tereshkova do after the spaceflight?

(a) She gave a speech during her award ceremony.
(b) She helped with the later Soviet space programs.
(c) She wrote a book about her space travel.
(d) She accepted a position at a space museum.

57. 테레시코바는 우주 비행 후 무엇을 했나?

(a) 그녀는 그녀의 시상식에서 연설을 했다.
(b) 그녀는 이후 소련의 우주 프로그램을 도왔다.
(c) 그녀는 우주 여행에 관한 책을 썼습니다.
(d) 그녀는 우주 박물관에서 직책을 수락했다.

> **해설**
> 마지막 단락에서 그녀가 다시 비행을 하지는 않았지만 계속해서 소련 우주 프로그램에서 일했다는 내용을 통해 **(b) She helped with the later Soviet space programs**가 정답임을 알 수 있다.

> **단어**
> award ceremony n. 시상식   museum n. 박물관

58. In the context of the passage, record means _____.

(a) history
(b) journal
(c) transaction
(d) album

58. 글의 문맥에 따르면, record는 _____를 의미한다.

(a) 이력
(b) 저널
(c) 거래
(d) 앨범

> **해설**
> 문맥상 그녀의 낙하 기록과 경험이 그녀의 소련 우주 프로그램 자원을 받아들이게 했다는 내용이므로 record는 과거의 경험을 나타내는 '기록, 이력'을 의미한다는 것을 알 수 있다. 이 때, history는 일반적으로 '역사'를 의미하지만 (개인, 가정, 장소의) '**이력/내력**'이라는 의미도 있다. 따라서 **(a) history**가 정답이다.

59. In the context of the passage, handle means _____.

(a) operate
(b) hold
(c) survive
(d) govern

59. 글의 문맥에 따르면, handle은 _____를 의미한다.

(a) 운영하다
(b) 보류하다
(c) 생존하다
(d) 통치하다

> **해설**
> 문맥상 오랜 시간을 혼자서 견딜 수 있는지를 알아내기 위한 테스트들을 거쳤다는 내용이므로 handle은 '**견디다, 생존하다**'를 의미한다는 것을 알 수 있다. 따라서 **(c) survive**가 정답이다.

PART 2. Read the following magazine article and answer the questions. The underlined words in the article are for vocabulary questions.

60~66

DOGS MOVE QUICKLY TO HELP THEIR OWNERS

60) A study published in *Learning and Behavior* has found that dogs are more likely to come up to a person who is crying than to a person who hums a tune. Additionally, dogs display quicker actions when assisting people in distress.

The recent study was conducted 61) to determine the dogs' capacity for pro-social behavior. Researchers examined how the dogs delivered comfort and attention, and 61) if they were capable of providing substantive help to humans in need. For the experiment, the researchers observed 34 dogs of various ages, sizes, and breeds, along with their respective owners.

The members of the first group were asked to make crying sounds and say "help" in a distressed tone every 15 seconds. 62) Meanwhile, the members of the second group were told to hum the tune of *Twinkle, Twinkle, Little Star* and say "help" using a 65) normal tone at the same interval. Researchers chose humming among other actions because it is a sound that the dog participants usually had not been exposed to.

개는 주인을 돕기 위해 빠르게 움직인다

『Learning and Behavior』에서 발표된 한 연구에 따르면 개는 노래를 흥얼거리는 사람보다 울고 있는 사람에게 다가갈 가능성이 더 높다는 것을 발견했다. 게다가, 개는 곤경에 처한 사람들을 도울 때 더 빠른 행동을 보인다.

최근의 연구는 61) 친사회적 행동에 대한 개의 능력을 알아내기 위해 수행되었다. 연구자들은 어떻게 개가 위로와 관심을 전달하는지, 61) 그리고 그들이 도움이 필요한 인간에게 실질적인 도움을 줄 수 있는지 조사했다. 실험을 위해, 연구원들은 각각의 주인과 함께 다양한 연령, 크기 그리고 품종의 34 마리의 개를 관찰했다.

첫 번째 그룹의 구성원은 15초마다 울음소리를 내고 괴로운 어조로 "도와줘"라고 말하도록 요청받았다. 62) 한편, 두 번째 그룹의 멤버들은 『반짝 반짝 작은 별』 곡을 흥얼거리며, 같은 간격으로 65) 보통의 어조를 사용하여 "도와줘"라고 말하라는 지시를 받았다. 연구자들은 참가견들이 평소에 노출된 적이 없었던 소리이기 때문에 다른 행동들 중에서 콧노래를 선택했다.

One by one, the dog owners were asked to sit behind a clear plastic door that could be easily opened by a dog's nose or paw. The dogs, on the other hand, were positioned in a room where they could see and hear their owners cry or hum. The dog owners had been classified into two groups. After the experiment, it was found that although the number of dogs that opened the door was quite similar in both groups, there was a significant difference in how quickly the dogs in each group "rescued" their owners in the other room.

63) **The dogs in the crying group opened the door and** 66) <u>rushed</u> **to their owners within 23.43 seconds, while the dogs whose owners hummed took three times longer—95.89 seconds on average.** It was also noted that the dogs' ages, sizes, and breeds did not affect how they responded in the experiment.

Overall, the *Learning and Behavior* 64) **study reinforced the idea that dogs are capable of detecting human emotions. It also advanced the notion that dogs can be an even greater help to humankind, particularly during therapy.**

한 몇씩 차례로, 견주들은 개의 코나 앞발로 쉽게 열 수 있는 투명한 플라스틱 문 뒤에 앉도록 요청받았다. 반면에, 개들은 주인이 울거나 콧노래를 하는 것을 보고 들을 수 있는 방에 배치되었다. 견주는 두 그룹으로 분류되었다. 실험 후, 비록 문을 연 개들의 수는 두 그룹에서 상당히 비슷했지만, 각 그룹의 개들이 다른 방에서 주인을 얼마나 빠르게 "구출"했는지는 상당한 차이가 있는 것으로 밝혀졌다.

63) 울고 있는 그룹의 개들은 문을 열고 23.43초 안에 그들의 주인에게 66) 달려갔고, 주인이 콧노래를 부른 개는 평균 95.89초로 3배 더 오래 걸렸다. 또한 개의 나이, 크기 및 품종이 실험에서 그들이 반응하는 방식에 영향을 미치지 않는 것으로 나타났다.

전반적으로, 「Learning and Behavior」의 연구는 64) 개가 인간의 감정을 감지할 수 있다는 생각을 강화했다. 또한 개가 특히 치료 중에 인류에게 훨씬 더 큰 도움이 될 수 있다는 개념을 발전시켰다.

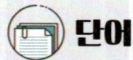 **단어**

publish v. 발표하다
display v. 보이다, 보여주다
capacity n. 능력, 역량
substantive adj. 실질적인
breed n. 품종, 번식
distressed adj. 괴로운
expose v. 노출시키다
paw n. 앞발
classify v. 분류하다
participant n. 참가자
reinforce v. 강화하다
emotion n. 감정

come up to phr. ~에 다가가다, 이르다
assist v. 돕다, 보조하다
pro-social behavior n. 친사회적 행동
observe v. 관찰하다
respective adj. 각각의
interval n. 간격
hum v. (콧노래를) 흥얼거리다
position v. 배치하다
significant adj. 상당한
note v. 주목하다, 언급하다
be capable of phr. ~을 할 수 있다
advance v. 발전시키다, 진보하다

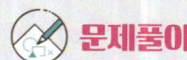 **문제풀이**

60. What is the article all about?
(a) the effects of receiving comfort from dogs
(b) how dogs react when someone needs help
(c) the differences between crying and humming sounds
(d) why people prefer dogs for emotional support

60. 기사는 모두 무엇에 관한 것인가?
(a) 개에게 위로를 받는 것의 효과
(b) 누군가가 도움을 필요로 할 때 개들이 반응하는 방법
(c) 울음 소리와 흥얼거리는 소리의 차이점
(d) 사람들이 정서적 지지를 위해 개를 선호하는 이유

해설

제목과 글의 서두에서 사람이 도움을 필요로 할 때 개의 행동이 달라짐을 언급하고 있으며, 이를 증명하는 실험이 뒤이어 나온다. 즉, 글의 내용은 누군가가 도움을 필요로 할 때 개들이 어떻게 반응하는지에 관한 내용임을 알 수 있다. 따라서 **(b) how dogs react when someone needs help**가 정답이다.

paraphrasing point

display quicker actions when assisting people in distress → react when someone needs help

단어 receive v. 받다   prefer v. ~을 좋아하다, 선호하다   emotional adj. 정서의, 감정의

61. Why did the researchers **conduct the study**?

(a) to determine whether dogs have emotions
(b) to estimate how much comfort dogs provide to humans
(c) to prove that dogs are incapable of ignoring their owners
(d) to know whether dogs would actually help people in need

61. 왜 연구자들이 **연구를 했는가**?

(a) 개에게 감정이 있는지 알아내기 위해
(b) 개가 인간에게 얼마나 많은 위안을 제공하는지 추정하기 위해
(c) 개가 주인을 무시할 수 없음을 증명하기 위해
(d) 개가 실제로 도움이 필요한 사람들을 도울 수 있는지 알기 위해

 **Tip!** 연구 계기를 묻는 질문이므로 지문의 상단 쪽에서 실험의 목적을 언급하는 곳을 찾는다.

해설

연구는 개의 친사회적 행동 능력을 알아내기 위해 수행되었으며, 도움이 필요한 인간에게 실질적인 도움을 줄 수 있는지를 실험했다는 내용을 통해 **(d) to know whether dogs would actually help people in need**가 정답임을 알 수 있다.

paraphrasing point
providing substantive help to humans in need → actually help people in need

단어
conduct v. (특정한 활동)을 하다   comfort n. 안락, 편안, 위안
incapable adj. ~을 할 수 없는   whether conj. ~인지 아닌지

---

62. How was **the second group** of owners prepared for observation?

(a) They were asked to hum a lullaby.
(b) They were instructed to cry for help.
(c) They were told to ignore their pets.
(d) They were advised to calm the dogs.

62. **두 번째 주인 그룹**은 관찰을 위해 어떻게 준비되었는가?

(a) 그들은 자장가를 흥얼거리도록 요청받았다.
(b) 그들은 도와달라고 외치라는 지시를 받았다.
(c) 그들은 반려동물을 무시하라는 말을 들었다.
(d) 그들은 개를 진정시키라는 조언을 받았다.

 **Tip!** 문제에서 언급한 the second group을 본문에서 찾아 읽는다.

해설

두 번째 그룹을 언급한 단락에서 구성원들이 「반짝 반짝 작은 별」 곡을 흥얼거리며, 같은 간격으로 보통의 어조를 사용하여 "도와줘"라고 말하라고 지시를 받았다는 내용을 통해 **(a) They were asked to hum a lullaby**가 정답임을 알 수 있다.

paraphrasing point were told to hum → were asked to hum

단어
observation v. 관찰, 관측   instructed adj. 교육을 받은, 교양이 있는

63. Why most likely did dogs respond faster with the first group?

(a) because the dogs are racing with other dogs
(b) because dogs take the time to enjoy tunes
(c) because dogs want to save their owners
(d) because dogs are irritated by the crying sounds

63. 왜 개들이 첫 번째 그룹에서 더 빨리 반응했을 것 같은가?

(a) 개가 다른 개와 경주를 하고 있기 때문에
(b) 개는 음악을 즐기는 데 시간을 할애하기 때문에
(c) 개는 주인을 구하고 싶어하기 때문에
(d) 개가 우는 소리에 짜증을 내기 때문에

해설

첫 번째 그룹의 주인은 15초마다 울음소리를 내며 괴로운 어조로 도와달라고 요청을 했고, 이에 콧노래를 흥얼거린 두 번째 그룹과 비교해 개들이 3배나 더 빨리 반응했다는 내용을 통해 개가 주인을 구하고 싶어하기 때문임을 알 수 있다. 따라서 **(c) because dogs want to save their owners**가 정답이다.

단어

tune n. 곡, 음, 선율   irritated adj. 짜증이 난

---

64. What could be the study's significance in the field of medicine?

(a) The study will encourage using dogs in treatment programs.
(b) The study will foster better understanding of pet ownership.
(c) The study will urge further research on dogs' emotions.
(d) The study will promote training dogs as house helpers.

64. 의학 분야에서 이 연구의 중요성은 무엇인가?

(a) 이 연구는 치료 프로그램에 개를 사용하는 것을 장려할 것이다.
(b) 이 연구는 반려동물 소유권에 대한 더 나은 이해를 촉진할 것이다.
(c) 이 연구는 개의 감정에 대한 추가적인 연구를 촉구할 것이다.
(d) 이 연구는 훈련견을 집 도우미로 홍보할 것이다.

해설

이 연구는 개가 인간의 감정을 감지할 수 있다는 생각을 강화시켰으며, 개가 특히 치료에서 인류에게 더 큰 도움이 될 수 있다는 개념을 발전시켰다는 내용을 통해 **(a) The study will encourage using dogs in treatment programs**가 정답임을 알 수 있다.

paraphrasing point

during therapy → in treatment programs

단어

treatment n. 치료, 처치   foster v. 장려하다, 조성하다, 발전시키다

65. In the context of the passage, <u>normal</u> means _____.

(a) healthy
(b) ordinary
(c) accepted
(d) right

65. 글의 문맥에 따르면, <u>normal</u>은 _____을 의미한다.

(a) 건강한
(b) 보통의
(c) 인정된
(d) 옳은

> 해설

두 그룹 중 첫번째 그룹은 우는 소리와 괴로운 어조를 사용한 반면 두번째 그룹은 노래를 부르며 normal한 어조를 사용했다는 대조 표현을 통해 normal이 '보통의, 평범한'의 의미임을 유추할 수 있다. 따라서 **(b) ordinary**가 정답이다.

66. In the context of the passage, <u>rushed</u> means _____.

(a) pushed
(b) delayed
(c) hurried
(d) flowed

66. 글의 문맥에 따르면, <u>rushed</u>는 _____을 의미한다.

(a) 밀었다
(b) 지연했다
(c) 서둘러 갔다
(d) 흘러갔다

> 해설

대조 그룹은 95.89초가 걸렸지만 울고 있는 그룹의 개들은 23.43초만에 주인에게 rushed했다는 내용을 통해 rush가 '달려 갔다, 서둘러 갔다'는 의미임을 유추할 수 있다. 따라서 **(c) hurried**가 정답이다.

PART 3. Read the following encyclopedia article and answer the questions. The underlined words in the article are for vocabulary questions.

67~73

THE ELIZABETH TOWER

67) **The Elizabeth Tower is a clock tower in London famous for** being **the most accurate chiming clock in the world.** The tower is commonly referred to as "Big Ben," a nickname that pertains to the tower's main bell.

68) **After the old Palace of Westminster had burned down in 1834, architects in England were invited to submit a design for a new palace.** After careful selection, the British government chose English architect Charles Barry's 72) **proposal**, which initially did not include a clock tower. It was only after two years that the clock tower was added to his design with the help of architect Augustus Pugin, who also designed its Gothic interior.

The tower's construction began in September 1843, but it rapidly fell behind the original schedule of completion. The tower was only completed after 15 years, and there was no ribbon-cutting ceremony to celebrate its opening. In 1858, the tower chimed for the first time, and it has become a daily time signal since 1924.

The tower was branded as the "Clock Tower" or "St. Stephen's Tower" during Queen Victoria's reign, and 69) **was later renamed the "Elizabeth Tower" to mark Queen Elizabeth II's 60th year on the British throne in 2012.**

엘리자베스 타워

67) 엘리자베스 타워는 세계에서 가장 정확한 차임벨 시계로 유명한 런던의 시계탑이다. 그 타워는 일반적으로 타워의 주요 종과 관련된 별명인 "빅 벤"으로 불린다.

68) 1834년에 옛 웨스트민스터 궁전이 불타버린 후, 영국의 건축가들은 새로운 궁전의 디자인을 제출할 것을 요청받았다. 신중한 선택 끝에, 영국 정부는 영국 건축가 찰스 배리의 72) 제안을 선택했는데, 처음에는 시계탑이 포함되지 않았다. 고딕 양식의 인테리어도 설계했던 건축가 아우구스투스 푸긴의 도움으로 시계탑이 그의 설계에 추가된 것은 불과 2년 뒤였다.

탑의 건설은 1843년 9월에 시작되었지만, 원래의 완공 일정보다 심하게 늦어졌다. 탑은 15년 만에 완공되었으며, 개관을 기념하는 리본 컷팅식은 없었다. 1858년, 탑이 처음으로 울렸고, 1924년부터 매일 시간을 알리는 신호가 되었다.

타워는 빅토리아 여왕의 통치 기간 동안 "시계탑" 또는 "세인트 스티븐스 타워"로 불렸고, 69) 이후 2012년 엘리자베스 2세 여왕의 영국 왕위 60주년을 기념하기 위해 "엘리자베스 타워"로 개명되었다.

The Elizabeth Tower stands over 315 feet high and is composed of stone walls and iron frames. It 73) **houses** the largest bell in the tower, Big Ben, which weighs at least 13 tons and chimes every hour. It also features a public clock with faces that can be seen from all four sides of the tower.

The Elizabeth Tower's reliable timekeeping depends on weight and gravity. 70) **Engineers use a stack of old pennies to adjust the clock.** If they add a penny on the pendulum, the clock will tick faster. If the penny is removed, then the clock will slow down.

The clock has been stopped by heavy snow, German bombing raids during WWII, and the breakdown of mechanical components used for more than a hundred years. But it has become 71) **a point of national pride to keep the clock running dependably.** To date, the Elizabeth Tower remains a British cultural icon, an enduring symbol of the United Kingdom and parliamentary democracy.

엘리자베스 타워는 높이가 315피트에 달하며 돌담과 철제 뼈대로 구성되어 있다. 그것은 가장 큰 종인 빅 벤을 타워 안에 73) 수용하고 있으며, 이는 최소 13톤의 무게에 달해 그 매시간 종을 울린다. 또한 타워의 네 면 모두에서 볼 수 있는 앞면들을 가진 공공 시계가 있다는 특징을 가졌다.

엘리자베스 타워의 신뢰할 수 있는 시간 측정기는 무게와 중력에 의존한다. 기술자들은 70) 시계를 조정하기 위해 오래된 페니(영국의 작은 동전) 더미를 사용한다. 시계 추에 페니를 추가하면, 시계가 더 빨리 똑딱거리게 될 것이다. 페니가 제거되면, 시계가 느려지게 될 것이다.

시계는 폭설, 제2차 세계대전 중 독일의 폭격, 100년 이상 사용된 기계 부품의 고장으로 멈춘 적이 있다. 그러나 71) 시계를 믿을 수 있게 작동하도록 유지시키는 것은 국가적 자부심의 포인트가 되었다. 현재까지, 엘리자베스 타워는 영국과 의회 민주주의의 영원한 상징인 영국의 문화적 아이콘으로 남아 있다.

단어

chime v. 종을 울리다
burn down v. 소실되다, 전소되다
submit v. 제출하다
fall behind v. 늦어지다
ceremony n. 기념식, 의식
reign n. 통치
mark v. 기념하다, 표시하다
feature v. 특징으로 삼다, 특징을 갖다

pertain to v. ~와 관계가 있다
architect n. 건축가
initially ad. 초기에는, 처음에는
complete v. 완공하다
brand v. 이름을 붙이다
rename v. 개명하다
weigh v. 무게를 달다
dependably ad. 믿음직하게

 **문제풀이**

67. What is **most remarkable** about the Elizabeth Tower?

(a) **its precision in telling the time**
(b) having a wrong nickname
(c) its very large bells
(d) being the world's first clock tower

67. 엘리자베스 타워에서 가장 주목할 만한 것은 무엇인가?

(a) **시간 알림에 있어서의 정확성**
(b) 잘못된 별명을 가짐
(c) 매우 큰 종
(d) 세계 최초의 시계탑

 엘리자베스 타워의 정의를 묻는 문제로 첫 단락에서 most remarkable의 대응 표현인 famous for을 찾는다.

엘리자베스 타워는 세계에서 가장 정확한 차임벨 시계로 유명한 런던의 시계탑이라는 언급을 통해 (a) its precision in telling the time이 정답임을 알 수 있다.

▶ paraphrasing point

the most accurate chiming clock → its precision in telling the time

단어   precision n. 정확, 정밀

---

68. **When** did the **need to build** a palace arise?

(a) after British officials had ordered renovations
(b) **after** the edifice was **destroyed by fire**
(c) after the original construction plan took so long
(d) after architects proposed new building designs

68. 언제 궁전을 지을 필요가 생겼는가?

(a) 영국 관리들이 수리를 명령한 후
(b) **건축물이 화재로 파괴된 후**
(c) 원래 건설 계획이 너무 오래 걸린 후
(d) 건축가가 새로운 건물 설계를 제안한 후

해설
1834년에 옛 웨스트민스터 궁전이 불타버린 후, 영국의 건축가들은 새로운 궁전의 디자인을 제출할 것을 요청받았다는 내용을 통해 건물이 화재로 파괴된 후 궁전을 지을 필요가 생겼다는 것을 알 수 있다. 따라서 (b) after the edifice was destroyed by fire가 정답이다.

▶ paraphrasing point

burned down → destroyed by fire

단어   official n. 공무원   renovation n. 혁신   edifice n. 건축물

69. Why was the clock tower **renamed** as Elizabeth Tower **in 2012**?

(a) to remember the British queen's birthday
(b) to proclaim the tower's first-ever chime
(c) to celebrate the clock's 15 years of completion
(d) to honor a ruler's 60-year reign in England

69. 시계탑이 2012년에 엘리자베스 타워로 이름이 변경된 이유는 무엇인가?

(a) 영국 여왕의 생일을 기억하기 위해
(b) 탑 최초의 종소리를 선포하기 위해
(c) 시계의 완성 15주년을 축하하기 위해
(d) 영국 통치자의 60년 통치를 기리기 위해

 Tip! 본문에서 2012년을 찾아 주변부를 읽는다.

해설

2012년에 엘리자베스 2세 여왕의 통치(영국 왕위) 60주년을 기념하기 위해 "엘리자베스 타워"로 개명되었다는 내용을 통해 **(d) to honor a ruler's 60-year region in England**가 정답임을 알 수 있다.

▸ paraphrasing point

to mark Queen Elizabeth II's 60th year on the British throne → to honor a ruler's 60-year reign in England

단어 chime n. 종소리

---

70. What most likely are the **pennies used for**?

(a) to control the clock tower's gravity
(b) to serve as tokens to keep the clock going
(c) to adjust the mechanism with their weight
(d) to set its time with British history

70. 페니(동전)는 무엇을 위해 **사용되는** 것 같은가?

(a) 시계탑의 중력을 제어하기 위해
(b) 시계가 계속 움직인다는 징표 역할을 하기 위해
(c) 무게로 기계 장치를 조정하기 위해
(d) 영국 역사에 맞춰 시간을 설정하기 위해

 Tip! 페니가 언급된 곳을 찾아 주변부를 읽는다.

해설

기술자들이 시계를 조정하기 위해 오래된 페니 더미를 사용하는데, 페니의 추가/제거에 따라 시계의 속도를 조절한다는 내용을 통해 페니의 무게로 시계의 기계 장치를 조정한다는 것을 알 수 있다. 따라서 (c) to adjust the mechanism with their weight가 정답이다.

단어 mechanism n. 기계 장치, 기구

71. Why most likely are British people **proud of the clock tower**?

(a) It went undamaged during WWII.
(b) It has stood tall for almost a hundred years.
(c) It can be trusted to display the time.
(d) It never stops working.

71. 영국인들이 시계탑을 자랑스럽게 여기는 이유는 무엇일까?

(a) 제2차 세계 대전 동안 손상되지 않았다.
(b) 거의 100년 동안 우뚝 서있다.
(c) 시간 표시를 신뢰할 수 있다.
(d) 결코 작동을 멈추지 않는다.

> **해설**

시계를 안정적으로 작동시키는 것이 국가적 자부심의 포인트가 되었다는 내용을 통해 영국인이 시계탑을 자랑스럽게 여기는 이유가 시간을 신뢰할 수 있기 때문이라는 것임을 유추할 수 있다. 따라서 (c) It can be trusted to display the time이 정답이다.

> **paraphrasing point**

keep the clock running dependably → can be trusted to display the time

단어 undamaged adj. 손상되지 않은   display v. 전시하다, 내보이다

---

72. In the context of the passage, <u>proposal</u> means _____.

(a) program
(b) policy
(c) petition
(d) plan

72. 글의 문맥에 따르면, <u>proposal</u>은 _____을 의미한다.

(a) 프로그램
(b) 정책
(c) 청원
(d) 계획

> **해설**

영국의 건축가들은 새로운 궁전의 디자인을 제출할 것을 요청받았고, 그 중 찰스 배리의 proposal을 선택했다는 내용을 통해 proposal은 '**계획, 제안**'의 의미임을 알 수 있다. 따라서 **(d) plan**이 정답이다.

73. In the context of the passage, <u>houses</u> means _____. (a) conceals (b) limits **(c) contains** (d) guards	**73.** 글의 문맥에 따르면, <u>houses</u>는 _____을 의미한다. (a) 감추다 (b) 제한하다 **(c) 포함하다** (d) 지키다

> **해설**

엘리자베스 타워는 가장 큰 종인 빅 벤을 타워 안에 갖고 있는 것이므로 house가 '수용하다'는 의미로 쓰였음을 유추할 수 있다. 따라서 (c) contains가 정답이다.

PART 4. Read the following business letter and answer the questions. The underlined words in the letter are for vocabulary questions.

74~80

ATTENTION

To: ALL RESIDENTS OF SOUTHWOODS ESTATES
From: HOMEOWNERS ASSOCIATION BOARD (HOA)
Re: PREVENTIVE MEASURE AGAINST MEASLES

We are alarmed by the ongoing measles outbreak in the country. In our state alone, the number of measles cases has tripled from only five during the last month. While no case of the disease has been reported in Northville yet, we believe that keeping our neighborhood measles-free should still be our priority. Therefore, 75) **we should work together to prevent the disease before it** 79) **strikes, rather than cure it once it affects our families.**

In line with this, the HOA will be conducting a medical mission with the aid of volunteer doctors from the Iowa Medical Center. 76) **The mission will include an orientation regarding the infection, covering its causes, symptoms, and treatment.** 74),76) **All residents, especially parents, must attend the event to better understand measles and the risks it entails.**

알려드립니다

Southwoods Estates의 모든 거주자들에게

주택소유주 협회 이사회(HOA)로부터

홍역에 대한 예방 조치

우리는 이 나라에서 진행 중인 홍역 발생에 놀랐습니다. 우리 주에서만, 홍역 발병 건수는 지난 달 동안 5건에서 3배로 증가했습니다. 노스빌에서는 아직 이 질병의 사례가 보고되지 않았지만, 우리 동네에 홍역이 없는 상태를 유지하는 것이 여전히 우리의 최우선이라고 믿습니다. 75) 따라서 우리는 질병이 우리 가족에게 영향을 미칠 때 치료하기보다는, 그것이 79) 발병하기 전에 질병을 예방하기 위해 함께 노력해야 합니다.

이에 따라, HOA는 아이오와 의료센터의 자원봉사 의사 분들의 도움으로 의료 선교를 수행할 것입니다. 76) 선교에는 원인, 증상 및 치료법을 다루는 감염에 관한 오리엔테이션이 포함될 것입니다. 74), 76) 모든 거주자, 특히 부모님들은 홍역과 그것이 수반하는 위험을 더 잘 이해하기 위해 행사에 참석해야 합니다.

Apart from the briefing, residents will also be accommodated for medical consultations and physical examinations. Doctors will evaluate general health and check for symptoms of measles. [77] **Anyone found positive to the virus will be prescribed antiviral medicines and recommended for vaccination.**

While the consultations and assessments are free, [78] **the measles** [80] **shot will cost $75 and will be available at the pharmacist's table.** Have it administered by the attending doctor after the diagnoses.

The schedule and venues for the medical mission are as follows:
- **Briefing:** March 7, from 9:00 a.m. to 12:00 p.m. at the Club House
- **General Consultation:** March 7-8, from 8:00 a.m. to 5:00 p.m. at the Sports Complex

We are hoping for your full cooperation.

Anna Sue Bennett
HOA Chairperson

브리핑 외에도, 주민들은 의료 상담 및 신체검사를 제공받을 것입니다. 의사는 전반적인 건강 상태를 평가하고 홍역 증상을 확인할 것입니다. [77] 바이러스에 양성 반응을 보인 누구에게나 항바이러스제가 처방될 것이며 예방 접종이 권장될 것입니다.

상담 및 평가는 무료이지만, [78] 홍역 [80] 예방주사는 75달러이며 약사 진료대에서 구할 수 있습니다. 진단 후 주치의에게 투여 받으십시오.

의료 선교의 일정 및 장소는 다음과 같습니다.

- 브리핑: 3월 7일 오전 9시 ~ 오후 12시, Club House에서
- 일반 상담: 3월 7일-8일 오전 8시 ~ 오후 5시, Sports Complex에서

여러분의 적극적인 협조를 바랍니다.

Anna Sue Bennett 드림
HOA 의장

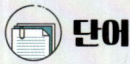 **단어**

measles n. 홍역
triple v. 3배가 되다
affect v. 영향을 미치다
medical mission n. 의료 선교
symptom n. 증상
apart from prep. ~와는 별개로
consultation n. 상담, 자문
examination n. 검사
prescribe v. 처방하다
recommend v. 권장하다, 추천하다
resident n. 주민, 거주자
assessment n. 평가
pharmacist n. 약사
diagnose n. 진단, v. 진단하다
cooperation n. 협조

outbreak n. 발생
priority n. 우선 사항
conduct v. 수행하다
infection n. 감염(병)
treatment n. 치료
accommodate v. 수용하다
physical adj. 신체의
evaluate v. 확인하다, 평가하다
antiviral adj. 항바이러스의
vaccination n. 예방접종
entail v. 수반하다
available adj. 이용할 수 있는
administer v. 관리하다
venue n. 장소

 **문제풀이**

74. What is the purpose of the letter?

(a) to warn homeowners against a contagious disease
(b) to call for participation in a medical program
(c) to remind residents about vaccination schedules
(d) to propose a campaign on ending an outbreak

74. 편지의 목적은 무엇인가?

(a) 주민들에게 전염병에 대해 경고하기
(b) 의료 프로그램에 참여할 것을 요청하기
(c) 주민들에게 예방 접종 일정에 대해 상기시키기
(d) 발병 종식 캠페인을 제안하기

해설

모든 거주자들은 홍역과 그것이 수반하는 위험을 더 잘 이해하기 위해 행사에 참석해야 한다고 권고하는 언급이 있으며, 글 하단에 의료 선교의 일정 및 장소도 알려주고 있다. 이를 통해 거주자들이 홍역 예방 프로그램에 참여하도록 하는 것이 이 편지의 목적임을 알 수 있다. 따라서 **(b) to call for participation in a medical program**이 정답이다.

단어 contagious disease n. 전염병   participation n. 참가, 참여   resident n. 주민, 거주자

75. How most likely can the community ensure they are measles-free?

(a) by treating measles cases immediately
(b) by kicking out affected families from the area
(c) by avoiding the infection before it spreads
(d) by transferring everyone to another neighborhood

75. 어떻게 지역에 홍역이 없도록 보장할 수 있는가?

(a) 홍역 환자들을 즉시 치료함으로써
(b) 지역에서 감염된 가족들을 쫓아냄으로써
(c) 전염되기 전에 감염을 피함으로써
(d) 모든 사람들을 또다른 지역으로 이주시킴으로써

> 해설

질병이 가족들에게 영향을 미칠 때 치료하기보다는 발병하기 전에 예방하기 위해 노력해야 한다는 내용을 통해 (c) by avoiding the infection before it spreads가 정답이다.

> paraphrasing point

to prevent the disease before it strikes → by avoiding the infection before it spreads

단어 immediately ad. 즉시   kick out v. 쫓아내다   infection n. 감염

---

76. Why should homeowners go to the **orientation**?

(a) so they can get used to the new facility
(b) so they can volunteer as doctors' assistants
(c) so they can study medical procedures
(d) so they can familiarize themselves with the infection

76. 왜 주택소유주들은 **오리엔테이션**에 가야 하는가?

(a) 그래서 그들이 새로운 시설에 익숙해질 수 있도록
(b) 그래서 그들이 의사 조수로 자원봉사 할 수 있도록
(c) 그래서 그들이 의료 절차를 연구할 수 있도록
(d) 그래서 그들이 감염에 대해 스스로 잘 알 수 있도록

 **Tip!** 오리엔테이션이 언급된 주변부를 찾아 읽는다.

> 해설

모든 거주자들은 홍역과 그것이 수반하는 위험을 더 잘 이해하기 위해 행사에 참석해야 한다는 내용을 통해 (d) so they can familiarize themselves with the infection이 정답임을 알 수 있다.

> paraphrasing point

better understand → familiarize

단어 facility n. 시설   assistant n. 보조원, 조수   procedure n. 절차

77. When will a patient probably NOT receive **prescription drugs**?

   (a) if one is found to have zero symptoms
   (b) if one is currently on prescription medication
   (c) if one has immediately caught the virus
   (d) if one has already been vaccinated

77. 언제 환자가 처방약을 받지 못할 것 같은가?

   (a) 증상이 없는 것으로 밝혀진 사람
   (b) 현재 처방약을 복용중인 사람
   (c) 즉시 바이러스에 감염된 사람
   (d) 이미 백신주사를 맞은 사람

> 해설

바이러스에 양성 반응이 발견된 사람은 누구나 항바이러스제가 처방된다는 내용을 통해 증상이 없는 사람은 처방을 받을 수 없다는 것을 유추할 수 있다. 따라서 **(a) if one is found to have zero symptoms**이 정답이다.

> paraphrasing point

prescribed antiviral medicines → prescription drugs

> 단어   prescription drugs n. 의사의 처방전이 필요한 약

---

78. What most likely should one do to get **the measles shot**?

   (a) purchase a vaccine from the pharmacist
   (b) finish the briefing given on the first day
   (c) consult with their private physician
   (d) visit both days of the medical mission

78. **홍역 예방주사**를 맞으려면 무엇을 해야 할 것인가?

   (a) 약사로부터 백신을 구입한다
   (b) 첫날에 주어진 브리핑을 마친다
   (c) 담당 의사와 상담한다
   (d) 의료 선교 중 이틀 모두 방문한다

 Tip! 문제의 shot을 본문에서 찾아 읽는다.

> 해설

상담 및 평가는 무료지만, 홍역 예방 주사는 75달러이며 약사 진료대에서 구할 수 있다는 언급을 통해 홍역 예방 주사를 맞으려면 약사에게 백신을 구입해야 한다는 것을 알 수 있다. 따라서 **(a) purchase a vaccine from the pharmacist**가 정답이다.

> paraphrasing point

will be available at the pharmacist's table → purchase a vaccine from the pharmacist

> 단어   pharmacist n. 약사, 약국

79. In the context of the passage, <u>strikes</u> means _____.

(a) collides
(b) arrives
(c) punches
(d) misses

79. 글의 문맥에 따르면, <u>strikes</u>는 _____을 의미한다.

(a) 충돌하다
(b) 도래하다
(c) 주먹으로 치다
(d) 놓치다

해설

질병이 strikes하기 전에 예방해야 한다는 내용을 통해 strike는 prevent와 대조된다는 것을 알 수 있다. prevent는 '예방하다'는 뜻이므로 strike는 '**발병하다**'로 유추할 수 있다. 따라서 **(b) arrives**가 정답이다. strike는 (재난, 질병 등이 갑자기) 발생하다, 덮치다는 의미로도 쓰인다.

80. In the context of the passage, <u>shot</u> means _____.

(a) picture
(b) explosion
(c) attempt
(d) injection

80. 글의 문맥에 따르면, <u>shot</u>은 _____을 의미한다.

(a) 사진
(b) 폭발
(c) 시도
(d) 주사

해설

바이러스에 양성인 사람은 처방약과 예방접종이 권장된다는 내용 뒤에 홍역 shot은 75달러라는 내용을 통해 shot이 '**주사**'를 나타낸다는 것을 유추할 수 있다. 따라서 **(d) injection**이 정답이다.

실전모의고사 <제2회>

53 (b)	54 (d)	55 (b)	56 (c)	57 (a)	58 (c)	59 (a)	60 (a)	61 (d)	62 (c)
63 (b)	64 (b)	65 (c)	66 (a)	67 (b)	68 (d)	69 (a)	70 (c)	71 (d)	72 (b)
73 (a)	74 (b)	75 (c)	76 (d)	77 (d)	78 (c)	79 (c)	80 (b)		

PART 1. Read the following biography article and answer the questions. The underlined words in the article are for vocabulary questions.

53~59

L. FRANK BAUM

L. Frank Baum was an American author [53] **best known for writing** The Wonderful Wizard of Oz. [53] **He is considered the "Father of the American Fairy Tale" for creating the Oz series, which ranks among the most famous and widely translated works of American literature.**

Baum was born in Chittenango, New York, on May 15, 1856. Young Baum was homeschooled during his early years. Due to health issues, he was unable to continue his formal education and earn a high school degree. [54] **At the age of 15, Baum took to writing stories. He later began self-publishing his own journals when his father brought home a printing press.**

While writing short stories for various magazines in his 20s, Baum ventured into acting in stage plays. Baum's father owned a theater company during that time and in 1880, his father [58] **delegated** the management of the company to him. Two years later, he would write and stage his first play, which became a modest success.

라이먼 프랭크 바움

라이먼 프랭크 바움은 「오즈의 마법사」를 저술한 것으로 [53] 가장 잘 알려진 미국 작가였다. 그는 미국 문학에서 가장 유명하고 널리 번역된 작품 중 하나인 오즈 시리즈를 창작한 "미국 동화의 아버지"로 불린다.

바움은 1856년 5월 15일 뉴욕의 치터냉고에서 태어났다. 어린 바움은 유년기에 홈스쿨링을 받았다. 건강상의 문제로 인해, 그는 정규 교육을 계속할 수 없었고 고등학교 학위를 취득할 수 없었다. [54] 15세에, 바움은 이야기를 쓰기 시작했다. 그는 나중에 아버지가 인쇄기를 집에 가져왔을 때 자신의 저널을 자체 출판하기 시작했다.

20대에 다양한 잡지에 단편 소설을 쓰면서, 바움은 무대 연극에서 연기하는 것에 도전했다. 바움의 아버지는 당시 극단 회사를 소유했고 1880년에 그의 아버지는 회사 경영을 그에게 [58] 위임했다. 2년 후, 그는 그의 첫 번째 연극을 쓰고 무대를 꾸몄는데, 이는 적당한 성공을 거두었다.

Unfortunately, [55)] **Baum's theater burned down in 1882 along with all of his costumes, props, and many of his manuscripts. Baum, disheartened, would search for a more** [59)] **stable job to support his family.** For the next two decades, he worked as a traveling salesman and then as a journalist for various magazines and newspapers.

In 1897, Baum wrote a collection of stories based on famous nursery rhymes entitled *Mother Goose in Prose*. [56)] **The book's reception allowed Baum to quit being a salesman and become a full-time writer.** Two years later, he followed it up with a poetry book, *Father Goose, His Book*, which became the best-selling children's book of the year.

Baum's next work, *The Wonderful Wizard of Oz*, was the first major American fairy tale during a time when most fairy tales were written by Europeans. [57)] **Following the fantastical adventures of his characters, the novel features a real American setting and a fictional world filled with talking trees and everlasting rainbows: the mystical Land of Oz.** Many children were captivated by the story, a fairy tale that was bright and playful when so many others were dark and grim, and they wrote letters to Baum requesting a sequel. Baum satisfied his fans by writing 13 sequels throughout the following years.

Baum continued writing stories in the Land of Oz until he passed away on May 6, 1919. After Baum's death, the Oz series remained so popular that it was continued by other authors, who produced an additional 26 books.

안타깝게도, [55)] 바움의 극장은 1882년에 그의 모든 의상, 소품, 그리고 많은 원고들과 함께 화재로 인해 소실되었다. 낙담한 바움은 가족을 부양하기 위해 더 [59)] 안정적인 직업을 찾아야 했다. 그 후 20년 동안, 그는 외판원으로 일하며 그 다음 다양한 잡지와 신문의 기자로 일했다.

1897년, 바움은 「엄마 거위 이야기」라는 제목을 붙인 유명한 동요를 바탕으로 한 이야기 모음집을 썼다. [56)] 이 책의 인기로 바움은 세일즈맨을 그만두게 했고 전업 작가가 되었다. 2년 후, 그는 그의 시집 「아빠 거위: 그의 책」을 출간했고, 이는 올해의 베스트셀러 아동 도서가 되었다.

바움의 다음 작품인 「오즈의 마법사」는 대부분의 동화가 유럽인에 의해 쓰여졌던 당시에 최초의 주요 미국 동화였다. [57)] 그의 캐릭터들의 환상적인 모험을 따라가는 소설은 진정한 미국의 배경과 말하는 나무와 영원한 무지개로 가득 찬 가상의 세계인 오즈의 신비한 땅을 특징으로 한다. 다른 많은 동화들이 어둡고 암울했을 때 다수의 아이들은 밝고 장난기 많은 그 동화 속 이야기에 사로잡혀서, 속편을 요청하는 편지를 바움에게 썼다. 바움은 이후 몇 년에 걸쳐 13편의 속편을 씀으로써 그의 팬들을 만족시켰다.

바움은 1919년 5월 6일 그가 세상을 떠날 때까지 오즈의 땅 속 이야기를 계속 썼다. 바움이 사망한 후에도, 오즈 시리즈는 계속해서 인기를 끌어서 26권의 추가적인 책을 제작한 다른 작가들에 의해 계속되었습니다.

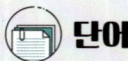 **단어**

rank v. 순위를 차지하다 n. 지위, 계급
literature n. 문학
formal adj. 정규의, 정식의
self-publishing n. 자체 출판
venture v. 도전하다
stage n. 무대
theater n. 극단, 극장
costumes n. 의상
manuscript n. 원고
stable adj. 안정된, 안정적인
nursery rhyme n. 동요, 자장가
reception n. 인기
fairy tale n. 동화
adventures n. 모험
novel n. 소설
fictional adj. 가상의, 허구의
captivate v. 매료시키다, ~의 마음을 사로잡다
grim adj. 냉혹한, 모진, 음침한, 단호한

translate v. 번역하다
homeschool n. 홈스쿨링(자택 학습)
degree n. 학위
printing press n. 인쇄기
management n. 경영
modest adj. 보통 정도의, 적당한
burn down v. 소실되다
prop n. 소품
dishearten v. 낙담시키다, 낙담하게 하다
collection n. 모음집
entitle v. ~에 제목을 붙이다, 자격을 주다
poetry n. 시
fantastical adj 환상적인
character n. 캐릭터, 주인공
feature v. 특징으로 하다 n. 특색, 특징
everlasting adj. 영원한, 변치 않는
playful adj. 장난스러운, 장난기 많은, 쾌활한
sequel n. (책·영화·연극 등의) 속편

 문제풀이

53. What is L. Frank Baum **most recognized for**?

(a) creating the fairy tale genre
(b) authoring a popular work of fiction
(c) being the Wizard of Oz
(d) translating American literature

53. 라이먼 프랭크 바움은 무엇으로 가장 잘 알려져 있는가?

(a) 동화 장르를 만든 것
(b) 인기있는 소설 작품을 저술한 것
(c) 오즈의 마법사가 된 것
(d) 미국문학을 번역한 것

해설

바움은 유명하고 널리 번역된 작품 중 하나인 오즈 시리즈를 쓴 것으로 유명하며, 미국 동화의 아버지라고 불린다는 언급을 통해 인기있는 소설 작품의 저작으로 가장 잘 알려져 있음을 알 수 있다. 따라서 **(b) authoring a popular work of fiction**이 정답이다.

paraphrasing point

best known for → most recognized for
writing → authoring

단어 create v. 만들다, 창조하다   author v. 쓰다, 저술하다   translate v. 번역하다, 통역하다

54. When did Baum start writing?

(a) after he began acting on stage
(b) as soon as his health improved
(c) when he published his father's journals
(d) before he received the printing press

54. 언제 바움은 글을 쓰기 시작했는가?

(a) 그가 무대에서 연기를 시작한 후
(b) 그의 건강이 좋아지자마자
(c) 그가 그의 아버지의 저널을 출간했을 때
(d) 그가 인쇄기를 받기 전에

 **Tip!** during his early years가 있는 두번째 문단에서 답을 찾는다.

해설

바움은 15세에 글을 쓰기 시작했고, 그 뒤 아버지가 인쇄기를 가져왔을 때 저널을 출간했으므로 그가 인쇄기를 받기 전임을 알 수 있다. 따라서 **(d) before he received the printing press**가 정답이다.

단어 improve v. 좋아지다, 개선되다, 나아지다, 향상시키다   receive v. 받다

---

55. Why did Baum decide to leave the theater and find a new **profession**?

(a) because he wanted to become like his father
(b) because his workplace was ruined
(c) because his first play wasn't liked by people
(d) because theater management was unprofitable

55. 바움이 극장을 떠나 새로운 직업을 찾기로 결정한 이유는 무엇인가?

(a) 그가 아버지처럼 되고 싶었기 때문에
(b) 그의 일터가 폐허가 되었기 때문에
(c) 그의 첫 연극은 사람들이 좋아하지 않았기 때문에
(d) 극장의 경영이 수익성이 없었기 때문에

해설

극장이 소실되었고, 낙담한 바움이 가족을 부양하기 위해 더 안정된 직업을 찾아야 했다는 내용을 통해 그의 직장이 폐허가 되었기 때문에 극단을 떠나 새로운 직업을 찾기로 결심했다는 것을 알 수 있다. 따라서 **(b) because his workplace was ruined**가 정답이다.

paraphrasing point

job → profession
burned down → ruined

단어 profession n. 직업, 직종   ruin v. 폐허로 만들다, 파멸시키다
management n. 경영, 운영, 관리   unprofitable adj. 수익을 못 내는, 이익이 없는

56. Why was Baum able to **work as a full-time writer**?

(a) because he wrote the best-selling children's book
(b) because he was good at selling his stories
(c) because his first book was successful
(d) because there was a big market for poetry

56. 왜 바움이 전업 작가로 활동할 수 있었는가?

(a) 그가 베스트셀러 아동 도서를 썼기 때문에
(b) 그가 자신의 이야기를 잘 팔았기 때문에
(c) 그의 첫 번째 책이 성공했기 때문에
(d) 시 시장이 컸기 때문에

해설

1897년 바움은 「엄마 거위 이야기」라는 유명한 동요를 바탕으로 한 이야기 모음집을 썼고, 이 책의 인기로 전임 작가가 되었다는 내용을 통해 (c) because his first book was successful이 정답이다.

paraphrasing point

become a full-time writer → work as a full-time writer

단어 successful adj. 성공한, 성공적인   poetry n. 시, 시가

---

57. Based on the text, what probably made *The Wonderful Wizard of Oz* successful?

(a) The adventures are fun and colorful.
(b) The author was not European.
(c) It is the original American fairy tale.
(d) It has many interesting sequels.

57. 본문에 따르면, 「오즈의 마법사」가 성공한 이유는 무엇일까?

(a) 모험이 재밌고 다채로워서
(b) 저자가 유럽인이 아니어서
(c) 본래 미국 동화여서
(d) 흥미로운 속편이 많아서

해설

바움의 다음 작품인 「오즈의 마법사」는 환상적인 모험을 따라가며 말하는 나무와 영원한 무지개로 가득 찬 가상의 세계인 오즈의 신비한 땅을 특징으로 한다는 내용을 통해 모험이 다채롭고 재미있기 때문에 성공했음을 알 수 있다. 따라서 **(a) The adventures are fun and colorful**이 정답이다.

paraphrasing point

talking trees and everlasting rainbows → fun and colorful

단어 author n. 저자, 작가   interesting adj. 흥미로운, 재미있는

58. In the context of the passage, <u>delegated</u> means _____.

(a) moved
(b) delivered
(c) assigned
(d) brought

58. 글의 문맥에 따르면, <u>delegated</u>는 _____을 의미한다.

(a) 이사했다
(b) 배달했다
(c) 부여했다
(d) 가져왔다

> **해설**
>
> 아버지가 극단을 소유했고, 회사 경영권을 그에게 delegate했다는 내용을 통해 delegate가 '**위임하다**', '**부여하다**'의 의미라는 것을 유추할 수 있다. 따라서 **(c) assigned**가 정답이다.

59. In the context of the passage, <u>stable</u> means _____.

(a) secure
(b) even
(c) balanced
(d) healthy

59. 글의 문맥에 따르면, <u>stable</u>은 _____을 의미한다.

(a) 안정적인
(b) 평편한
(c) 균형 잡힌
(d) 건강한

> **해설**
>
> 바움의 극장이 소실된 후 가족을 부양하기 위해 stable한 직업을 찾아야 했다는 점에서 stable이 '**안정적인**'의 의미라는 것을 유추할 수 있다. 따라서 **(a) secure**가 정답이다.

PART 2. Read the following magazine article and answer the questions. The underlined words in the article are for vocabulary questions.

60~66

FAR-UVC LIGHT HAS POTENTIAL TO CONTROL THE SPREAD OF DEADLY DISEASES

Scientists have identified that some wavelengths of ultraviolet C light, or UVC light, can safely limit the spread of diseases. UVC light is a certain range within the ultraviolet (UV) light spectrum. **60) A specific range of UVC light, which is called "far-UVC light," does not harm human skin and has shown potential to be effective against all microbes.**

UV light has long been used to 65) **disinfect** water, food, instruments, and other items by killing harmful bacteria. However, UV light is not recommended to kill airborne viruses in areas with people. It penetrates the outer layer of the skin and can cause skin-related illnesses such as premature aging and skin cancer. This is why public spaces have to be cleared of people first before being sterilized with UV light.

Researchers at the Center for Radiological Research at Columbia University Irving Medical Center have studied the possibility of using UV light to eliminate microbes safely and effectively. **61) They discovered that a low dose of far-UVC light, which measures 207 to 222 nanometers in wavelength, can safely kill germs on the human skin.** Far-UVC light is safe because it does not break through the skin's outer layer.

원단파장 광선은 치명적인 질병의 확산을 제어할 잠재력이 있다

과학자들은 자외선 C 광선 또는 단파장 광선의 일부 파장이 질병의 확산을 안전하게 제한할 수 있음을 확인했다. 단파장 광선은 자외선(UV) 광 스펙트럼 내의 특정 범위이다. 60) "원단파장 광선"이라고 불리는 특정 범위의 단파장 광선은 사람의 피부에 해를 끼치지 않으며 모든 미생물에 대해 효과적인 잠재력을 보여주었다.

자외선은 오랫동안 해로운 박테리아를 죽임으로써 물, 음식, 도구 및 기타 품목을 65) 소독하는 데 사용되어왔다. 그러나, 자외선은 사람이 있는 곳에서 공기 중 바이러스를 죽일 때에는 권장되지 않는다. 그것은 피부의 외층을 관통하여 조기 노화 및 피부암과 같은 피부 관련 질병을 일으킬 수 있다. 이것이 바로 공공 장소에서 자외선으로 살균하기 전에 먼저 사람이 없게 해야 하는 이유이다.

컬럼비아대학 어빙의료센터의 방사선 연구소 연구원들은 자외선 광선을 사용하여 미생물을 안전하고 효과적으로 제거할 수 있는 가능성을 연구했다. 61) 그들은 파장이 207~222 나노미터로 측정되는 소량의 원단파장 자외선 광선이 사람의 피부에 있는 세균을 안전하게 죽일 수 있음을 발견했다. 원단파장 자외선 광선은 피부의 외층을 통해 뚫고 들어오지 않기 때문에 안전하다.

Far-UVC light works by rendering bacteria and viruses inactive, [62)] **notably "superbugs," which are bacteria that have gained resistance to antibiotics over time.** Because superbugs are expected to kill an estimated 10 million people by 2050, far-UVC light is poised to be used in different applications to fight the bacteria. These include cleaning surgical wounds and sanitizing vulnerable body parts prior to medical procedures to avoid infection.

In particular, the researchers believe that [63)] **far-UVC light may be ideal for sterilizing indoor public spaces.** People interact the most in public locations such as airports and schools, making disease easy to [66)] **transmit** through coughing and sneezing. However, [63)] **far-UVC light could be applied in these spaces without inconveniencing people.**

For almost a decade, the researchers have been testing the safety of far-UVC light on humans as well as on the environment. [64)] **Experiments continue to be conducted** to confirm that far-UVC light is indeed efficient, and that it will not have short- or long-term undesirable effects on skin.

원단파장 자외선 광선은 박테리아와 바이러스, [62)] 특히 시간이 지남에 따라 항생제에 대한 내성을 얻는 박테리아인 "슈퍼버그"를 비활성화 시키는 작용을 한다. 슈퍼버그는 2050년까지 약 천만 명을 죽일 것으로 예상되기 때문에, 원단파장 자외선 광선은 박테리아와 싸우기 위해 다양한 용도로 사용될 만반의 태세를 갖추고 있다. 여기에는 감염을 방지하기 위해 의료 절차 전에 수술한 상처 부위를 깨끗하게 하고 취약한 신체 부위를 소독하는 것이 포함된다.

특히, 연구진은 [63)] 원단파장 자외선 광선이 실내 공공장소 살균에 이상적일지도 모른다고 믿는다. 사람들은 기침과 재채기를 통해 질병을 쉽게 [66)] 전파하며 공항과 학교와 같은 공공장소에서 가장 많이 상호 작용한다. 그러나, [63)] 원단파장 자외선 광선은 사람들을 불편하게 하는 일 없이 이러한 공간에 적용될 수 있다.

거의 10년 동안, 연구원들은 환경뿐만 아니라 인간에 대한 원단파장 자외선 광선의 안전성을 테스트해오고 있는 중이다. [64)] 원단파장 자외선 광선이 실제로 효율적이고, 피부에 단기 또는 장기적으로 바람직하지 않은 영향을 미치지 않는다는 사실을 확인하기 위한 실험이 계속 진행된다.

단어

UVC n. 단파장 자외선
identify v. 확인하다, 식별하다
ultraviolet n. 자외선
potential n. 잠재력
harmful adj. 해로운
penetrate v. 관통하다, 침입하다
cancer n. 암
eliminate v. 제거하다
nanometer n. 나노미터

far-UVC n. 원단파장 자외선
wavelength n. 파장
spectrum n. 스펙트럼, 분광
instrument n. 도구, 장비, 악기
bacteria n. 박테리아
premature n. 조기 노화
sterilize v. 살균하다
microbe n. 미생물
germ n. 세균

render v. ~하게 만들다, 주다, 제공하다
resistance n. 내성
notably ad. 특히, 두드러지게
be poised to v v. ~할 만반의 태세를 갖추고 있다
surgical adj. 외과의, 수술의
sanitize v. 소독하다
procedure n. 순서, 절차
interact v. 상호작용하다
sneeze v. 재채기하다
confirm v. 확인하다

inactive adj. 비활성의, 소극적인
antibiotic n. 항생제
estimate v. 예상하다, 예측하다
application n. 용도, 적용
wound n. 상처, 상해
vulnerable adj. 취약한
infection n. 감염, 전염
cough v. 기침하다
environment n. 환경

 문제풀이

60. What makes far-UVC light ideal for controlling the spread of diseases?

(a) It is harmless to the skin of people.
(b) It cures most human diseases.
(c) It has a wide range of wavelengths.
(d) It can reach bacteria located deep down the skin.

60. 무엇이 원단파장 자외선 광선을 질병의 확산을 제어하는 데 이상적으로 만드는가?

(a) 사람의 피부에 무해하다.
(b) 대부분의 인간 질병을 치료한다.
(c) 넓은 범위의 파장을 가진다.
(d) 피부 깊숙한 곳에 위치한 박테리아에 도달할 수 있다.

해설

원단파장 자외선 광선이 인간의 피부에 해를 끼치지 않으며 모든 미생물에 대해 효과적으로 잠재력을 보여주었다는 내용을 통해 **(a) It is harmless to the skin of people**이 정답임을 알 수 있다.

▶ paraphrasing point

does not harm → is harmless

단어 spread n. 확산, 전파   harmless adj. 무해한, 해가 없는

61. How can far-UVC light be used for medical treatment?

(a) by curing patients with skin cancer
(b) by preventing the skin from aging too early
(c) by letting patients endure high doses of UV treatment
(d) by getting rid of germs on the skin surface

61. 어떻게 원단파장 자외선 광선이 의학적 치료에 사용될 수 있는가?

(a) 피부암 환자를 치료함으로써
(b) 피부가 너무 일찍 노화되는 것을 방지함으로써
(c) 환자가 고용량의 UV 치료를 견디도록 함으로써
(d) 피부 표면의 세균을 제거함으로써

> 해설

저용량의 원단파장 자외선 광선이 사람의 피부에 있는 세균을 안전하게 죽일 수 있다는 것을 발견했다는 내용을 통해 **(d) by getting rid of germs on the skin surface**가 정답임을 알 수 있다.

> paraphrasing point

kill → getting rid of

> 단어

treatment n. 치료, 처치
get rid of v. 제거하다, 끝내다
endure v. 견디다, 참다
surface n. 표면

---

62. What makes "**superbugs**" stand out among microbes?

(a) being able to spread in the air more easily
(b) having immunity to the effects of ultraviolet light
(c) having higher tolerance to anti-bacterial drugs
(d) being able to pass through human tissue

62. 무엇이 "슈퍼버그"가 미생물 중에서도 부각되게 만드는가?

(a) 공기 중에 보다 쉽게 확산할 수 있는 것
(b) 자외선의 영향에 대한 면역력을 가지는 것
(c) 항생제에 대한 내성이 더 높은 것
(d) 인간 조직을 통과할 수 있는 것

 Tip! 바꿔 쓸 수 없는 표현 superbugs를 본문에서 찾아 읽는다.

> 해설

슈퍼버그를 시간이 지남에 따라 항생제에 내성이 생긴 박테리아로 묘사하는 내용을 통해 **(c) having higher tolerance to anti-bacterial drugs**가 정답임을 알 수 있다.

> paraphrasing point

resistance to antibiotics → tolerance to anti-bacterial drugs

> 단어

stand out v. 부각되다, 눈에 띄다, 빼어나다, 도드라지다
immunity n. 면역력
tissue n. 조직

63. Based on the article, why most likely is it **ideal** to use far-UVC light **to sterilize public locations**?

(a) It doesn't come into contact with people in these spaces.
(b) It doesn't require clearing these spaces of people first.
(c) These spaces attract all sorts of bacteria and viruses.
(d) These spaces can easily be rid of people first.

63. 기사에 따르면, **공공장소를 살균하기 위해** 원단파장 자외선 광선을 사용하는 것이 **이상적인** 이유는 무엇일 것 같은가?

(a) 이 장소들에 있는 사람들과 접촉하지 않는다.
(b) 이 장소들에서 사람들을 먼저 내보내는 것을 요구하지 않는다.
(c) 이 장소들이 모든 종류의 박테리아와 바이러스를 끌어들인다.
(d) 이 장소들이 사람을 먼저 쉽게 없앨 수 있다.

해설

다섯 번째 문단 첫째줄에서 '원단파장 자외선 광선이 실내 공공장소 살균에 이상적일지도 모른다'고 언급되어 있고, 특히 마지막 줄에서 '원단파장 자외선 광선은 사람들을 불편하게 하는 일 없이 이러한 공간에 적용될 수 있다'는 내용을 통해 사람들을 장소 밖으로 내보내는 불편함을 유발하지 않고도 공공장소를 살균할 수 있음을 추론할 수 있다. 따라서 (b) It doesn't require clearing these spaces of people first가 정답이다.

단어 come into contact with v. ~와 접촉하다, 만나다   clear A of B v. A에서 B를 치우다, 내보내다

---

64. When will experiments on far-UVC light probably conclude?

(a) if it proves effective against the most common microbes
(b) if its use shows no harm on the skin for any duration
(c) if regular UV light is no longer harmful on the skin
(d) if safer methods are found to kill superbugs

64. 원단파장 자외선에 대한 실험은 언제 끝날까?

(a) 가장 흔한 미생물에 대해 효과적인 것으로 입증된다면
(b) 어떤 기간에도 그것의 사용이 피부에 해를 입히지 않음을 보여준다면
(c) 일반 자외선이 더이상 피부에 해롭지 않다면
(d) 슈퍼버그를 죽이는 더 안전한 방법이 발견된다면

해설

원단파장 자외선 광선이 실제로 효율적이고, 피부에 해를 끼치지 않는다는 사실을 확인하기 위한 실험이 계속된다는 내용을 통해 이 실험은 어떤 기간에도 피부에 해를 끼치지 않을 때 종료된다는 것을 알 수 있다. 따라서 (b) if its use shows no harm on the skin for any duration이 정답이다.

▶ paraphrasing point

continue to be conducted → for any duration

단어 experiment n. 실험   conclude v. 끝내다, 마치다, 결론을 내리다   duration n. 기간

65. In the context of the passage, disinfect means _____.

(a) cure
(b) wash
(c) clean
(d) pollute

65. 글의 문맥에 따르면, disinfect는 _____을 의미한다.

(a) 치료하다
(b) 세척하다
(c) 소독하다
(d) 오염시키다

> **해설**
>
> 문맥상 자외선은 오랫동안 해로운 박테리아를 죽임으로써 물, 음식, 도구 및 기타 품목을 disinfect하는데 사용되었다는 내용을 통해 disinfect가 '**소독하다**'의 의미라는 것을 유추할 수 있다. 따라서 **(c) clean**이 정답이다.

66. In the context of the passage, transmit means _____.

(a) transfer
(b) control
(c) broadcast
(d) bring

66. 글의 문맥에 따르면, transmit은 _____을 의미한다.

(a) 전달하다
(b) 통제하다
(c) 방송하다
(d) 가져오다

> **해설**
>
> 사람들은 공공장소 기침과 재채기를 통해 질병을 쉽게 transmit한다는 내용을 통해 transmit이 '**전파하다, 전달하다**'의 의미라는 것을 알 수 있다. 따라서 **(a) transfer**가 정답이다.

PART 3. Read the following encyclopedia article and answer the questions. The underlined words in the article are for vocabulary questions.

67~73

FLEUR-DE-LIS

67) **The fleur-de-lis is an ancient symbol** resembling a lily flower composed of three petals bound together at their bases. Widely used as **a religious, political, and artistic symbol**, the fleur-de-lis has long been associated with the French crown, and has been used by French kings as **an emblem of their** sovereignty.

The fleur-de-lis's 72) association with the French monarchs may be rooted in the era of **Clovis** I, King of the Franks. 68) **Legend has it that the fleur-de-lis is the baptismal lily presented by an angel to Clovis as a symbol of his purity**. The lily is believed to have sprung from the tears of Eve, the first woman in the Bible, as she left Eden.

King Philip I has been depicted on his throne 69) **holding a short cane with fleur-de-lis on one end. A similar cane was seen in the Great Seal of Louis VII during the 12th century.** At the time, Louis VII also had little golden fleur-de-lis scattered on his blue shield. Since then, kings have used the scattered fleur-de-lis on their shields, armors, and coats of arms to emphasize their divine right to the throne.

백합 문양

67) 백합 문양은 세 개의 꽃잎이 밑 부분에 함께 묶여 구성된 백합 꽃을 닮은 고대 상징이다. 종교적, 정치적, 예술적 상징으로 널리 사용되는 백합 문양은 오랫동안 프랑스 왕관과 관련이 있어왔으며, 프랑스 왕이 주권의 상징으로 사용해왔다.

프랑스 군주와 백합 문양의 72) 관련성은 프랑크인의 왕 클로비스 1세 시대에 뿌리를 두고 있을 지도 모른다. 68) 전설에 따르면 백합 문양은 천사가 클로비스에게 순결의 상징으로 선물한 세례 백합이라고 한다. 백합은 에덴을 떠날 때 성경의 첫 번째 여인인 이브의 눈물에서 싹이 트는 것으로 믿어진다.

필리프 1세 왕은 재위 시절에 69) 한쪽 끝에 백합 문양이 있는 짧은 지팡이를 들고 있는 모습으로 묘사되어왔다. 비슷한 지팡이가 12세기 동안 루이 7세의 국새에서 발견되었다. 당시, 루이 7세는 파란 방패에 흩뿌려진 황금색의 작은 백합 문양이 있었다. 그때부터, 왕들은 왕좌에 대한 신성한 권리를 강조하기 위해 방패, 갑옷, 그리고 문장에 흩뿌려진 백합 문양을 사용했다.

The symbol has had different meanings throughout history. 70) **Some historians believe that the three petals represent the three social classes of medieval social hierarchy: the commoners, the clergy, and the nobility.** The modern fleur-de-lis has been said to stand for life, light, and perfection. 71) **Over time, the versatile symbol has retained a number of values, and has proven itself capable of evoking different feelings from different people.**

Between the classical and the modern periods, artists began to 71) adopt the shape of the fleur-de-lis and stylize it according to their patrons' 73) tastes. As the symbol's popularity increased, it began to appear in market stalls and shop windows. It has been used in architecture to adorn the tops of fences and roofs, and even in the military as a badge of honor. Versions of the fleur-de-lis have also become logos for many sports teams and universities.

그 상징은 역사를 통틀어 다른 의미를 가지고 있다. 70) 일부 역사가들은 세 개의 꽃잎이 중세 사회 계층의 세 가지 사회 계급인 평민, 성직자, 귀족을 대표한다고 믿는다. 현대 백합 문양은 생명, 빛, 완벽함을 상징하는 것으로 알려져 있다. 71) 시간이 지남에 따라, 다변하는 상징은 수많은 가치를 간직해왔으며, 그 자체로 다른 사람들의 다른 감정을 불러 일으킬 수 있음이 입증되었다.

고전과 현대 사이에서 예술가들은 71) 고객들의 73) 취향에 따라 백합 문양의 모양을 채택하고, 그것을 양식화하기 시작했다. 상징의 인기가 높아지면서, 그것은 가판대와 가게 진열창 나타나기 시작했다. 그것은 건축 분야에서 울타리와 지붕의 꼭대기를 장식하기 위해 사용되어왔으며, 심지어 군대에서도 명예 훈장으로 사용되어왔다. 백합 문양의 여러 형태들은 또한 많은 스포츠 팀과 대학의 로고가 되어왔다.

단어

ancient adj. 고대의
petal n. 꽃잎
emblem n. 상징
root v. 뿌리를 내리다
baptismal adj. 세례의
purity n. 순결, 순수성
depict v. 묘사하다
cane n. 지팡이
scatter v. ~을 뿌리다, 분산시키다
the Great Seal 국새

be composed of v. ~로 구성되다
religious adj. 종교의
sovereignty n. 주권
era n. 시대
lily n. 백합
spring v. 싹이 트다
throne n. 왕좌
the Great Seal n. 국새(국가를 상징하는 도장)
shield n. 방패
armor n. 갑옷

coats of arms n. 문장(국가나 가문 등을 상징하는 방패모양의 상징표)
divine right n. 왕권, 왕권 신수설(왕권에 대한 신성한 권리)
medieval adj. 중세의
commoner n. 일반인, 평민
nobility n. 귀족
evoke v. 불러일으키다, 환기시키다

emphasize v. 강조하다
historian n. 역사가
hierarchy n. 계층, 계급제도
clergy n. 성직자
versatile adj. 다변하는, 다재다능한
patron n. 후원자, 고객

문제풀이

67. What is the fleur-de-lis?

(a) a plant that is frequently used for decoration
(b) an ancient symbol that represents royalty
(c) a flower-like gem that is attached to crowns
(d) an old symbol for France's independence

67. 백합 문양은 무엇인가?

(a) 장식용으로 자주 사용되는 식물
(b) 왕권을 보여주는 고대 상징
(c) 왕관에 부착된 꽃과 같은 보석
(d) 프랑스 독립을 위한 오래된 상징

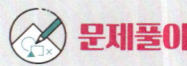 주제인 백합 문양의 정의를 묻는 질문이므로 첫 단락에서 확인한다.

백합 문양은 고대의 상징이자 종교적, 정치적, 예술적 상징이며, 프랑스 주권의 상징이라는 내용을 통해 왕권을 보여주는 고대 상징이라는 것을 알 수 있다. 따라서 **(b) an ancient symbol that represents royalty**가 정답이다.

▸ **paraphrasing point**
sovereignty → royalty

 frequently ad. 자주   **royalty** n. 왕권   **gem** n. 보석
crown n. 왕관   **independence** n. 독립

68. Why was **Clovis** given a lily during his **baptism**?

(a) because he resembled an angel from the heavens
(b) because he was a son of the first woman in the Bible
(c) because he was the first king of the Franks
(d) because he was purified by the event

68. 왜 **클로비스**는 그의 **세례** 때 백합을 받았는가?

(a) 그는 하늘에서 온 천사를 닮았기 때문에
(b) 그가 성경에서 첫 번째 여성의 아들이었기 때문에
(c) 그가 프랑크인의 첫 번째 왕이었기 때문에
(d) 그가 그 일로 인해 정화되었기 때문에

 클로비스가 언급된 곳을 찾아 읽는다.

해설

전설에 따르면 백합 문양이 천사가 클로비스에게 순결(purity)의 상징으로 선물한 것이라는 언급을 통해 그가 그 일로 인해 정화(purified)되었기 때문이라는 것을 알 수 있다. 따라서 **(d) because he was purified by the event**가 정답이다.

단어 baptism n. 세례 resemble v. 닮다, 유사하다
Bible n. 성경, 성서 purify v. 정화하다, 정제하다

---

69. How was the fleur-de-lis used around **the 12th century**?

(a) It was placed on kings' canes.
(b) It was scattered on royal seals.
(c) It was sewn on blue coats.
(d) It was printed on the king's throne.

69. 백합 문양은 **12세기**에 어떻게 사용되었는가?

(a) 왕들의 지팡이에 새겨져 있었다.
(b) 옥새에 흩뿌려져 있었다.
(c) 파란색 코트에 바느질되어 있었다.
(d) 왕의 보좌에 찍혀있었다.

 the 12th century가 언급된 곳을 찾아 읽는다.

해설

필리프 1세 왕 재위 시절에 백합 문양이 새겨진 지팡이를 들고 있는 모습이 묘사되어왔고, 그와 유사한 모양의 지팡이가 12세기 루이 7세의 국새에서도 발견되었다는 내용을 통해 백합 문양이 왕들의 지팡이에 새겨져 있었다는 것을 알 수 있다. 따라서 **(a) It was placed on kings' canes**가 정답이다.

단어 royal seal n. 옥새 print v. (자국·무늬 등을) 찍다, 새기다

70. What did the fleur-de-lis represent during **the medieval period**?

(a) the spread of power throughout France
(b) the religious beliefs of the people
(c) the social structure of that time
(d) the reign of fashionable nobility

70. 백합 문양은 중세시대에 무엇을 상징했는가?

(a) 프랑스 전역의 권력 확산
(b) 사람들의 종교적 신념
(c) 그 당시의 사회 구조
(d) 유행하는 귀족의 통치

 Tip! 중세시대를 언급하는 곳을 찾아 읽는다.

해설
역사가들이 백합 문양의 세 개의 꽃잎이 중세 사회의 계급인 평민, 성직자, 귀족을 대표한다고 믿는다는 내용을 통해 당시의 사회 구조를 나타냈다는 사실을 알 수 있다. 따라서 **(c) the social structure of that time**이 정답이다.

paraphrasing point
social hierarchy → social structure

단어 represent v. 상징하다, 나타내다   religious adj. 종교의   fashionable adj. 유행하는

---

71. Why most likely has the fleur-de-lis become **a popular symbol**?

(a) because artists can easily copy it
(b) because it was promoted by the military
(c) because its meaning is so consistent
(d) because it can be viewed in many ways

71. 백합 문양이 인기있는 상징이 된 이유는 무엇일 것 같은가?

(a) 예술가들이 쉽게 복제할 수 있기 때문에
(b) 그것은 군대에서 홍보되었기 때문에
(c) 그 의미가 매우 일관성이 있기 때문에
(d) 그것은 다양한 방식으로 보여질 수 있기 때문에

해설
백합 문양은 시대에 따라 다변하는 상징을 지녀왔고, 예술가들은 고객들의 취향에 따라 다르게 양식화 할 수 있었으며 인기가 많아졌다는 내용이 있다. 즉, 백합 문양이 고객들의 취향에 따라 다양한 방식으로 보여질 수 있으므로 인기가 많아졌음을 유추할 수 있다. 따라서 **(d) because it can be viewed in many ways**가 정답이다.

paraphrasing point
a number of values → many ways

72. In the context of the passage, association means _____.

(a) society
(b) connection
(c) alliance
(d) friendship

72. 글의 문맥에 따르면, association은 _____을 의미한다.

(a) 사회
(b) 연결
(c) 동맹
(d) 우정

> **해설**
> 문맥상 프랑스 군주와 백합 문양의 '**관계, 관련성, 연관성**' 등을 나타내므로 **(b) connection**이 정답임을 알 수 있다.

73. In the context of the passage, tastes means _____.

(a) likings
(b) flavors
(c) experiences
(d) samples

73. 글의 문맥에 따르면, tastes는 _____을 의미한다.

(a) 선호
(b) 풍미
(c) 경험
(d) 샘플

> **해설**
> 문맥상 예술가들이 후원자의 입맛(tastes)에 따라 백합 문양을 채택하고 스타일을 지정했다는 내용을 통해 tastes가 후원자의 **취향, 선호도**'를 의미함을 알 수 있다. 따라서 **(a) likings**가 정답이다.

PART 4. Read the following business letter and answer the questions. The underlined words in the letter are for vocabulary questions.

74~80

Mr. Barry Carney
Accounting Manager
Falcon Industries

Dear Mr. Carney:

74) **Please accept this letter as a notice of my resignation from my position as an accounting associate at Falcon Industries.** My last day of employment at the company will be on the 7th of January.

I recently received an offer from the company that I have always dreamt of joining. After careful 79) <u>consideration</u>, I have decided to accept the offer.

75) **Falcon Industries is the first company I have ever worked for, so my three years of work with you have been truly memorable.** I am grateful for having been part of the then newly formed digital accounting department, which was entrusted with the responsibility of digitizing the company's financial records.

76) **I am proud of my tenure at the department because we have successfully improved the accuracy of the company's accounting system. As a result, the company's credit rating increased, which attracted new investors.**

Mr. Barry Carney
회계팀장
팔콘 인더스트리

Carney씨께:

74) 팔콘 인더스트리의 회계부 사원 직책에서 사임한다는 통지로서 이 편지를 받아주시기 바랍니다. 저의 회사에서 마지막으로 일하는 날은 1월 7일이 될 것입니다.

저는 최근에 제가 항상 입사를 꿈꾸던 회사로부터 제의를 받았습니다. 신중한 79) 고려 끝에, 제안을 수락하기로 결정했습니다.

75) 팔콘 인더스트리는 제가 지금까지 일해왔던 첫 회사이기에, 당신과 함께 한 3년간의 일이 정말 기억에 남습니다. 회사의 재무 기록을 디지털화하는 책임을 맡았던, 당시 신생 부서인 디지털 회계 부서의 일원으로 받아주셔서 감사합니다.

76) 저는 우리가 회사 회계 시스템의 정확성을 성공적으로 개선했기 때문에 부서에서 근무한 것이 자랑스럽습니다. 그 결과, 회사의 신용 등급이 올랐고, 이는 새로운 투자자를 유치해냈습니다.

I am confident that the accounting team can handle the transition with ease. Nonetheless, [77] **I would still like to help with the turnover of work** to my replacement. As such, I am [80] willing to train the new employee on my responsibilities. I will also ensure that all of my pending reports are completed immediately to make the transition as smooth as possible.

Thank you again for the opportunity to work for Falcon Industries. [78] **I wish for more success for the company, and I look forward to keeping in touch with you.** You can email me anytime at sharmainelance@gmail.com or call me at my personal number, 317-573-9250.

Sincerely,
Sharmaine Lance
Accounting Associate

저는 회계 팀이 회계팀에서 쉽게 인수인계를 처리할 수 있다고 확신합니다. 그럼에도 불구하고, [77] 저는 여전히 제 후임자에게 업무를 인계하는 것을 돕고 싶습니다 그리하여, 저는 [80] 기꺼이 신입 사원에게 제 책무를 교육할 의향이 있습니다. 또한 가능한 한 원활하게 인수인계가 이루어지도록 저의 보류 중인 모든 보고서가 즉시 완료되도록 하겠습니다.

팔콘 인더스트리에서 일할 수 있는 기회를 주셔서 다시 한 번 감사드립니다. [78] 회사의 더 많은 성공을 기원하며, 앞으로도 계속 연락 드리겠습니다. 언제든지 sharmainelance@gmail.com으로 이메일을 보내시거나 제 개인번호인 317-573-9250으로 전화주실 수 있습니다.

Sharmaine Lance 드림
회계부 사원

 단어

notice n. 통지, 공지
work for v. ~에 근무하다
entrust v. 맡다, 위임하다
improve v. 개선하다
credit n. 신용
confident adj. 확신하는
transition n. 전환, 교체, 인수인계
responsibility n. 책임
pending adj. 보류의, 미결의
keep in touch with v. ~와 계속 연락하다

resignation n. 사임
accounting department n. 회계부서
tenure n. 근무, 재직
accuracy n. 정확성
rating n. 등급
handle v. 처리하다, 다루다
turnover of work n. 업무의 인계
ensure v. ~하게 하다, 보장하다
opportunity n. 기회

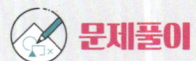 문제풀이

74. Why is Sharmaine Lance writing to Barry Carney?

(a) to negotiate the terms of her resignation
(b) to notify him of her departure from the company
(c) to accept a job offer in her dream department
(d) to request an interview with his accounting firm

74. Sharmaine Lance가 Barry Carney에게 편지를 보내는 이유는 무엇인가?

(a) 그녀의 사임 조건을 협상하기 위해
(b) 그에게 그녀의 퇴사를 알리기 위해
(c) 그녀의 꿈의 부서의 일자리 제안을 수락하기 위해
(d) 그의 회계 법인과의 인터뷰를 요청하기 위해

 Tip! 첫 단락에서 편지의 목적과 이유를 확인할 수 있다.

 해설

첫 문장에서 회계 담당자에게 사임 통지로 받아 달라는 편지의 내용으로 보아 퇴사를 알리기 위해 편지를 보낸다는 사실을 알 수 있다. 따라서 **(b) to notify him of her departure from the company**가 정답이다.

▸ **paraphrasing point**
resignation → departure

단어 negotiate v. 협상하다   notify v. 알리다, 통지하다   request v. 요청하다, 요구하다

---

75. Why does Lance consider her stay in Falcon Industries **unforgettable**?

(a) She had the chance to form a new department.
(b) Falcon Industries is her dream company.
(c) She received her first job opportunity there.
(d) Falcon Industries developed digital accounting.

75. 왜 Lance는 팔콘 인더스트리에 머무르는 것을 잊을 수 없다고 생각하는가?

(a) 그녀는 새로운 부서를 구성할 기회가 있었다.
(b) 팔콘 인더스트리는 그녀의 꿈의 회사이다.
(c) 그녀는 그곳에서 첫 번째 취업 기회를 얻었다.
(d) 팔콘 인더스트리는 디지털 회계를 개발했다.

해설

팔콘 인더스트리가 처음 일한 회사이기 때문에 함께 일한 3년이 기억에 남는다는 내용을 통해 **(c) She received her first job opportunity there**이 정답이다.

> **paraphrasing point**

memorable → unforgettable

the first company → the first job opportunity

단어 unforgettable adj. 잊을 수 없는   form v. 형성하다, 구성하다

---

76. What is probably one of Lance's greatest contributions to the company?

(a) helping the company gain more business
(b) creating a new fiscal system from scratch
(c) assessing the credit rating of the business
(d) locating investors for the company

76. Lance가 회사에 기여한 가장 큰 성과로 적절한 것은 무엇인가?

(a) 회사가 실적을 더 늘리도록 지원하는 것
(b) 처음부터 새로운 재정 시스템을 만드는 것
(c) 사업의 신용 등급을 평가하는 것
(d) 회사의 투자자를 찾는 것

해설

부서에서 근무하며 회계 시스템의 정확성을 개선해서 회사 신용등급이 올라 새 투자자들을 유치했다는 내용을 통해 Lance가 회사에 기여한 것이 회사 투자자 찾기라는 것을 알 수 있다. 따라서 **(d) locating investors for the company**가 정답이다.

> **paraphrasing point**

attracted new investors → locating investors

단어 contribution n. 기여   fiscal adj. 재정상의
locate v. ~을 위치시키다, 찾다, 발견하다   investor n. 투자자

77. How does Lance **plan to aid** with the turnover?

(a) by suggesting applicants for her replacement
(b) by allocating her pending tasks to her teammates
(c) by creating a timetable of her report deadlines
(d) by providing guidance to her replacement

77. Lance는 어떻게 인수인계를 도울 계획인가?

(a) 그녀의 후임자를 위한 지원자들을 제안함으로써
(b) 그녀의 보류 중인 작업을 팀원에게 할당함으로써
(c) 보고서 마감일의 시간표를 작성함으로써
(d) 그녀의 후임자에게 지침을 제공함으로서

해설

후임자에게 업무를 인계하는 것을 돕고 싶고, 기꺼이 신입 사원에게 자신의 책무를 교육할 의향이 있다는 내용을 통해 **(d) by providing guidance to her replacement**가 정답임을 알 수 있다.

paraphrasing point

help → aid
train → providing guidance

 aid v. 돕다   replacement n. 대체, 교체, 후임자   deadline n. 마감 시간

---

78. What is Lance's wish for Falcon Industries?

(a) for it to finally gain success
(b) for it to keep contacting former employees
(c) for it to achieve further success
(d) for it to succeed without her services

78. 팔콘 인더스트리에 대한 Lance의 소망은 무엇인가?

(a) 회사가 결국 성공하기를
(b) 회사가 이전 직원들과 계속 연락하기를
(c) 회사가 더 많은 성공을 거두기를
(d) 회사가 그녀의 도움 없이 성공하기를

해설

마지막 문단에서 회사의 더 많은 성공을 기원한다는 내용을 통해 **(c) for it to achieve further success**가 정답임을 알 수 있다.

paraphrasing point

more → further

achieve v. 달성하다   further ad. 더 이상의, 추가의

79. In the context of the passage, consideration means _____.

(a) attention
(b) sympathy
(c) thinking
(d) doubting

79. 글의 문맥에 따르면, consideration은 _____을 의미한다.

(a) 주의
(b) 동정
(c) 생각
(d) 의심

> **해설**
>
> 문맥상 신중한 consideration 끝에 제안을 수락하기로 결정했다는 내용을 통해 consideration이 '고려, 생각'을 뜻한다는 것을 알 수 있다. 따라서 **(c) thinking**이 정답이다.

80. In the context of the passage, willing means _____.

(a) hesitant
(b) prepared
(c) fortunate
(d) satisfied

80. 글의 문맥에 따르면, willing은 _____를 의미한다.

(a) 망설이는
(b) 준비된
(c) 행운의
(d) 만족하는

> **해설**
>
> 문맥상 자신의 대체자인 신입 사원에게 자리를 넘겨줄 것을 도울 것이고, 따라서 신입 사원을 교육시키겠다는 내용을 통해 willing이 '의향이 있는, 준비된'의 의미임을 알 수 있다. 또한 be willing to~는 '기꺼이 ~하다'라는 표현으로 사용된다. 따라서 **(b) prepared**가 정답이다.

지텔프 공식 교육사이트

지텔프는 지텔프에듀
G-TELP EDU
www.gtelpedu.com

경찰, 공무원, 군무원, 자격증, 취업 – 합격영어 지텔프!
본 교재에 대한 MP3 파일, 온라인 강의, 무료학습자료는
지텔프에듀 웹사이트에서 확인하실 수 있습니다.

G-TELP KOREA 출판사업본부